Children of a New Fatherland

CHILDREN OF
A NEW FATHERLAND

Germany's Post-War
Right-Wing Politics

J.H. BRINKS

Translated by Paul Vincent
Foreword by David Binder

I.B. Tauris *Publishers*

LONDON · NEW YORK

First published in 2000 by I.B.Tauris & Co Ltd,
Victoria House, Bloomsbury Square, London WC1B 4DZ
175 Fifth Avenue, New York NY 10010
Website: http://www.ibtauris.com

In the United States of America and in Canada distributed by
St Martin's Press, 175 Fifth Avenue, New York NY 10010

A shorter version of this book was published as *De Rechterflank
van Duitsland* by BOOM Publishers, Amsterdam, in 1994.

A full CIP record for this book is available from the British Library
A full CIP record for this book is available from the Library of
Congress

ISBN 1 86064 458 9 (hardback)

Library of Congress catalog card number: available

Set in Monotype Dante by Ewan Smith, London
Printed and bound in Great Britain by WBC Ltd, Bridgend

Contents

Preface

What prompted me to write this book in the first place was the desire to know why, almost immediately after German reunification, there was a veritable boom in attacks on foreigners, often associated with Nazi symbolism.

After the attacks in Hoyerswerda in East Germany in 1991 and in Rostock in the autumn of 1992, it was clear that many people felt a need for background information on these events. How could it be, one was frequently asked, that such scenes were taking place in a country that had always prided itself on being 'anti-fascist' and was also regarded as such by many people in the West. But it was impossible to view these trends separately from the situation in the old Federal Republic. Here too violence against foreigners, particularly against asylum-seekers, experienced a revival that was given worldwide attention after the attacks in Mölln in West Germany in 1992 and Solingen in 1993. However, these attacks were not isolated incidents but the extremist expression of a 'swing to the right' among the population that was reflected in German politics. I have tried to map out a few of the political and ideological roots of this *Rechtsruck*. The relatively large number of notes offers interested readers the opportunity of researching things for themselves.

Xenophobia and a 'swing to the right' have not been exclusive to Germany since the implosion of party communism. Elsewhere in Europe too, since the fall of the Iron Curtain, it is possible to identify an increase in racist violence and right-wing authoritarian sentiments among the population and in politics.[1]

However, there seems to me to be little point in invoking a 'European question' if this is meant to imply that detailed research is thereby rendered unnecessary. For example, in 1997 the European Parliament debated respect for human rights in the European Union in the year 1995. Various abuses were listed, but references to abuses in individual countries had to be omitted. In the case of Germany, this meant the omission of any of the violent attacks on centres for asylum-seekers.[2]

I have chosen Germany as a case study because in many respects it is Europe's engine room. Through German reunification the country has again become a fully fledged partner. Germany had been divided into three and occupied, but this unnatural situation has ended. This, in my view, calls for certain trends in Germany to be subjected to a thorough critical examination, without this automatically fuelling outdated anti-German sentiments or resentments.

My German colleagues, both journalists and historians, have been extraordinarily helpful to me in my research. I should like to take this opportunity of expressing my thanks to Roger Eatwell (Bath), Kurt Goldstein (Berlin), Professor Walter Grab (Tel Aviv), Gerke Hoekstra, the late Dr Lieuwe Hornstra (Freie Universität), Professor Georg Iggers (Buffalo), Monika Kadur and other staff of Amnesty International in Berlin, Josh Klemkow, Simon Wiesenthal, Ralf Wolz, Professor Wolfgang Wippermann (Freie Universität, Berlin), the former Akademie der Wissenschaften (East Berlin) and to the Presse- und Informationsamt der Bundesregierung.

I am particularly grateful to my teachers and friends, Sheila Browne (Oxford) and Professor Paul Valkenburgh (Vries). Without their co-operation, which was often accompanied by lively discussion, this book would not have been written. The findings are of course entirely the responsibility of the author.

This book was completed during the author's tenure of the Charlemagne Institute Fellowship.

Birkbeck College

Foreword

Germany has been ruled with brief interruptions by the political right wing for nearly all of the twentieth century: as monarchists, as Nazis and, after the Second World War, as Christian conservatives. Indeed, the very creation of the German national state in the late nineteenth century was performed by the right wing. (The German left, powerful as it sometimes became, was born in internationalism and became national only under the aegis of foreign occupation powers after the second great war.)

That lengthy history of the right wing has given it a primary role in the ever-developing German sense of national identity in all its aspects – from symbols like flags, salutes, anthems and uniforms to deciding fundamental matters such as who is authorised to be a German citizen and what territory must be considered inviolably 'German'. It lies at the heart of such tortured moments but also euphoric moments of the post-war era as the great national debate at the beginning of the 1970s over *Ostpolitik*. Again, the ever unresolved identity issue was reflected in the *Historikerstreit* nearly a decade later, in which historians fiercely debated the nature and degree of German guilt for the crimes of the Hitler regime.

One must acknowledge, however, that the political right was not all bad for Germany – that its representatives did much to build and consolidate a nation that once seemed almost hopelessly divided against itself, to preserve virtues such as diligence, public service and rectitude, and to erect a social system that blazed trails in looking after the underprivileged, to serve as a balance against anarchy and revolutionary chaos.

Furthermore, as Richard Lowenthal, the journalist and political thinker who was close to the Social Democratic Party for much of his career, once observed, what made the German Federal Republic work was 'that the German right finally accepted democracy'. Indeed, the evolution of the Federal Republic is unthinkable without the massive contributions of the right, however grave its shortcomings or faults. The problem was that the mainstream of the German right continually flirted with and sometimes fostered the extreme right, whether the outright anti-Semites of the Kaiser era, the Nazis in the inter-war period or, during the last decade, the various brands of neo-Nazis. In the case of Hitler, his rise to power could hardly have taken place without the massive assistance of Germany's bankers, industrialists and, ultimately, its conservative politicians.

That pattern was not repeated in the Federal Republic during the Cold War. Indeed, the extreme right was largely repressed by Federal authorities in West Germany and of course by the Communist Party in East Germany.

Only recently, since the fall of the Berlin Wall and unification of the two Germanys, has the extreme right re-emerged in more or less full flower – often with the ugliest sorts of manifestations such as brutal killings of foreigners and Hitlerite political revivals. The cynical formula of the mainstream conservatives – the Christian Democratic Union and its Bavarian partner, the Christian Social Union – was *rechts überholen*, overtaking on the right, which is fraught with danger in politics and in highway driving.

As the extreme right-wing groupings marched, rallied and promoted their xenophobic programmes, the Union parties, to the revulsion of many Germans, simply digested their ravings and regurgitated them in 'acceptable' formulas under their mainstream banners. Even the Social Democratic Party proved a bit susceptible to the siren songs of the rightists.

For its part, East Germany under the Communists perversely

preserved some rightist elements in its system, from Volksarmee uniforms and drills that strongly resembled those of the Wehrmacht to exaggerated nationalist pronouncements by politicians and historians in its latter years, as means to represent itself as genuinely 'German' to the broad public. Yet, politically stunted by four decades of one-party rule, East Germany became a fertile field for rightist extremist activities after the collapse of the Berlin Wall.

Now that a centrist–leftist coalition has taken the helm in national politics it may be possible to view the current role of the right and its extremist fringe a bit more dispassionately. We have J. H. Brinks to thank for a fresh and thorough analysis of this essential German problem.

David Binder

Introduction

In the first two years after the *Wiedervereinigung* (German Unification), racist violence and anti-Semitism assumed such alarming forms in Germany that the World Jewish Congress seriously considered whether punitive measures should be taken against the newly united Germany.[1] It struck many observers both inside and outside Germany as remarkable that things should have reached this point. It is true that racist violence and anti-Semitism are not an exclusively German preserve, but since the implosion of party Communism they are back on the agenda in Europe. However, the striking aspect of the violence in Germany is that it often goes hand in hand with a number of features that evoke grim memories. The fact is that many outrages against foreigners are often linked to Nazi views or symbolism. Violence against foreigners is obviously also a barometer for German reunification, in which the National-Socialist inheritance still plays a significant part.

The old Federal Republic had not also always found it easy to deal adequately with the legacy of the Third Reich. But all in all it can be argued that most young people in West Germany had certainly subjected the National-Socialist past to critical examination. The majority of West Germans became convinced that this legacy was not just a footnote in German history. The demonstrations against xenophobia and right-wing extremism that took place in Germany in 1992 also showed that many people were aware of their responsibility. These demonstrations came late, but they did come, and they showed that many Germans had sought a rapprochement with liberal and Western values such as were once expressed in the slogan of the French Revolution: *liberté, égalité, fraternité*.

However, and this was overlooked by many observers, those mass protests were directed not only against a racist undercurrent in both German societies: they also specifically targeted the conservative German politicians who for so long had avoided taking a stand against right-wing extremist violence. Many demonstrators accused the politicians of carrying a share of the responsibility for the escalating racist violence. Was this accusation justified? For some years there do indeed seem to have been processes at work in West German society that point to the increasing influence of right-wing authoritarian views. These developments do not date only from *after* German reunification.

In the old Federal Republic, right-wing radical views, of which racism is only one component, were promulgated mainly by a movement sometimes given the label 'New Right'. This largely publicity-oriented network believes, for example, that it is time to draw a line under the Third Reich. According to New Right, the way in which the National-Socialist past is dealt with in Germany is unrealistic and a 'gift' of the victorious Allies. They tend to play down the importance of the Third Reich to a large extent; sometimes they even deny its crimes. Second, the New Right sees the present German unification only as the second phase of the real reunification that is still to come. They believe that the true *Wiedervereinigung*, namely of the former Eastern territories of East Prussia, Pomerania and Silesia, is still imminent. That means that they do not recognise Poland's western border and see it as a kind of demarcation line. Third, New Right authors profess a form of racism. While they do not do so publicly and maintain that every race has a right to its own territory, in effect they are preaching a type of apartheid: a 'liberationist nationalism' is bound to lead to what they call 'ethnopluralism', a multiplicity of nations.

One may well say that these are right-wing Utopians, such as one finds in every country, and they have no social support, so what are we getting worked up about. But that is only partly true, because it looks as though in recent years some New Right views and sentiments have been increasingly widely adopted, especially by German conservatives. The Christlich Demokratische Union (CDU) and Christlich Soziale Union (CSU) were afraid of otherwise losing voters to the major New Right political grouping disseminating new-right ideas, namely to Franz Schönhuber's Republikaner. The German conservatives are tidying up some of New Right's manifesto points, after which they will be presented in an 'acceptable' way. The CSU in particular applied this technique with so much success that the Republikaner in 1998 felt obliged to respond with the slogan 'we keep the promises of the CSU'. But it is doubtful whether the ideas of Schönhuber and supporters can be neutralised in this way. Through this policy the conservatives appear to have helped prepare the fertile soil in which right-wing radical and extremist activities could flourish, and some points of view even gained a certain respectability.

Not entirely without justification, German critics of the conservative philosophy argued that the epicentre of right-wing violence committed since reunification seemed to be located very much in the centre of German society. Particularly in the *Historikerstreit*, a debate among academics on whether the Third Reich was 'unique' or not, in Chancellor Kohl's initial refusal to recognise the western Polish border, and during the 'asylum debate' in 1991 and 1992, it emerged that that the views of the Republikaner were lurking in the background. And, particularly after German reunification, it became clear that some sentiments and manifesto points of the Republikaner after all had wider public support than might have been assumed at first sight.

Not only did the German conservatives respond to right-wing authoritarian sentiments in the public at large, but the behaviour of the Sozialdemokratische Partei Deutschlands (SPD) does not inspire much confidence either. Under pressure from their rank and file, the Social Democrats collaborated in the indirect abolition of the right of asylum. In the light of these developments, the German writer

Günter Grass left the SPD in 1993. Grass, who nevertheless campaigned for the SPD in the 1998 Bundestag elections, and many other
German democrats seemed to realise that this 'pull to the right'
among the grass roots, which was followed by a 'pull to the right'
among the political elite, could jeopardise democratic structures. And
indeed the amendment of the German right to asylum was *partly* a
consequence of the attack in Rostock in East Germany.

The images of the violence in Hoyerswerda in 1991 and Rostock
in 1992 showed that xenophobic trends found fertile soil in the former
GDR. After the collapse of the Wall there was a huge upsurge of
xenophobia in East Germany. Here too the National-Socialist legacy
plays an important part, because it is especially in the former GDR
that the ethnically coloured violence, mostly carried out by young
people, goes hand in hand with Nazi symbols or ideas. Why is that?
There are many explanations, all of which are incomplete. Nevertheless I shall attempt to identify a number of possible motives for
this behaviour. It was mainly the German 'two-tier society' and the
disappointment of many East Germans at the failure of the promised
prosperity to materialise, which led younger people particularly to
resort to certain values and standards from their upbringing. There is
a relationship between the political culture in which these East Germans had grown up and right-wing authoritarian ideas.

The GDR tried to design a new 'socialist personality'. However,
this New Man was a theoretical construct, which had to be brought
to life by the imposition of a party line in East Germany. This social
regimentation was reminiscent of the Third Reich in its use of mass
symbols and political rituals and its close association with militarism.
The official military and paramilitary upbringing given to every East
German was on the Prussian, militaristic model. The Spartan upbringing began in the nursery and continued during paramilitary
training at primary and secondary school. After the collapse of the
Wall it seemed to some a small step from a *Wehrspartakiade*, a GDR
sports demonstration in various disciplines, to a paramilitary *Wehr-
sportgruppe*, a right-wing extremist militia.

In the GDR German identity and German nationalism were for a long time inseparable. One could even speak of an East German National Bolshevism. The East German Communist Party tried to create a synthesis of elements of nineteenth-century German nationalism and modern party Communism. However, particularly after the collapse of the Wall, it emerged that latent anti-Semitic and anti-Slav sentiments had been preserved in this combination. In the view of the film director Konrad Weiss, the 'violence principle' played an important part in East German society. In the GDR this 'violence principle' was elevated to a national virtue. Humanistic, liberal or democratic traditions did not seem to be really developing here. If these words had any meaning, it was often only in the service of the authoritarian state or of the party.

The GDR always propagated fairly authoritarian standards in its methods of upbringing. Values regarded as essentially socialist included the old 'Prussian virtues': order, discipline, punctuality, a sense of duty, cleanliness and physical toughness. These Prussian *Tugenden*, which were originally quite ascetic, were converted by the East German state into submissive virtues and they were often the *same* virtues that the New Right has been advocating for some years in West Germany. For some East Germans, joining forces with right-wing radical and 'national-revolutionary' groups was relatively easy, because in part the same values were being propagated in them as they were familiar with from their own training, namely authoritarian, nationalistic, 'socialist', anti-capitalist and revolutionary manifesto points.

Like the New Right and many a conservative politician, many young East Germans were anxious to draw a line under the legacy of the Third Reich as soon as possible after the collapse of the Wall. But, in part, these young people had other motives than right-wing radicals in West Germany.

What had happened to the legacy of the Third Reich in the GDR? One of the pillars of the first 'workers' and farmers' state on German soil' was 'anti-fascism'. Shortly after the Second World War the GDR had proclaimed itself the 'better Germany'. After all it was primarily the German Communists who had paid a heavy price in the struggle against National Socialism. The humanistic traditions of German history would have to be turned into reality in the German Democratic Republic. However, this legitimate anti-fascist claim quickly changed into a legitimising state dogma. East German 'anti-fascism' became a myth, or in the words of the Belgian historian Verbeeck, a 'foundation myth'.[2] The fact was that the East German state used 'anti-fascism' to justify the state and to legitimise itself in the eyes of its own population and of the outside world. The East German people as a whole were declared co-victors in the Second World War. This was not a case of 'inability to mourn' as was once observed in the old Federal Republic by the West German psychoanalysts Alexander and Margarete Mitscherlich, but rather an official prohibition. The official line, considered suitable for both domestic and foreign use, was more or less: 'Our Goethe, your Mengele.'

Even under the GDR dictatorship, some young people came to the conclusion that the system could be provoked and sabotaged by adopting a kind of anti 'anti-fascist' role. This was not surprising. From an early age small children were forced to visit the former concentration camps. There they were also, like soldiers in the former East German army, the Nationale Volksarmee, sworn in as 'socialists' in an 'anti-fascist' ritual. This latent anti 'anti-fascism' surfaced particularly after the collapse of the Wall, and was able to flourish, reinforced by the two-tier sciety and the 'asylum-debate'. The German government, unknowingly and unintentionally, further encouraged this by the wholesale renaming of streets and squares in the former GDR, which had been named after 'anti-fascist' party members. This policy was subsequently interpreted by some as an invitation to embark on their own anti 'anti-fascist' iconoclasm.

It is no easy task to account briefly for these trends in the reunited Germany. It seems clear that this 'pull to the right' at the grass roots should not be answered by a 'pull to the right' in the political establishment. This may, as many Germans feel, indeed subvert Germany's democratic political culture. Such a development would be particularly unfavourable for the East Germans because they have as yet scarcely become acquainted with democracy, and had not had sufficient time to identify with it.

Not only in the former GDR but also in the old Federal Republic, there is an observable increase in right-wing authoritarian sentiments, particularly among young people. One should not underestimate these developments. It is true, history does not repeat itself. But if one refuses to face the present and come to terms with the past some will be inclined to give old responses to new challenges.

Abbreviations and Acronyms

BvS	Bundesanstalt für vereinigungsbedingte Sonderausgaben
CDU	Christlich-Demokratische Union
CSU	Christlich-Soziale Union
DM	Deutschmark
DTSB	Deutscher Turn-und Sportbund
DVU	Deutsche Volksunion
EKD	Evangelische Kirche in Deutschland
EU	European Union
FAP	Freiheitliche Arbeiter Partei
FAZ	*Frankfurter Allgemeine Zeitung*
FDJ	Freie Deutsche Jugend
FDP	Freie Demokratische Partei
GDR	German Democratic Republic
GPU	Gosudarstvennoe Politiceskoe Upravlenie (name of Soviet secret police until 1934)
GST	Gesellschaft für Sport und Technik
IM	*Inoffizieller Mitarbeiter*
KPD	Kommunistische Partei Deutschlands
MfS	Ministerium für Staatssicherheit
NDPD	National Demokratische Partei Deutschlands
NSDAP	Nationalsozialistische Deutsche Arbeiterpartei
NVA	Nationale Volksarmee
PDS	Partei des Demokratischen Sozialismus
SA	*Sturmabteilung*
SD	*Sicherheitsdienst* (of the SS)

SED	Sozialistische Einheitspartei Deutschlands
SPD	Sozialdemokratische Partei Deutschlands
SS	*Schutzstaffel*
SZ	*Süddeutsche Zeitung*
TAZ	*Die Tageszeitung*

I

Background

1

German Partition: A Failed Judgement of Solomon and the Myth of the Class State

MOST West Germans equated the national identity of the former Federal Republic with the German constitution, the Deutschmark and a Western view of democracy. For the young offspring of the economic miracle of the 1950s and 1960s, national identity and constitutional patriotism were often one and the same. With this generation there was generally scarcely any question of an identification with Germany within its borders of, for example, 1871, 1937 or 1938. The majority of them seemed to have accepted German partition. As a result of this, for these young West Germans, Mallorca was much closer than Potsdam. They were often ignorant about the conditions under which the inhabitants of the 'first workers' and peasants' state on German soil' had to live.

But in large sections of the conservative West German political establishment the cry was: 'Germany divided into three? Never!' Despite the changed political map of Europe after 1945, West Germany kept on its long-term agenda the aim of reuniting the German territories within the borders of 31 December 1937. But it seemed as though German partition was final. It is often assumed that this division was purely the result of the policies of the Soviet Union. That is only partly true; partition was also maintained by the West. In fact, it is not impossible to see the West as responsible in the first instance for the division. In the view of the German journalist

3

Wolfgang Venohr, all the steps that led up to German partition originated from the Western and not from the Eastern side.[1] The Allies found their most loyal confederate in the conservative politician Konrad Adenauer. It was this Christian Democrat who was to tie the Western part of Germany closely to the West.

What was the thrust of this Western policy? To give a number of examples: on 20 June 1948 the old Reichsmark was abolished in the Western zones of Germany and the Deutschmark (DM) introduced. The Soviet Marshal Sokolovsky was bound to react to this, and did so three days later by introducing the Ostmark. This was just what the three Western Allies had been waiting for: the Deutschmark was now immediately introduced into the three Western sectors of Berlin. As is well known, Stalin reacted by blockading Berlin. He was afraid, not entirely without justification, that this Western enclave might disrupt the economy in the part of Germany occupied by the Soviet Union. On 23 May 1949 the West German constitution was proclaimed, forming the basis for the Federal Republic. On 15 September 1949 Konrad Adenauer became its first chancellor.

The reaction was not long in coming. On 7 October 1949 the German Democratic Republic was founded. Its first president was the Communist Party member Wilhelm Pieck, and the Social Democrat Otto Grotewohl was appointed prime minister. A few days later, on 10 October 1949, the head of the Soviet military administration, General Chuikov, transferred his authority to the government of the GDR. But these were all reactive measures from the Eastern side. For a long time the Soviet Union had pursued an active policy aimed at the restoration of German unity. On 10 March 1952 Stalin presented the famous memorandum which bears his name. This offer meant that German unity could be realised in exchange for a neutral and non-aligned Germany. But in response to this proposal, the Federal Republic signed the European Defence Community treaty in May of that year. This implied a clear rejection of Stalin's plan.

If one looks at the facts it does indeed look as if the West took the initiative in the whole process leading up to German partition. The

Western powers found their most important ally in Konrad Adenauer. In his book *Die roten Preußen*, Venohr described how Ernst Lemmer, a member of the executive of the West German and West Berlin Christian Democratic Union (CDU), told him as early as November 1951, 'Believe me, Mr Venohr, this Adenauer is a wicked, wicked man! He's fighting against everything that is Protestant and Prussian; he is fighting against Berlin! This man is determined to prevent the reunification of Germany with all the means at his disposal!'[2]

It was true that for Adenauer Protestantism and Prussian values were the seedbed of much national misery. Even at the time of the Weimar Republic he made it clear that as far as he was concerned the Prussians could be excluded from Germany. Adenauer also identified Prussia with National Socialism and with Communism. Both dictatorships had in his view originated in Prussia, which was later to be located mainly in the GDR. Adenauer's nightmare was that Germany might one day give up its link with the West. The West German ambassador in London, Hans Herwarth von Bittenfeld, stated in 1955 to the Minister of State at the British Foreign Office, Sir Ivon Kirkpatrick, that Adenauer had no confidence in the German people. He was reportedly very concerned that after he had disappeared from the political stage a future German government might ally itself with Russia to the detriment of Germany.[3] Adenauer preferred to identify himself completely with the Western Rhine Union traditions and the partition and occupation of Germany gave him the means to do this. Nor was it necessary for Berlin to become the capital of Germany again because for him that would be equivalent to a spiritual restoration of Prussia.

However, none of this prevented him from proclaiming the ultimate goal of German unity. Meanwhile West German political culture was changing at a great rate. The old Federal Republic always regarded itself as a German country, but nationalistic jingoism had quickly disappeared. In its place an Atlantic culture, which owed its existence in no little measure to the policies of Konrad Adenauer, grew up. In the Federal Republic an Americanised culture emerged, a Coca-Cola culture, as some critics maintained. Consequently, for some West Germans a stay in the GDR was like a rendezvous with the German past.

The course of East German history had been totally different from that of the old Federal Republic. In 1946, in the Soviet zone of occupation, the predecessor of the German Democratic Republic, the German Communist Party (KPD) and the German Social Democratic Party (SPD) merged to become the Sozialistische Einheitspartei Deutschlands (SED). Total power was centred in the hands of the Stalinist Walter Ulbricht. In the Eastern part of the defeated German Reich, the 'dictatorship of the proletariat' was put into practice under the leadership of a 'revolutionary elite party'. But in fact this meant simply the dictatorship of the party. As early as the third SED party rally in 1950 the East German Communist Party circulated a song with the refrain: 'The party, the party, it is always right'.[4]

The German Communists identified themselves with the tradition of their classic theorists. Marx, Engels and Lenin, but also Karl Liebknecht, August Bebel and many others, had once made an impressive plea for the revolutionary class state. 'The workers have no fatherland', as Marx and Engels had maintained in their Communist Manifesto, published in the revolutionary year of 1848. So it seemed that the German Democratic Republic could be grafted on to this pronouncement. But at the same time the founding fathers of the Communist Party had already at a very early stage come out in favour of a united Germany. For later East German Communists this meant a split national consciousness. Consequently, it is not surprising that this national double book-keeping led to a double morality on the national question. Whatever path the East German Communists followed, that of German unity, or of the German class state, which would imply partition, a dilemma of a bad national conscience lay in wait: either united, but not truly revolutionary, or revolutionary, but not really united.

Moreover, the national identity of the Germans had frequently been the subject of critical and gloomy reflection. Even the question of where Germany was could not always be answered satisfactorily. Goethe once summarised this question succinctly: *Deutschland? Aber wo liegt es?* ('Germany? But where is it?'). Karl Marx pointed out at an early date the lack of a national identity among his compatriots. In March 1843 he went so far as to maintain, 'The most insignificant Dutchman is still a citizen compared with the greatest German.'[5] This outburst portrayed a typical phenomenon which can be characterised as German self-hatred. This self-hatred and the double morality relating to national identity were never entirely overcome by the German Communists and by some Social Democrats. On the one hand these *Vaterlandslose Gesellen* (fellows without a fatherland) promoted the idea of the class state, which was intended to initiate a revolutionary Germany. On the other hand, they could not entirely abandon the idea of pan-German unity. Consequently, it was not surprising, in view of these characteristics of the 'workman without a country', that 'left-wing' and 'right-wing' manifesto points could sometimes be united in a single person.

During a discussion in 1987 with a senior SED official at the Humboldt University in East Berlin, I was confronted with this dichotomy. With an expansive gesture of his hand my interlocutor maintained that the GDR was a *weltoffenes Land*, a 'country open to the world'. He probably assumed that I would not contradict him: after all I was being allowed to carry out research in the GDR. And presumably he was expecting some expression of thanks, at least in the form of a decorous silence. However, I interrupted him and, pointing in the direction of the Brandenburg Gate, said, 'Yes, and it ends there!' To my astonishment he broke into a smile and said, almost with relief, 'That's a good one! That's a good one! All that left-wing nonsense! It's all pointless!' He had, as was clearly apparent, a conservative mentality. And this attitude was shared by many of his compatriots. It was a time when Franz Josef Strauss was the most popular German politician in the GDR.

The theme of German unity occupied even the most convinced Stalinists. It was not only the conservative West German establishment that persisted in its demand for the undoing of German partition. The Eastern part of Germany also emphatically demanded a united Germany up to the mid-1950s. Despite, and after 1961 perhaps partly because of, the Wall, the East Germans developed into 'more German' Germans than the citizens of the Federal Republic. In East Germany, not only many aspects of German-ness, the sense of being German, but of nationalist jingoism had been well preserved. The majority of East Germans were constantly aware of being German, not least to remind the West and the Russian occupier that East Germans were of German origin. In this way one could point out to both of them that German division was something unnatural. But not only the grass roots but also East German politics had deliberately kept the sense of German-ness alive. At the beginning of the 1950s, in his 'turn towards nationalism', the then party leader Ulbricht had even used German nationalism to legitimise the party and the state. In those years the official East German demand was emphatically: 'Germans around a single table'.[6]

Ulbricht regarded himself as an historian. In 1963 the party leader went so far as to declare in the central organ of the SED, *Neues Deutschland*, that 'history has for a long time so to speak been my third profession' (he was also party leader and earlier he had worked as a carpenter).[7] For Ulbricht, West Germany was a 'zone in which the law of the jungle prevailed' in which 'the honest labour of the workers counted for little and the black marketeers prospered. Here a kind of nature reserve was created for war criminals and enemies of the people, for junkers and war profiteers.'[8] With his hand on the historical atlas he constantly demanded German unity. One of his most important demands was that the American occupiers should withdraw from German soil. The renowned East German historian Albert Norden went so far as to appeal to the most recent anti-Americanism of the Germans. In his book *Um die Nation* (*Concerning the Nation*) of 1952 he stated that 'The strategy of the USA' was based 'on the crushing of Germany'. Therefore, in Norden's view, 'for the decent former German officer and NCO and for every

German there is only one alternative: he must resist and oppose the Americans who are intent on causing a world conflagration with the same courage with which he once waged war'.[9] In order to add force to this demand Ulbricht appealed to German history. For example, he maintained, following Engels and Fichte, that the ancient Germans had fought against foreign domination ever since the battle against the Roman legions in the Teutoburg Forest. The Germans, he argued, were 'free people whose personal industry and courage were far superior to those of the Roman troops. They fought for the liberation of their country.'[10] Ulbricht was still largely in the jingoistic tradition of nineteenth-century German nationalism.

Particularly after 1815 a political philosophy developed in the German territories that appealed to traditions of mystification. Germany was to be found, in the view of these romantics, wherever German culture prevailed and wherever German was spoken. An important aspect of this nineteenth-century German nationalism was the exclusion from the concept of German of 'identifiable' non-Germans living on German territory. This mainly applied to the Slav peoples: Czechs, Poles and Russians were often ruled out as 'lazy' and 'dirty'. These rulings also served to camouflage social oppositions within Germany. Like nationalism, this is not an exclusively German phenomenon, but an important subsidiary function of all nationalism, particularly the kind formulated in 'ethnic' terms.

The romantic myths developed in the nineteenth century were adopted by nationalistic German historians and politicians. They tried to forge into a congruent unity German culture, the German nation and the German state. Not only anti-Slav sentiments but anti-Semitism increased, and, particularly after the foundation of the Reich by Bismarck in 1871, anti-Semitism often became an accepted and *salon-fähig* phenomenon, a topic of conversation in society drawing rooms.

In the 1950s the East German party historians were still largely rooted in the nationalistic traditions of the nineteenth century. One of them, Leo Stern, defined quite precisely the historic mission of German history. He maintained that it was the task of East German historical scholarship to show 'that German history is rich in great and shining examples of courage, heroism, patriotism and devotion to the great cause of the German people'.[11] The GDR began to cultivate more and more actively a German national consciousness, and the 'nation' and the willingness to defend it gained great social importance.

This was an event of considerable significance. The fact was that after 1945 a large proportion of East Germans suffered from the shattered sense of national identity. As early as the 1950s, this new East German feeling of *Heimat* led to familiar formulations. In 1954, for example, the GDR historian Ernst Engelberg maintained that the miners in the Erz mountains in the nineteenth century had a '*gesundes Volksempfinden*', that is an expression of *lingua tertii imperii* or 'language of the Third Reich', for 'healthy national sense'.[12] The East German historian Max Steinmetz spoke in 1965 in relation to the German contemporaries of Dürer of the 'high degree of mental originality of Germans'.[13] Such statements did not seem to worry Ulbricht. On the contrary, the head of the party and the head of the state went so far as to stimulate this German nationalism.

The importance of German history for the East German Communist Party can scarcely be overestimated. The role of Marxist-Leninist historical scholarship in the GDR was like that of theology in a theocracy. Every political measure was given an historical basis. Conversely, (German) history was written in such a way that it could be seen only as a prelude to the SED and the GDR.

For Marxist-Leninist historians the dominant view of history was the completely politicised view of Ernst Thälmann, the leader of the Kommunistische Partei Deutschlands (KPD) in the Weimar Republic, who once maintained that 'politics is history that takes place in the present. One must try to get closer to the essence of history if one is to understand the essence of politics.'[14] For the East German Communists there was only one politically correct line, which was also projected back into the past.

Meanwhile Adenauer persisted in his wish to keep 'red Prussia' out of West Germany. After the failure of the Geneva Conference in 1955 Khrushchev had also had enough. During a stop-over in East Berlin in 1955, he and Bulganin announced that the Soviet Union would support an independent GDR as well as its good 'socialist' achievements. Probably both Adenauer and Ulbricht breathed a sigh of relief, but Ulbricht particularly must have felt that a great weight had been lifted from his shoulders. He had after all seen that the Kremlin had been prepared to drop him. Particularly after the popular uprising of 17 June 1953, the East German Communist Party gradually accepted the German partition as a *fait accompli*, although a back door to 'German unity' remained open.

Ulbricht never lost his German nationalism. For him, national identity and nationalism were synonymous. Honecker immediately and drastically changed his predecessor's 'German nationalist' policies. He tried to give shape to the concept of a 'socialist nation'. For a definition of the GDR, which was characterised as a 'nation of the new type', it was no longer ethnic (German) but mainly social and economic criteria that applied. In other words, a state becomes a state only through social and economic organisation and not through its ethnic constitution.[15] In this system the concept 'German' even became taboo for a number of years, and the Federal Republic for some time was explicitly designated as a foreign country. After Honecker's assumption of power in 1971 there was an 'anti-German' campaign among the GDR's officials. Wherever possible the term 'German' was removed from names. It was no longer permitted even to sing the text of the national anthem, since that referred to 'Germany, united fatherland'. This led to the grotesque situation that one could now solemnly begin the national anthem with 'Mmm Mmm Mmm'. Many East Germans probably regarded this course of events as a great humiliation.

Honecker was not able to maintain this 'anti-German' campaign for long. On 12 December 1974 he returned to his old principles and again made a distinction between citizenship and nationality. It was not right, said Honecker, that there should be ambiguity in the filling

in of forms. From now on the rule was 'unambivalently: citizenship
– GDR, nationality – German. That's how things are.'[16]

That was indeed how things were. Honecker had to acknowledge
the German *identity* of his citizens. This identity was German and
could not be sacrificed to an empty formula that was removed from
reality. Later Honecker even promoted the formula of 'socialism in
the colours of the GDR'. In this way he wanted once more to
emphasise German identity, and for the time being the desire for a
reunified Germany seemed to have had its day.

After Honecker became the head of the party and state in 1971 the
GDR appeared finally to have resigned itself to German partition. Yet
after a number of years something strange happened to East German
national identity. This first became apparent when the official evalu-
ation of German history changed. The Germans in the GDR followed
this change very closely. From 1976/77 onwards the GDR again
emphatically considered itself a *German* state. It even resorted to the
whole and *undivided* history of Germany, formally to legitimise the
divided German nation. And it was the arch-enemies of Adenauer,
namely the old Prussians and Lutheranism, who again took centre
stage: Luther, Frederick II and Bismarck were once more completely
salonfähig in East Germany. It was obvious that this trend would
encourage a feeling of inter-German solidarity. But might it not also
reactivate nationalist sentiment and resentment?

Most East Germans felt a desire to be reunified with the Federal
Republic, but this was considered to be no longer a political reality.
After the collapse of the Wall the *Wiedervereinigung* (German unification) was given a heartfelt welcome by the great majority of Germans
in the GDR. The national consciousness of the East Germans was
after all rooted in a *single and undivided* German history. Many
Germans in both East and West also probably regarded unification in
its first hours as a spiritual symbiosis. However, this union was soon
followed by a new kind of partition. The bitterness that occurs when
a desire for such a bond fails might help to explain why the dis-
appointments, particularly for the weaker party, were so intense.

2

The Two-tier Society: A New Partition?

Morality can never be achieved through the device of institutions: and, because socialism strives for institutions, it remains political; it can criticise, abolish abuses, attain rights: it will never be able to change life on earth because that power is reserved for philosophy, faith, the transcendental idea. However, when the shortcomings of socialism become clear it should be no cause for rejoicing among those who oppose it from a facile preference for the existing order, from fear of having to make sacrifices and out of emotional laziness. (Walther Rathenau, *Von kommenden Dingen*, 1918, p. 15)

THE joy on both sides at inter-German unity turned out to be of short duration. Almost a year after the *Wende*, or turning point, the West German Emnid Institute came to the conclusion that almost one in three West Germans was against reunification. And, of the new Federal citizens, 78 per cent felt that in the long run they would be treated as second-class citizens.[1] At the end of 1997 three out of four East Germans still believed they were second-class citizens. Indeed, it was striking that this feeling had grown stronger.[2] At grass-roots level particularly, increasing dissatisfaction with the unpleasant consequences of reunification led some younger East Germans to become receptive to types of xenophobia and to identify with right-wing authoritarian points of view. As an outsider, one could easily point to Central and Eastern European neighbours whose situation was far worse than that of the new Federal citizens. This did not

13

detract from the fact that, after the unification, many East Germans
found that Communist Party propaganda about the West turned out
to be partly true.

A high level of unemployment, feelings of pointlessness and
violence became part of the new social and intellectual reality. The
majority of East Germans still welcomed the fall of the Wall, but the
state treaty concluded in 1990 gave insufficient protection to the rights
of the new Federal citizens. This *Einigungsvertrag* between West and
East Germany was felt by many new Federal citizens to be a *diktat*.
For example, quite soon after the introduction of the Deutschmark,
the *Handelsorganisationen* (HOs) introduced a policy based on no
longer buying any GDR products. Instead, West German goods were
bought. Cows were reared with their own milk, whole herds were
slaughtered, and eggs and many other products were recycled. A
consequence of this market policy was that unemployment rose much
higher among the population of the new Federal territories than had
been originally predicted. The number of unemployed rose daily –
more or less camouflaged by concepts such as 'a part-timer working
zero hours per week', work creation measures, retraining, early-
retirement schemes, and so on. By mid-1991 there were over three
million unemployed and part-timers in the former GDR. As early as
August 1991, the West Berlin political scientist Hajo Funke stated
that experts expected that the percentage of unemployed part-timers
would rise to between 40 and 60 per cent by mid-1992.[3] And indeed,
according to the weekly *Der Spiegel,* by mid-1992 between 40 and 50
per cent of employees in the new Federal territories had no regular
employment.[4] Serious experts, said Funke as early as 1991, cannot
assess whether or when there will be a recovery.[5]

Since German unification there has been a constant rise in the
number of unemployed. In December 1997 in the whole of Germany
a total of 4,521,583 people were unemployed. The percentage of
unemployed for the whole of the Federal Republic was 11.8 per cent.
In the former GDR, however, unemployment was almost twice as
high, totalling 19.4 per cent as opposed to 9.9 per cent in the West.

This was the highest number of unemployed in the history of the Federal Republic.[6]

Every month 9,000 jobs were lost in East Germany in 1997.[7] Many East Germans probably understand that this situation will have to continue for some time in order to create prospects for the future. Nevertheless there are aspects of reunification that most East Germans simply fail to understand.

To take another example: Article 41 of the Unification Treaty contained the provision that all citizens who had left the GDR between 1949 and 1961, and their descendants, could assert their rights to their previous property. Many descendants of East Germans who had been expelled or had fled discovered that there was something to be gained in the new Federal territories. Hundreds of thousands now demanded through their lawyers land and buildings in places where they themselves had often never been, despite the compensation that previous owners had received from the West German government for the loss of their property. Partly because of this they were able to integrate in West German society and identified with Atlantic and Western values. The principle of 'restitution overrides compensation' that prevailed in the Unification Agreement was in fact somewhat unjust – all the more so since for a long time GDR citizens had to make reparations to the Soviet Union for the World War they had lost, while West Germany was already receiving Marshall Aid.

The fury of many East Germans at the (imminent) surrender of hearth and home was considerable. During a television report in 1992 on the East Berlin village of Klein Machnow, the mood was so hostile that during the filming my film crew and I were jeered at by inhabitants. That was not surprising, because the villagers thought we were employees of agents who came to film or photograph their future property with great regularity. In total there are over one million claims to 1.5 million properties. In communities like Klein Machnow, Teltow or Stansdorf, south of Berlin, 70 per cent of the houses are being claimed by West Germans. It is quite possible that a large number of these requests will be honoured.

The effect this had and continues to have on the East German population is dire. A considerable majority of East Germans literally retreated into their own homes and summerhouses during the SED regime. In a kind of *innere Emigration*, all their time, energy and money were invested in the improvement of their own living conditions. Now many people were threatened with having to leave and this course of events naturally caused a lot of bad blood. As a result, the minister of employment, the Christian Democrat Norbert Blüm, spoke quite soon after the *Wende* of an approaching social catastrophe in the new Federal territories.

One of the reasons why there is only a laborious recovery in the ex-GDR is the uncertainty about who are to be the new owners of land and properties. Partly as a result of this, the West German Treuhandanstalt, the body that managed the bankrupt property of the former GDR, did not operate efficiently.[8] This was because it could not sell any land or property before ownership was clear. This is also one of the reasons why the new Federal territories are an uncertain and unattractive area for investment. The large companies that are investing in the former GDR are meanwhile pocketing large sums in investment incentives. It would have been more socially just to use this money to reform East German companies. However, that would imply that for a long time to come many companies would make very little or no profit. Meanwhile it was very difficult to persuade West German workers to move to the new Federal territories. Some of them even preferred to commute daily to the West by aeroplane.

But unemployment and questions of property ownership were not the only burden on reunification. Rents rose and many new Federal citizens were afraid that they would not be able to afford the increases. Some East Germans could see no future for themselves. These fears, real or otherwise, led to alienation, despair and sometimes even suicide. They again tried to get out of this new impoverishment by using the Deutschmark as a vehicle of national and personal identity. This sometimes led to an unbridled money fetishism, an anti-social, nineteenth-century *laissez-faire* capitalism. The German writer Günter

Grass spoke in this connection of 'the new Manchester-style capitalism'.

An important question is whether these problems could have been
foreseen – and, if so, why almost no one pointed out these transitional
phenomena of German unity to the East Germans. During the
process of German reunification and even afterwards, the fear of
Germany becoming larger and more powerful was often exorcised
with the formula: we need not be afraid because history will not
repeat itself. At the same time, however, many people assumed that
the history of the economic miracle *would* repeat itself. This was a
daring assumption, in view of the predicted collapse of Central and
Eastern European markets, since they had been the most important
economic partners of the former GDR.

In addition, wages were adjusted too quickly to the West German
level and were completely detached from the increase in productivity.
Excessive wage costs and low productivity compared with West Germany, together with a lack of know-how on the part of entrepreneurs
and often an insufficient supply of capital, also contributed to the
loss of many tens of thousands of jobs in East Germany in 1997.

The possibility, to use an historical analogy, that for example a
Gründerkrach might take place, was not contemplated. (The *Gründerkrach* was the great and protracted economic crisis that took place
after the foundation of the Reich in 1871.) But it was not the done
thing to criticise German reunification. When Günter Grass was asked
in a television interview what gave him the right to oppose unification, he replied in annoyance that it was the right of freedom of
expression.

One of the critics of the course of events was Wolfgang Herles.
Herles is one of the most renowned West German political television
journalists. Literally and figuratively, he had a front-row seat at the
process of German reunification. The title of his 1990 book, *Nationalrausch (National Intoxication)*, indicated the tenor of his findings.[9] His
conclusion was that through unification with the GDR a nationalist
virus would spread through the whole of Germany. Almost no one

had considered the possibility of a federation, confederation or 'Austrian' model. His point was not that the unification should actually have happened in one or other of those ways. The cardinal point of his argument was that these options were not up for debate and were as little open to discussion as the great economic problems that could be expected.

The chief news editor of the West German TV station WDR, Fritz Pleitgen, went so far as to maintain at a press conference: 'We haven't the courage to discuss German unity, nor dare we say anything about the heroic people of the GDR. We trumpet what Kohl and Vogel say. We practise jovial journalism. On German unity, we've gone along with the tide out of pure fear.'[10]

There were a number of policy-makers who had reservations about rapid German unification because of its negative consequences. The president of the Bundesbank, Karl-Otto Pöhl, described the introduction of the Deutschmark in the new Federal territories as a 'failure' and resigned in 1991. Meanwhile Chancellor Kohl remained optimistic. 'No one will be worse off,' he stated in the spring of 1990, 'but many people will be better off.' In October of that year he went so far as to maintain that East Germany would be a 'blossoming landscape' within a few years and he maintained that he knew 'dozens not to say hundreds of entrepreneurs' who were 'on the point of investing in the new Federal territories'. He asserted that 'in the Federal Republic nobody has to give up anything because of Germany's unification'.

The chancellor made a further pronouncement, which was to have far-reaching consequences for inter-German relations. He announced that taxes would not be raised. This also turned out to be too optimistic, although this was not just because of the 'solidarity contribution' that West Germans had to pay for reunification.

According to Klaus Dreher, who for many years led the *Süddeutsche Zeitung* team in Bonn, Kohl knew as early as 19 December 1989, when he visited the GDR for the first time since the collapse of the Wall, that the GDR was in serious economic difficulties. At the moment when Kohl addressed his audience in front of the Frauen-kirche in Dresden, he had just had a discussion with Hans Modrow, the then prime minister of the GDR. Modrow had asked him for a loan of DM 15 billion, because otherwise public life in the GDR would collapse. A little later Modrow travelled to Moscow. Because Kohl also had good relations with Gorbachev, the chancellor knew at an early stage that the GDR was bankrupt. Kohl knew that the SED leaders had asked the Soviet Union in vain for help. His later assertion that the collapse of the economy of the Eastern bloc states could not be foreseen at the time was wrong. In the view of Dreher, whose biography of Kohl appeared in 1998, no one was better informed than Kohl.

On 30 January 1991 Kohl admitted to the Bundestag that the costs of German unity could no longer be financed without tax rises. The 'solidarity supplement' was introduced on 1 July.[11] In September 1997 the German national debt totalled DM 2.13 trillion, a new post-war record.[12] Both West and East Germans should have been made aware from the beginning of the long-term economic, social and psychological difficulties of the unification. They were foreseeable.

It is important to consider the psychological dimension. The East German psychiatrist Hans Joachim Maaz maintained in his study, *Der Gefühlsstau. Ein Psychogramm der DDR*, of 1990, on the 'pent-up emotions' of his compatriots, that there was no question of a revolution in the GDR.[13] In his view the necessary 'psychological revolution' had failed to materialise and all the old psychological structures were still intact. He believed that people had not distanced themselves sufficiently from authoritarian structures. The revolution in the GDR turned out to be a package of demands formulated in a negative way. The small group of genuine revolutionaries, including the East German opposition movement Neues Forum, which stressed the importance of sincere changes, ended up together with the GDR on the rubbish heap of history when they had fulfilled their very short-lived function as a revolutionary avant-garde. To put it briefly, the ex-GDR citizen has only two options: either there is a process of

absorption and grieving, during which many people will come to the
conclusion that they are both the culprits and the victims; or, in
order to ward off this unpleasant conclusion, they may have to find
a new target for their rage, which might present itself in the form of
new enemies. The old target, the SED, is no more. Since the *Wende*,
in the face of threatening material and non-material problems, many
younger East Germans have resorted to an extremely aggressive
racism. Maaz, following Bertolt Brecht, maintains that the womb of
the monster which bore National Socialism is still fertile.[14] Indeed,
the restorationist tendencies of the only partially successful revolution
in the GDR must not be underestimated. But even if the wish is
there, the opportunities for the new Federal citizens to concern
themselves actively with the National Socialist and Communist past
are, at present, very scarce. From the look of it people will have
other concerns for many years to come.

A 'psychological revolution' in the former GDR would, however,
need to go hand in hand with a shift in consciousness in West
Germany. This applies not only to the obvious arrogance of some
West Germans towards their new compatriots.[15] For many years the
GDR also offered an excuse for not facing one's own past, which
sometimes had not yet been dealt with. As early as 1967 the West
German husband-and-wife writing team of Alexander and Margarete
Mitscherlich argued that the Federal Republic and the GDR were
blaming each other for the legacy of the Third Reich. There was not
sufficient real confrontation of the past. The result of this was that
both Germanys saw in each other's existence a legitimisation of their
own suppression. Therefore it was, in the opinion of the Mitscher-
lichs, questionable how Germany would react if there was also a
question of a severe economic burden.[16] The mutual excuse for not
coming to terms with the past has now disappeared and, moreover,
economic prospects are less rosy than expected.

The new Germany was regarded by many people not only *de jure*,
but also *de facto* as a continuation of the Federal Republic with five
new states. It was to be expected that in the former GDR there could

not be an immediate identification with a democratic political culture. According to representative surveys in 1994, half of East Germans were not satisfied with 'democracy on the West German model'. The majority of East Germans, it is true, accepted the new political system (in 1994, 52 per cent judged this system in a positive way, while in 1990 the figure was 75 per cent), but many people, according to Professor Rolf Reißig of the Institute for Social Sciences in East Berlin, accepted it 'only because of its efficiency or as a matter of adaptation rather than of conviction'.[17] This trend has continued, particularly among younger people. In 1997 most East Germans were of the opinion that it had been basically right to transfer the West German political order to the new Federal territories. However, in reply to the question whether the 'democracy that we have in the Federal Republic' is the 'best political system', 60 per cent of West Germans gave a positive answer in 1997, while only 26 per cent of East Germans in the same age group (14–29) shared this opinion.[18]

For many East Germans, Western liberal democracy has only a relative value. This emerged at an early date when in July 1992 the 'committees for justice' were set up in the new Federal territories, which had the protection of Manfred Stolpe, the Social Democrat prime minister of Brandenburg. One of the intellectual fathers of these 'committees for justice' was the East German historian Ernst Engelberg. Engelberg put his definition of democracy clearly into words in 1965. At the time he maintained that 'democracy and dictatorship are not opposites. The question is always: Democracy for whom? Dictatorship against whom? ... In reality parliamentary bourgeois democracy is on the one hand a means of balancing the interests of various factions of the urban and national capitalists; on the other hand, it is a means of suppressing the workers and other employees.'[19]

But this formulation of Engelberg's showed great similarities with the views of the conservative revolutionary theoretician Carl Schmitt, active in the Weimar period. Schmitt is now often regarded as one of the precursors and fellow-travellers of the Third Reich. This political commentator also maintained that dictatorship and democracy are not opposites. On the contrary, in his view dictatorship was in fact the most consistent realisation of democracy, and 'in this sense ... every genuine state is a total state'.[20]

Democracy consists of two components: on the one hand a political democratic culture, and on the other hand, democratic institutions. The latter, as has been shown by German unification, can be introduced relatively quickly. The former, however, will take much longer. The tense situation, particularly in the new Federal territories, was partly inevitable. The people and the politicians had decided that there should be a rapid German reunification. However, what could have been avoided was the way in which this proceeded. Populism, jingoism and false promises by politicians created much resentment. After the *Wende* this resentment was vented on 'foreigners'. But xenophobia was not solely a result of reunification. It was also a product of East German society.

3

Xenophobia and Right-wing Radical Tendencies among Young People in East Germany

IN the study of right-wing extremism and militant racism in the former GDR two things strike one immediately. On the one hand, the manifestations are much more violent in the new Federal territories than in the old Federal Republic.[1] On the other hand, there are clear quantitative differences between East and West Germany. The internal security service, the Bundesamt für Verfassungsschutz, stated in relation to the year 1997 that 45 per cent of all right-wing radical crimes of violence were committed in the East, though only 17 per cent of Germans live there.[2] This is very remarkable, especially as the proportion of foreigners in the former GDR in 1998 was less than 2 per cent of the population.

Such differences between East and West are also reflected in a tendency among young people to vote for right-wing radical parties. While in 1998 in Western Germany 'only' one in ten young persons said, in answer to a survey by Forsa, that they would be prepared to vote for a right-wing radical party, in the former GDR one in six said they were willing to do so. This means that the pool of youngsters willing to vote for a right-wing party has almost doubled since 1995. In the old Federal Republic 23 per cent of the young interviewees argued that it should be possible to deport foreigners any day, whereas in the new *Länder* every third youngster held this opinion.[3] How can this be explained?

A considerable time before the collapse of the Wall it was apparent that many East Germans had an ambivalent attitude towards 'foreigners'. On the one hand, their views were largely determined by a mixture of jealousy and feelings of inferiority in respect of Westerners, who were by definition affluent – and they often behaved accordingly. On the other hand, the foreigner was regularly identified as one of the contract workers originating from Africa and Asia. These *Vertragswerktätige*, also popularly known as 'VWs', worked in East Germany for very low wages. There was scarcely any contact between East Germans and these guest workers; they were ostracised by the native population. There were never expressions of real solidarity between the two population groups. One of the reasons for this dismissive attitude of many East Germans towards Africans and Asians turned out to be latent racism. After the *Wende* this racism became particularly apparent in young East Germans.

In 1990 the Deutsche Jugendinstitut in Munich came to a number of remarkable conclusions. In the territory of the former GDR 40 per cent of those interviewed regarded foreigners as 'a nuisance', while in the former Federal Republic this was 'only' 25 per cent.[4]

A survey in Leipzig also seemed to confirm this tendency. In the months of November and December 1990 a study was conducted under the title: 'East German Youth: Attitudes to Foreigners and to a Number of Topical Political Problems'. It emerged in this survey that approximately half of the young people interviewed believed that there were too many foreigners living in East Germany. This view was particularly widespread among young trainees (70 per cent). Forty-five per cent of school children held this opinion, and 31 per cent of students agreed. Therefore 55 per cent believed that 'the proportion of foreigners in East Germany must be reduced'. Only 17 per cent did not share this opinion. These results are striking because in 1990 foreigners made up only approximately 1 per cent of the East German population.

Young East Germans generally had strongly ethnocentrically coloured likes and dislikes. But there was a particularly 'negative, hostile attitude' to Vietnamese, gypsies and Turks. Turks particularly had a very hard time and were described as decidedly 'unpleasant'.[5] And this in spite of the fact that before the collapse of the Wall most East Germans had scarcely, if ever, met a Turk. This attitude was not without consequences. Since unification, many Turks have refused to move to the *neue Länder* for fear of being attacked by right-wing extremists. After reunification the Vietnamese were the main target of East German racism. The conditions under which they had to live and work in the former GDR were mostly degrading. For example, in its treaties with Vietnam, the GDR had included the provision that Vietnamese women could not have any children in East Germany or live there with their families. During their stay in the GDR they were accommodated in unpleasant tenement blocks that East Germans usually avoided.

Soon after the *Wende*, racist sentiments were expressed more in the new Federal territories than in the former Federal Republic. But the prime minister of Saxony, Kurt Biedenkopf, who originated from West Germany, believed that things would not get out of hand. In his view it was only a 'marginal phenomenon of the upheaval'.[6] However, racist agitation in East Germany does not date from the collapse of the Wall. A considerable time before this turning point, young East German right-wing radicals agitated against Turks (*Kanaken*), Africans (*Kohle*) and Vietnamese (*Fidschis*). Russians and Poles were not spared this fate either. The aggression of these right-wing radicals was also focused on 'left-wing swine', homosexuals and punks – in short, against everyone who in their eyes had an 'un-German' appearance. There was also resentment against Jews, which resulted in some desecration of Jewish graves.

As early as the beginning of the 1980s, the police in the GDR registered the rise of right-wing radical activities. Various sub-cultures – Nazi skinheads, hooligans and Nazi heavy metal groups – organised themselves into associations that resembled semi-military *Wehrsportgruppen*. No publicity was given to the phenomenon in the GDR. Reports on them remained top secret. After all, the GDR had legitimised the building of the Wall in 1961 as an 'anti-fascist bulwark' against the West and therefore it was simply impossible for 'fascism' to exist in the GDR and hence it did not exist. Before the building of the Wall, fascist activities in East Germany could still be dismissed with the assertion that they were a provocation by the West. After 1961 the motto seemed to be: What isn't allowed does not exist. There was then, it is true, only a very small group of younger people with right-wing radical sympathies without any political significance. But from an early period their activities were observed by some average East German citizens (*stinknormale Bürger* or *'Stinos'*) with a certain passive tolerance, a clandestine pleasure. At least these young right-wing radicals had the nerve to rebel against the state and the party: most citizens did not have this kind of courage.

Shortly after the collapse of the Wall, the aggression and intolerance spread throughout the GDR. In an informal conversation in 1990, a minister from the transitional government of the East German prime minister, Hans Modrow, gave a number of examples. There appeared to be, the politician maintained, a constant stream of bomb alerts and death threats to members of the government and their families. Alarming forecasts were circulating of the problem of right-wing extremism. Once again these did not attract the attention they deserved. Usually they were not talked about, or people pointed to the imminent reunification, which would solve everything. But by now there was a serious problem. At the end of 1991 it became clear from the study 'Right-wing extremism and neo-Nazism among young East Berliners' that over 30 per cent of those aged between 15 and 20 who were interviewed had a 'worrying right-wing extremist stance'. Ten per cent considered themselves as belonging to the right-wing radical sub-culture or were in sympathy with it. The same number were of the opinion that Germany again 'needed a strong leader'. Almost 25 per cent wanted to keep the German nation pure. One-quarter of those included in the survey went so far as to believe that the use of violence against property or persons could be effective. Ten per cent believed that attacks were a legitimate means of political debate.[7]

It became clear during the first anniversary of German unity that these results were not purely paper tigers. Such a wave of racist violence swept through Germany that the Federal president, Richard von Weizsäcker, felt obliged to make a statement in which he reminded his compatriots of the first article of the German constitution. This article maintains that human dignity is inviolable. And that applied, said von Weizsäcker, to all human beings: 'Foreigners are just as much human beings as Germans. It is a human duty to respect their dignity.'

At the height of the right-wing extremist violence in 1992, 2,639 violent crimes were recorded. According to the internal security service, there has been a drop of 70 per cent if one compares those figures with 1996. The number of non-violent crimes fell by 5 per cent compared to its highest number (8,329) in 1993.[8] But the actual numbers are probably much higher, not only because victims often do not dare to report them for fear of reprisals. According to the newspaper *Der Tagesspiegel*, German security services recorded for the year 1997 11,720 offences with a right-wing and xenophobic background, that is the highest number since German unification. The number of violent crimes was estimated at 1,092.[9] However, according to some officials, the minister of the interior, Manfred Kanther, was delaying the publication of these figures.[10]

These are alarming figures for the united Germany, but the situation is particularly acute in the new Federal territories. Sometimes the authorities in East Germany even advise people from ethnic minorities not to go out in the evenings, or in any case not alone.

The crude manifestation of racism in the ex-GDR was also initially facilitated by a power vacuum. The police had been discredited because of their SED past and if they did intervene, they ran the risk of physical injury. In addition they turned out not to be prepared for social phenomena whose existence they knew of only through television. A notorious example were the riots in Magdeburg during the celebration of the East German *Herrentag* on Ascension Day in 1994. During this public holiday Africans were chased through the town centre by East German right-wing radicals. The chief of police played down these attacks by calling them *ausgeufertes Brauchtum*, that is 'customs that have got out of hand'.[11]

Were the police actually prepared to intervene when right-wing radicals attacked ethnic minorities? Bernd Wagner, the former head of the state security section of the Joint Criminal Investigation Department of the five new Federal states, believed that this was not always the case. Asked in 1992 whether the police sympathised with right-wing radical structures, he said: 'Yes. It can be shown that there were some police stations in the five new Federal states where policemen were good friends with skinheads of right-wing extremist orientation, and sometimes looked the other way when violent campaigns were going on.'[12] This behaviour was probably inspired by racist motives. As early as October 1991, a working party of critical police officers had maintained that the police force should investigate itself scrupulously for racism. This advice turned out to be not entirely unjustified. Amnesty International criticises the German police almost every year for their hostile attitude and sometimes violent behaviour towards foreigners.[13]

However, violence was committed not only by young right-wing extremists. Violent conflicts also took, and continued to take place between 'left-wing' groups and young right-wing radicals. In Halberstadt in East Germany in April 1992, for example, between five and six hundred skinheads came to blows with the police and left-wing *Autonomen*. In 1998 such conflicts are no longer the exception, but particularly in East Germany are part of everyday reality. In such scenarios the left wing uses slogans like 'better into the street than *Heim ins Reich*' (back home to the Reich). The right-wing retorts with the famous '*Rot Front Verrecke*' (death to the Red Front). Occasionally, however, the strangest monstrous alliances were struck between these two youth cultures. In Cottbus in East Germany there was a joint football match between the two groups. The young right-wing radicals presented the *Reichskriegsflagge*[14] from the German empire, which for them in a certain sense is a symbolic equivalent of the swastika flag. Their counterparts wore the old GDR flag. But mostly their confrontations were less peaceful and playful.[15]

At the end of 1996 the German security services had records of 45,300 (in 1995: 46,100) persons with right-wing extremist views, who belonged to 108 (in 1995: 96) organisations and groups.[16] According to the German authorities, 6,400 people were prepared to use violence (in 1995: 6,200).[17] Since 1992 the German government has banned 12 neo-Nazi organisations, including the Nationalistische Front, the Deutsche Alternative, the Wiking Jugend and the Nationale Offensive. However, the members of these groups, especially former Freiheitliche Arbeiter Partei (FAP) supporters, soon reorganised into so-called *Kameradschaften*, mainly in Berlin, Brandenburg and Sachsen-Anhalt. Since these scattered organisations have no rules of association, address lists or members' lists, it is very difficult for the German authorities to tackle them.[18]

In 1991 an amorphous group of approximately 20,000 mostly young people with militant right-wing extremist views were recorded in the five new Federal states. They were not neo-Nazis and they were not constantly committing crimes and violence, but their energy could be mobilised at any moment.[19] For these young people National Socialism played an important part, and it will not cause any surprise that they often argued for this ideology. On this point they could rely on broader social support. In a survey of 1992 by the Research Centre for Social Analysis in Leipzig, for example, it emerged that 40 per cent of trainees in Saxony believed that National Socialism 'also had its good side'. Eleven per cent of young people in industrial apprentice-ships even argued for 'a new National Socialist party to take over power'.[20] Such views were also translated into action. In 1996, in Saxony alone, 993 crimes with a right-wing extremist background were recorded. That constitutes an increase of 32.4 per cent compared with 1995. For the first six months of 1997 the rise was as high as 41 per cent.[21] In Saxony the right-wing extremist National Demokratische Partei Deutschlands (NDPD) had more than 1,000 members in 1998 – more than Bündnis 90 (the Greens).[22]

Since the *Wende* there has been a flourishing right-wing radical youth culture in the new Federal states. For example, in Berlin one constantly found the word *Hass* (hate) on walls in a number of suburbs. The last two letters of this slogan were often written in the form of runes, and whole walls were daubed with swastikas. This was mostly the work not of neo-Nazis but of young hooligans or fellow travellers without any 'party agenda' of their own. However, right-wing radicals and extremists were recruited from such groups. The 'hatred' among these young people was often unfocused, but as early as 1992 there were signs that seemed to indicate that their resentment was becoming less and less diffuse and nihilistic. The aggression was focused increasingly on the groups of earlier victims of the Third Reich. Not only the 'left', homosexuals and 'punks', but also alcoholics, people on social security and disabled persons are a target described as *Zecke* (tick) and *Assel* (woodlouse). Most of these young right-wing radicals, however, saw particularly in the large number of asylum-seekers a further legitimisation of their *raison d'être*. In this respect they are following a core element of National Socialism which in the 'twenty-five-point programme' of the NSDAP (Nationalsozialistische Deutsche Arbeiterpartei) is formulated as follows: 'Only a *Volksgenosse* [lit. national comrade] can be a citizen. Only those of German blood whatever their denomination can be *Volksgenosse*. A Jew can therefore not be a *Volksgenosse*.'[23]

Many of these young people wear the outfit of the skinheads. They dress in bomber jackets, jeans with turn-ups, and Doc Marten shoes or boots (so-called *Springerstiefel*). They often have crew-cut hair or shaven heads. The exchange of information and the establishing of contacts usually takes place via so-called 'fanzines' (fan magazines) or during concerts. In 1997 there was a large influx into various movements including the 'Hammer Skins' and the group 'Blood and Honour', which originated in Great Britain. In the meantime, the dissemination of right-wing radical messages via CDs, music cassettes and the Internet has also become very important. Rock music is at present the most important means of propaganda for neo-Nazis. In the months of July and August 1997 alone, the police confiscated 47,000 CDs and music cassettes with racist lyrics.[24] The *Landeskriminalamt* in Kiel reported in October 1997 that the police in Northern Germany had confiscated 260,000 illegal audio-tapes containing right-wing extremist texts.[25]

The lyrics of this music are particularly aggressive. Some examples follow. The group Kahlkopf, in its song 'The Pig Next Door', proclaims: 'I see a little girl standing by the kiosk / I jump right in her face / Now she's lying there and I have to go on / I am the pig, she didn't know.' The band Tonstörung proclaims in its song 'There Must be Masses of Blood': 'In the synagogue hangs a black pig / You must throw hand grenades into the parliaments.'[26] The group Die Zillertaler Türkenjäger sing in 'Kreuzberger Nächte': 'They lie there in their blood, I must tell you that the sight does me good.'[27] And the band Landser, from Berlin, sings: 'Africa for apes, Europe for Whites. Put the apes in the loo / flush them away like shit.'[28] There are now also countless web sites which proclaim anti-Semitic and racist messages with names such as 'Thule', 'White Aryan' and 'Jew-Watchers'.[29] Here, too, National Socialism and its genesis is of major importance. The name 'Thule', for example, refers to the 'Thule Gesellschaft', an occult society founded at the end of the First World War by Rudolf Freiherr von Sebottendorff, among whose members were Alfred Rosenberg and Rudolf Hess.

It can no longer be maintained that the spread of right-wing radicalism in the new Federal states is a marginal phenomenon. According to the criminologist Bernd Wagner, in 1998 almost one-third of East German youth had right-wing extremist orientations. Headteachers complain that in some parts of the former GDR the majority of the pupils have a 'right-wing extremist attitude'.[30] Annetta Kahane, who is in charge of the regional departments for matters relating to foreigners in the former GDR, stated in 1997: 'There is at present in East Germany a development of which one can say that the number of so-called "national liberated zones" is increasing.' Asked what such 'national liberated zones' are, she replied: 'The right-wing uses this phrase to describe certain areas, for example the Muldental near Wurzen, but also certain institutions, for example youth clubs or radio stations ... in those places the only ideology is right-wing radicalism.'[31]

The majority of East German right-wing radicals are adolescents or have just been through adolescence. Their willingness to use force in this context is extremely great. They are reminiscent of characters from the novel *Die Geächteten* (*The Pariahs*), written by Ernst von Salomon at the end of the 1920s. This author was one of the terrorists who assassinated the German foreign minister Walter Rathenau in 1922. He describes in detail the psychology of a disillusioned and embittered youth. These young people, who were generally organised into *Freikorpse*, were in the first instance interested in violence. Many of them could not stomach the German defeat in the First World War. For them the political left and right wings seemed to be fluid concepts. It was not only the proto-Nazi von Salomon who allied himself in his book with a Communist Party member. Before Hitler's assumption of power Honecker also made common cause with Nazis against Social Democrats. Many of these young front-line soldiers became absorbed in an obscure hatred and *Blut-und-Boden* mythology. Such a diffuse hatred seemed also to play a significant part with some young East Germans after the Wall came down. It seems that these young people embody right-wing extremist *tendencies*, although in far from all cases are all characteristics of a right-wing extremist philosophy present.

What is right-wing extremism? The German social scientist Richard Stöss defined right-wing extremism as a social model, which is opposed mainly to liberal and socialist traditions. Central to it is an ethnocentric, *völkisch* nationalism, and all other values and aims are subordinated to this basic principle. No attention is paid to the universal rights of man – freedom, equality and social justice; all these are rejected. One right-wing extremist ideal is the hierarchically structured German *Volksgemeinschaft*. This 'national community' must be expressed in a powerful authoritarian state. Outwardly it pursues expansionist or revisionist goals.[32] A racist image of the enemy is a significant part of a right-wing extremist philosophy. After the collapse of the Wall, this image seemed to be embodied mainly in the 'asylum-seeker' and the 'foreigner'. Such a construction seems to be necessary for group cohesion. Right-wing extremists generally express racist views much more militantly and aggressively than right-wing radicals. One could argue that the right-wing radical may harbour the same ideas as the extremist but does not resort to violence. In most cases, however, he will not hesitate to lend a helping hand.

In the right-wing extremist philosophy people, race, nation and state are more or less congruent concepts. Right-wing extremists often regard themselves as the people who have to do 'history's dirty work'. Their 'programme' seems to be determined to a large extent by their antipathies: against foreigners, an aversion to the current government, a radical dislike of left-wing politics in general and of militant *Autonomen* in particular. They are also opposed to an escapist *Null-Block* mentality and against Western hedonism. This last point may explain why West Germans are the main target of constant attacks by right-wing radicals on camp sites, particularly in Mecklenburg and Brandenburg.

A factor that must not be underestimated is the irrationality of right-wing radical and extremist views. Ernst von Salomon expressed this irrationality back in the 1920s. Asked about the motives for the murder of von Rathenau, the murderer replied that it was not because he did not have Germany's best interests at heart that he had to die. On the contrary. And he explained, 'I couldn't stand it if greatness were to emerge again in this fragmented and accursed time'. For him, von Rathenau was only the preserver of *old* Germany, whereas what mattered was the *new* Germany. In her study *The Meaning of Treason*, Rebecca West aptly expressed the psychopathology of such youngsters:

> Most parents and children contrive to gentle their relationship by tolerance of each other's wills so that it serves them well, and most citizens make the claims of the state and their individualities balance

on their books. But there are those who never persuade the love and
hatred they feel for their parents to sign a truce; and these often find
themselves compelled to spend their lives in love and hatred of the
society of which they are a part, striving to make it more beautiful
and noble, but insisting that the prerequisite of its reform is its destruction. The extreme case is the revolutionary, who clothes his desire
to establish a nihilist balance of forces, which is the most abstract of
lusts, the most metaphysical of murders, with the dedication of the
whole being seen in a baby sucking a nipple or kicking and howling
when its mother lifts it from its cot.[33]

It is often argued that the increase in right-wing extremist groups
is mainly a result of unemployment and economic crisis. This is only
partly true. Most young right-wing extremists have jobs. The German
educationalist Wilhelm Heitmeyer argued as early as 1991 that right-
wing extremism was conceivable even without unemployment.[34] The
problem of right-wing extremism can probably not be solved purely
by an economic revival in the new Federal states. Apart from their
racist activities, many right-wing extremists often display well-adjusted
behaviour. This is also one of the reasons why they are often able to
count on the sympathy of their neighbours while, for example, punks
and other sub-cultural groups are less able to do so.

For some young people right-wing radicalism, and to a lesser
extent right-wing extremism, offer a kind of reference point. As the
state took care of them all day they often have not been able to
identify with their parents. Besides, there is a generational conflict,
with the older generation often being accused of having colluded in
Communist Party rule. Nevertheless, some young right-wing radicals
were able to rely on the tacit support of their parents, support that
after the *Wende* often turned to open applause. A glaring example of
this was when the mayor of Herzsprung in Brandenburg personally
tried to stop the police winding up a Nazi meeting in a marquee. The
day ended with three casualties and the arrest of 13 men – including
the mayor.[35] Skinheads and the better adjusted *Faschos* seemed to be
expressing radical attitudes latent in large sections of the East German
population.

Since the Wall came down there has been a severe psychological crisis in the new Federal states. The right-wing radical sub-cultures seem to have overcome this to some extent. Right-wing radical agitation indeed seemed capable of giving people's lives new meaning in the German 'two-tier society'. Partly for this reason, they were also admired and envied by some bourgeois elements. In the past these average citizens did not have the courage to express in public their dissatisfaction with the regime, and right-wing radicals did this for them. Bernd Wagner, who in 1998 worked for the Zentrum Demokratische Kultur in Berlin, argued as early as 1992 that right-wing extremism in East Germany was more of a social movement with wide influence on attitudes and behaviour; it is less linked to party structures.[36] However, in April 1998 there was a turn of the tide. In the 1998 state elections in Saxony-Anhalt, 30 per cent of the voters under the age of 30 voted for the right-wing radical Deutsche Volksunion (DVU) of Gerhard Frey, who received 12.9 per cent of the total vote.[37] Immediately after his election victory, Frey explained: 'We have touched the life and soul of the East German people.'[38] But there were also others who indicated that this might be the case. Richard Stöss, for example, argued that these results could happen anywhere in East Germany: 'There is a risk that the dam may burst.'[39] Can one really speak of a 'right-wing social movement' in the new Federal states?

4

National-revolutionary Sentiments in the Former GDR?

IN October 1991 the East German writer Stephan Hermlin compared the 'German autumn' of that year with the beginnings of the Nazi era. Referring to the large numbers of attacks on foreigners, Hermlin argued: 'The events take us back almost sixty years, when Germany plunged into the abyss and when in Germany the light of humanism was extinguished.' One now often hears the slogan 'resist the beginning' and, according to the writer, the question was, 'whether we haven't already gone beyond the beginning'.[1] Politicians also implicitly referred to the Weimar period in relation to racist violence. The prime minister of Brandenburg, Manfred Stolpe, went so far as to maintain that this course of events testified to a mentality which had once ended in Auschwitz. Were the attacks indeed partly politically motivated? Was it possible that these were echoes of the national-revolutionary street-fighters of Hitler's *Sturmabteilung* (SA)? And how should the relatively large degree of social support enjoyed by right-wing radicals and even neo-Nazis in East Germany be explained? For in the new Federal states they were sometimes allowed to go their own way without hindrance.

It is worth examining the programme of the neo-Nazis. Until the beginning of the 1980s Adolf Hitler was the great example for most German neo-Nazis. There were also, however, neo-Nazis who were critical of Hitler. Their greatest reproach was that he had abandoned,

36

in their view, his early national-revolutionary ideals. These national-revolutionary ideas dated back to the dawning of National Socialism and were embodied in Otto and Gregor Strasser, and the Chief of Staff of the SA, Ernst Röhm. At that time the Strasser brothers and Röhm represented the 'left' wing of the National Socialists.[2] But as early as 4 July 1930, Otto Strasser and his followers had left the party on the principle that 'socialists leave the NSDAP'. As far as Hitler was concerned, the 'left', 'National-Bolshevist' or national-revolutionary plans of the Strasser brothers and Röhm had gone too far. In 1934 Röhm and Gregor Strasser were eliminated in the so-called Night of the Long Knives, which meant the end of the second, that is social revolution. However, the SA remained part of the National Socialist movement. These old national-revolutionaries, who were also described as social-revolutionaries or occasionally as the 'Trotskyists' of National Socialism,[3] were, among other things, anti-democratic, anti-capitalist, pro-Russian and on the left of National Socialism. This movement had a strong 'socialist' and revolutionary character. An important plank in the platform of these old National-Bolshevists was their anti-capitalism. In 1932 Gregor Strasser even spoke of an *anti-kapitalistische Sehnsucht* (an anti-capitalist yearning) that allegedly ran through the German people.[4] These ideas found great support at the time among the many workers who belonged to Röhm's SA who, in 1936, were characterized by the American author and journalist John Gunther as a motley collection of 'hooligans, clerks, half-trained boys, *Lumpenproletariat* off the streets'.[5] Because of this 'left-wing' programme it was also easy for many ex-German Communist Party members to be accepted into the NSDAP. In the elections of March 1932 more than a million Communist voters of Ernst Thälmann defected to Hitler's camp.[6] GDR historians always characterised these defectors as a negligible quantity. In their view they were a bunch of 'merely unemployed and classless proletarians'.[7] East German historians maintained quite apologetically that:

The majority of the petite bourgeoisie felt that only the Nazi party could save them. They were not capable of seeing through its social and national demagogy. That was the reason why the bourgeois middle classes, and large sections of the peasant class, who were also faced with bankruptcy, were receptive to the party of monopolistic capital, Hitler's party.[8]

However, the GDR Communist Party denied that it was precisely these classes who *in part* were the *conscious supporters and advocates* of National Socialism.

The implicit apology for the 'merely unemployed and classless proletarians' was for that matter not surprising. Both the National Socialists and the Communist Party were trying to win votes from these social target groups. And *both* ideologies were linked in their struggle for the favour of the electors by anti-democratic, anti-capitalist and 'socialist' views. However, these three elements had not only been important characteristics of the old national-revolutionaries around Röhm and the Strassers. These aspects – despite the very large programmatic differences with the national-revolutionaries – had also been characteristic of the German Communist Party, and were preserved in the political culture of the GDR.

In 1961, Peter Viereck argued in his book *Metapolitics. The Roots of the Nazi Mind*:

Today the Nazi 'second revolution' – i.e., into national bolshevism – is partly resumed in the Russian-sponsored Socialist Unity Party in East Germany. This party combines Communist and anti-western Nazi slogans and emotions under Soviet control. It welcomes former SS officers to create, in partnership with the Kremlin, a second totalitarian Germany. ... Let us be equally alert for Communism's ex-Nazis in Russia's East German puppet state. Hitler's famous remark about Communists becoming Nazis, a remark basic to national bolshevism, also works in reverse today, from nazism back to Communism: 'There is more that binds us to Bolshevism than separates us from it. There is, above all, genuine revolutionary feeling. ... I have always made allowance for this circumstance and given orders that former Communists are to be admitted to the Party at once. The petit-bourgeois Social Democrat and the trade-union boss will never make a National Socialist, but the Communist always will.'[9]

Rauschning (quoted in the Viereck extract above) had probably not been exaggerating when he cited Hitler's relative preference for German Communists. After all, in *Mein Kampf* Hitler had noted with satisfaction that from the very early years of the NSDAP 'tens of thousands of seduced Marxists made their way back to the *Volksgemeinschaft* to become fighters for an imminent and free German Reich'.[10]

In spite of the enormous differences of programme, there was indeed a connection, an affinity, between National Socialism and party Communism. This had already come to the surface in the 1920s and 1930s, as seen in the so-called 'Schlageter course', inaugurated in 1923 by the Comintern functionary Karl Radek, and in the case of Lieutenant Scheringer, who was converted from a National Socialist into a Communist in 1931.

In 1923, the 'fascist' Albert Leo Schlageter was sentenced to death and executed by the French occupying forces of the Ruhrgebiet because he had committed sabotage. Karl Radek, who was a member of the presidency of the Executive Committee of the Comintern and was responsible for the instruction of the KPD, described Schlageter at the assembly of the enlarged executive of the Comintern on 20 June 1923 as a 'martyr of German nationalism' and a 'courageous soldier of the counterrevolution'. Radek's argument was: 'If the people matter to the nation, then the nation will matter to the people'.[11]

This 'Schlageter course' lasted only a few months and was abandoned for the benefit of Soviet foreign policy. It was the period when Communists and nationalists proclaimed a 'people's war' against France. The KPD set up discussion groups in which Communists and National Socialists met to prepare for the struggle against France. The KPD's youth groups made contact with National Socialist student organisations. In July 1923 Radek published a pamphlet entitled *Schlageter – A Dispute*, in which he, the *völkisch* nationalist Reventlow and Arthur Moeller van den Bruck discussed the future of National-Bolshevism.

The KPD tried to gain control of nationalist sentiments. Within the KPD, a 'national Communist' wing formed around Heinz Neumann, who tried to establish contact with forces on the right. These attempts are known by the name of 'Scheringer-line' after the famous incident involving Lieutenant Scheringer, who in 1931 was sentenced to imprisonment for high treason. He was imprisoned in the fortress of Gollnow, where he had to serve his *Ehrenhaft*, or sentence of honour, together with his sworn enemies, that is Communists, who were imprisoned on the same floor. The Communists who worked to win over Scheringer were ultimately successful, using this achievement in their agitation and propaganda. 'It was especially the demands of the Communist "Programme of the Social and National Liberation" that very soon brought about political points of contact with the National Socialists,' writes Margarete Buber Neumann:

> The dismissal of the 'scandalous *diktat* of Versailles' and the 'smashing of the capitalist system in Germany' as it was called in the programme, conquered Scheringer's heart. When the Communists convinced him that Germany could liberate itself from the chains of the Peace Treaty of Versailles only by making a close pact with Soviet Russia and with the help of the Red Army, the Nazi lieutenant sympathized more and more with their arguments; soon Communism seemed to him a more promising ideal than did National Socialism.[12]

There were also other examples that indicated a certain political affinity between the KPD and the NSDAP. There was the so-called '*Rot-brauner Volksentscheid*' (red–brown plebiscite) in August 1931, when both National Socialists and Communists tried in vain to dissolve the Prussian convention that was dominated by the Social-Democrat Braun/Severing government. Another prominent example of mutual collaboration was the strike at the Berlin Public Transport Company in November 1932, led more or less jointly by the National Socialists and the Communists, that is by Josef Goebbels and Walter Ulbricht.[13]

Although this red–brown collaboration was only temporary, serving short-term aims, there obviously existed a certain affinity between National Socialists and party Communists that was also preserved in the political culture of the GDR.

Modern right-wing radicals and extremists therefore saw an opening, particularly in the former GDR. It seemed to offer the best possible seedbed for their 'national-revolutionary' ideas. And it was probably no coincidence that it would appeal strongly to the recent political past of the new Federal citizens. Many right-wing radicals and extremists, for example, were not emphasising for nothing the *socialist* component of their movements. One of the extremists who had understood this well early on was the West German neo-Nazi, Michael Kühnen. Kühnen was the founder of the Deutsche Alternative, a right-wing group banned in 1992. Together with his party members, he celebrated on 1 May 1990 in Neukirchen near Eisenach the 'day of German Labour'. The 'socialist' component was emphasised because the 'day of labour' is a socialist holiday in origin. Their Freie Gewerkschaftsbewegung showed a certain affinity with the GDR trade union Freier Deutscher Gewerkschaftsbund.[14] The deputy chairman of the right-wing extremist National Demokratische Partei Deutschlands (NPD) in Saxony, Jürgen Schön, also emphasised the party's 'socialist' character. According to Schön, the NPD is a 'revolutionary organisation' whose members share a 'common destiny as victims of capitalism' and who fight for the right to work.[15]

Despite their agitation and propaganda, the number of actual right-wing extremists in East Germany immediately after the *Wende* was negligible. But since the collapse of the Wall it is a cause for concern that many losers in German reunification appear to be obviously identifying themselves with *sections* of the right-wing extremist package of demands. They sympathise with the 'socialist', authoritarian, anti-capitalist and racist vision of society, and although the majority of these malcontents is not violent in itself, the militant actions of right-wing extremists are often viewed with passive approval.

The small number of members of the right-wing extremist subculture in East Germany is not necessarily a measure of its actual importance. The journalist Burkhard Schröder argued that in due course right-wing extremist circles could produce people capable of developing political theories. In his view, 'true "new" Nazi ideology [could] be developed that was fascist and nationalistic but at the same time appealed to the "modern" legacy of "real socialism"'.[16] Whether this gloomy prospect will prove true remains to be seen, but as yet it has not materialised. More worrying is that some citizens of the *neue Länder*, partly consciously, partly unconsciously, identify with certain components of right-wing authoritarian programmes. This identification may have been the result of the legacy of a political and social culture, with which they had not yet come to terms, and which was virtually unknown to the West before the collapse of the Wall.

II

History and Political Culture of the GDR: Right-wing Author–itarian Views in a Nutshell

5

Imposition of the Party Line and the Militarisation of East Germany

We believe that it would be a wrong course to impose the Soviet system on Germany, because this course does not accord with the present state of development in Germany.[1]

Our socialist state embodies the continuity of everything which is good, just as it represents the radical break with everything that is reactionary in German history.[2]

THE East German film director Konrad Weiss once called the 'violence principle' a striking feature of East German society. From the very beginning this violence was an integral part of the development of East German society. Immediately after 1945 the East German Communists tried to construct an image of tolerance and freedom. But the first party leader of the GDR, Walter Ulbricht, expressed their true intentions to his close associate Wolfgang Leonardt, 'It must appear democratic, but we must have everything firmly in our hands.'[3] From 1948 onwards the Soviet zone of occupation was normalised according to the Stalinist model. Within the party there were soon purges and show trials, just as in the Soviet Union, and the GDR became more and more a Soviet satellite. The cult of Stalin too reached unprecedented heights in about 1952 and 1953. The 'brilliant Field Marshal Generalissimo Stalin' was also praised as 'a brilliant teacher and leader'.

In 1953 the administrative system of the Soviet Union had been in general terms transposed to East German society. The Sozialistische Einheitspartei Deutschlands (SED) achieved this by means of the party, the state apparatus and the party-led mass organisations. It used a trio of repressive methods to maintain its administration. The law and the secret services focused on political opposition within the country. Opponents were first isolated, criminalised and later sometimes 'exported' to the Federal Republic in return for payment. Those who were not very interested in politics were neutralised with a diet of bread and circuses. The party ensured that the primary necessities of life could be adequately satisfied. Finally, young people were subordinated to the authority of the party and the state through an extremely ingenious system of political indoctrination.

The National Socialist dictatorship was succeeded almost immediately in the East of Germany by a Stalinist regime. During the transition from the Third Reich to the GDR the 'violence principle' and intolerance remained an important feature of everyday life. This was facilitated partly by the activities of former National Socialists. Their influence was apparent, for example, in the setting up and organisation of the East German army. Vincenz Müller was the founder of the Nationale Volksarmee (NVA) which was set up in 1956 from units of the *Volkspolizei*. In the Third Reich, Müller had occupied a senior post as a lieutenant-general in the *Wehrmacht*. During the summer of 1944 he was taken prisoner by the Red Army, after which he offered his services to the Soviet Union. It was Müller who ensured that this East German army had a 'national' complexion. In party circles there was a fear that East Germans would otherwise not be able to identify at all with this army. Through Müller's involvement the external characteristics of these armed forces attached directly to the traditions of the *Reichswehr* from the Weimar period and the *Wehrmacht*. The NVA was the only army in the Warsaw Pact that did not wear the olive green of the Red Army, but the traditional field grey of the *Wehrmacht*.

Particularly after the construction of the Wall in 1961 the NVA and the border troops became disciplined instruments for maintaining domestic and foreign order. No means was shunned to achieve this. The soldiers chosen to guard the borders did not know each other personally. So, by definition, they found themselves in the company of a colleague who could never be completely trusted. That was the intention of the commanders. Whenever a soldier refused to fire on a *Republikflüchtling*, it cost him not only a long stay in a military prison, but it was also reflected in the treatment of members of his family by the East German authorities. This sort of phenomenon looks like *Sippenhaft*, which essentially means that the family is punished for the 'failure' of one of its members.

The NVA's military exercises took place in the Soviet Union, mainly in Kazakhstan. Discipline and order were particularly strict here. For example, I once heard of a case where soldiers' cheeks were rubbed with a piece of cotton wool during morning parade to check whether they had shaved thoroughly. Until the fall of the Wall every soldier was obliged to take the oath of allegiance to the flag, the *Fahneneid*. This contained among other things the following words: 'I swear to be an honest, courageous, disciplined and watchful soldier, who will obey his military superiors unconditionally and carry out their orders with resolve … '.[4]

The *curricula vitae* of the founders of the NVA give an impression of where these practices derived from. In 1943 the Nationalkomitee Freies Deutschland was set up in Krasnogorsk in Soviet Russia. This was an assembly consisting of interned German prisoners-of-war whom the Red Army tried to convert into active Communists. The future senior political and military ranks of the GDR were to be recruited from their midst. When in 1943 General von Paulus was taken prisoner after the defeat at Stalingrad, he could probably not have dreamed that he would be able to spend his old age peacefully and with a good pension in the 'first-workers'-and-peasants'-state-on-German-soil'. Presumably the East German government made use of his expertise right up to his death in 1957. Both General Field-Marshal von Paulus and Vincenz Müller had been members of the Nationalkomitee.

In the GDR Prussian militarism had retained its *raison d'être* throughout the four decades of its existence. The change of flag turned out to be only a short intermezzo. The word 'peace' was – literally or figuratively – given the prefixes 'triumphant' and 'socialist', otherwise there was no question of a *real* peace. The GDR tried to design a new Socialist human being. This new man, however, was a theoretical construct, which had to be brought to life through social normalisation. The form of that normalisation was very reminiscent of the Third Reich: mass symbols and political rituals. But many other symbols were also often taken directly from the Third Reich. Victor Klemperer had suggested this affinity between party Communists and National Socialists in terms of language as early as 1946 in his book *Lingua Tertii Imperii*, on the language of the Third Reich.[5]

The affinities between the Third Reich and the GDR were not only at the level of idiom. This link applied particularly to the militaristic character of East German society. The official military and paramilitary upbringing which every East German was given from cradle to grave was based on the Prussian militaristic model. This upbringing began in the nursery and was continued during paramilitary training at primary and secondary school. Boys and girls were obliged to participate in the so-called Civil Defence Camps. In these camps the boys practised, among other things, using hand grenades. The girls learned how they could protect themselves against chemical weapons, and how they could disarm various kinds of NATO mines. Schoolchildren were also given paramilitary training in the GST, the Gesellschaft für Sport und Technik. This was done, for example, through great sporting manifestations in various disciplines, the so-called *Wehrspartakiaden*.

The GST was set up in 1952 and tried to prepare young people for military service. Important components of the training were shooting, combat sports, parachute jumping and diving. These activities were certainly not unpopular among many young East Germans. In addition, there was the Deutscher Turn-und Sportbund, the DTSB. After the collapse of the Wall for some young people it had turned out to be only a short step from a *Wehrspartakiade* to a paramilitary *Wehr-sportgruppe*. Perhaps the emergence of these right-wing extremist militias, which at present are active mainly in Brandenburg, was partly the result of the authoritarian mentality of organisations like the NVA, the GST and the DTSB.

Parallel to these organisations, which were geared to a physical and fighting culture, were the Junge Pioniere, the Thälmannpioniere and finally the FDJ, the Freie Deutsche Jugend. The FDJ in particular showed similarities with the Hitlerjugend from the Third Reich, which were sometimes reflected in sarcastic jokes about the (F)rühere (D)eutsche (J)ungvolk.[6] The individual's progress in society was to a large extent determined by countless politicised and militarised mass organisations.

All of this was subsequently monitored by the secret service, the Ministerium Für Staatssicherheit (MfS), whose practices did not date from the Third Reich but went all the way back to Kaiserism. Already in 1918 the American ambassador to the German imperial court in Berlin, James W. Gerard, argued that 'poisonous propaganda and spying are the twin offspring of Kaiserism'. He claimed that the Germans 'use more spies than all the other nations together' and sharply observed: 'Spy spies on spy – autocracy produces bureaucracy where men rise and fall not by the votes of their fellow citizens but by back stairs intrigue.'[7] This tradition was carried on and brought to perfection by the MfS. The MfS was ubiquitous, even if it was not physically present. This organisation had been set up on the model of the Soviet secret service, and called itself 'the shield and sword of the state and the party'. Almost everyone in the GDR was – directly or indirectly – connected with it. The mental terror which it spread was extremely effective. After the collapse of the Wall it was possible to gain an impression of the scope of this bureaucratic apparatus.[8] The real politics of the SED was expressed in this Kafkaesque bureau-cracy: the development of a completely processed mass human being. And furthermore, this policy was effective. At least the chance of someone's activities remaining undiscovered was relatively slight. This applied particularly to the older generation, who had for years had to reconcile themselves to 'the system'. They now ran the risk of being blamed for this, either by young East Germans who did not appreciate such behaviour, or by the new German government. Many former GDR citizens prefer to draw a line as soon as possible under their GDR past. There might still be statements in the files which could put somebody in a questionable light.

The way that the German authorities had dealt with these files deserves some comment. It was, for example, striking that some East German politicians were unmasked as *Inoffizielle Mitarbeiter* (IMs), after they had played their part in the reunification. Such a course of events took place with Wolfgang Schnur, Martin Kirchner, Ibrahim Böhme and Lothar de Maizière. Some East German critics find it hard to accept that the GDR past obviously has more consequences than the National Socialist past has for many West Germans, and they dispute West Germany's *moral* right to judge the GDR.

Earlier activities on behalf of the *Firma* have great repercussions today. Old Stasi workers are the great losers of reunification because they are barred from public posts. They are very embittered about this. 'When the Wall fell,' the wife of a Stasi employee once complained to me, 'the unanimous cry of the people was "Stasi into production". Many people meant by this that the MfS must be abolished and that the employees must do ordinary work. But now the former employees have been dismissed from all public offices and can't find a job anywhere.' Ex-Stasi staff or dismissed NVA officers do indeed sometimes appear to be the new pariahs. Given their ideological background they could also form an attractive reservoir for right-wing groups.[9]

Such an alliance between Stasi employees and right-wing radical young people is not completely new. The East German secret service had good contacts with right-wing radical young people even before 1989. The meeting centres of the latter were sometimes located close to the headquarters of the Ministry for State Security. Here they were left in relative peace. Often right-wing radical young people even came from Communist Party circles, and not infrequently from circles of the MfS itself.[10] Both professed a similar kind of catechism of social values and norms: obedience, discipline, order, punctuality and elements of the old German jingoism in the service of an authoritarian state. The big difference between the two was, however, that many of these right-wing young people from the ex-GDR believed that the East German state did not go far enough in this. Despite sometimes strict penalties for vandalism, the GDR legal system often ignored the political nature of right-wing radical offences.[11] On the other hand, their opponents, such as *Grufties*, *Müslis* and punks could be sure of heavy sentences for minor misdemeanours. Because they were on the margins of the asocial and anti-social elements.

In East Germany 'right-wing' norms and institutions were preserved under a 'left-wing' banner. Not only did the violence against foreigners shock many people in and outside Germany, but right-wing radicals also rediscovered the psychological effect caused by desecrating Jewish graves. That was an alarming development. Not only because it defiled the memory of the victims of the Holocaust, or because in this way they expressed their contempt for one of the roots of our culture. Experience teaches us that people first desecrate the dead and afterwards the living. And in relation to this anti-Semitic violence too, the GDR past sometimes turned out to be less 'anti-Fascist' than one might suspect at first sight.

6

The Language of the Third Reich and Anti-Semitism in the GDR

> There is a lot of talk today about exterminating the Fascist mentality; so much is done to achieve it. War criminals are sentenced, 'minor PGs' – *Parteigenossen* – [the language of the Fourth Reich!] are being removed from their posts, nationalist books are being taken out of circulation, Hitler place names and Goering Streets are being renamed. Hitler oaks are being felled. But it seems as though the language of the Third Reich in some characteristic expressions is bound to survive. These have established themselves so strongly, that they seem to have become a permanent feature of the German language. (Victor Klemperer, *LTI*, 1946, p. 20)

AT the time of the trial of the war criminal Adolf Eichmann in April 1961, the East German jurist Professor Friedrich Kaul came out with a remarkable statement. At a press conference in Jerusalem he answered the question why the GDR did not pay any reparations to the victims of Nazi rule. He maintained: 'The German Democratic Republic makes reparations in a particular way. This is consistent with the fact that we have removed the Nazis from their positions and that a Nazi cannot achieve a leading post in the GDR.'

On 6 September 1968 Simon Wiesenthal gave the lie to this statement in his report 'The Same Language: first for Hitler – now for Ulbricht'.[1] Wiesenthal demonstrated in his report that there were personal continuities between the GDR and the Third Reich. He published his findings a propos of the outbreak of the Arab–Israeli

War of 1967. During this Six Day War the decidedly pro-Arab and anti-Israeli attitude adopted by the whole Eastern bloc from 1952 onwards was given extra emphasis in the press. For that matter, this line was maintained for years afterwards. But the reporting in the GDR press was particularly partisan and anti-Israeli.

It quickly struck Wiesenthal that the use of language in the press and the propaganda of the GDR was different from the commentary in the other Socialist countries. In his view, certain statements corresponded almost literally with expressions in former National Socialist newspapers and magazines. Next, Wiesenthal conducted an experiment. In former National Socialist papers such as the *Völkischer Beobachter* and the *Schwarze Korps*, he replaced the word 'Jew' with 'Zionist'. He also replaced 'National Socialism' with the words 'the peace camp' or 'Socialist camp'. One now had the impression that these articles had not been written 30 years previously but that they were only six months or a year old. It soon emerged that these anti-Jewish writings had often been written by the same people who published on the 'Jewish menace' under the Third Reich. For example, on 14 July 1967 a cartoon appeared in the *Berliner Zeitung* showing a flying Moshe Dayan stretching out his hands to guard Jerusalem. Next to him stood Adolf Hitler, in an advanced state of decomposition. He was encouraging Dayan with the words 'You go right ahead, friend Dayan!' According to Wiesenthal, it emerged that there were Nazi groups in the editorial boards of magazines like *Neues Deutschland* and *Deutsche Außenpolitik*.

There follows a small sample from the list presented by Wiesenthal. In 1968 Doctor Richard Arnold was editor in chief of *Der nationale Demokrat*, the organ of the National Demokratische Partei Deutschlands (NDPD). In the GDR he was held in high regard, as was apparent, for example, from the high decoration he had been awarded, the *Vaterländischer Verdienstorden*. Arnold became a member of the NSDAP, on 1 April 1933. In his own words, in a *curriculum vitae* for the NSDAP he was 'responsible for the complete *Entjudung* of German intellectual life'. This *Entjudung* (in Arnold's words), 'must be carried out not only in relation to staff – by the removal of all Jews and Jewish lackeys from scholarship and the training and up-bringing of the people. It is a matter of exterminating every trace of *Judengeist* from German culture.' Kurt Herwart Ball was another journalist in the East German NDPD press. In 1968 he was also a member of staff of the Bureau for Propaganda of the GDR. Ball joined the NSDAP on 1 May 1933 and for a long period had been editor in chief of the SS magazine *Hammer*. His books were praised in 1936 as 'militant writings of the northern spirit'. Johannes Caspar was editor of the GDR newspaper *Mitteldeutsche Neueste Nachrichten*. He became a member of the NSDAP on 1 April 1930. As editor of the *Waldheimer Tagblatt* he had defended the racial laws of Nurem-berg, by designating them as a 'necessary surgical operation'.

In 1968 Doctor Karlheinz Gerstner worked as the chief reporter of the *Berliner Zeitung*. In 1963 he had been awarded the *Verdienst-medaille der DDR*. Gerstner too had joined the Nazi Party on 1 May 1933. During the war he wrote among other things a pamphlet entitled 'Negro-infected France'. Reimund Schnabel was editor of the *Neue Zeit* and worked for the Deutschland-Sender. He joined the Nazi Party on 1 November 1936. In July 1938 Schnabel, who worked in the *Reichsjugendführung* as a *Bannführer,* was praised by his then chief. It was to his credit that in 'four cases he had unmasked Jewish elements that had infiltrated the leadership of the Hitler Jugend. And dutifully surrendered them to their punishment.' It emerged from Wiesenthal's list that former National Socialists certainly did work in the press and the propaganda industry of the GDR. And some of them continued their anti-Jewish attitude under the flag of anti-Zionism. As a result, however, ideological elements of National Socialism were preserved in the GDR.

The GDR's way of dealing with the Holocaust was indeed one-sided and partisan. Jews were given the status of 'victims of Fascism'. Communist Party members, however, were consistently referred to as 'fighters against fascism'. Little attention was paid to the persecu-tion of Jews in the *Mahn-* and *Gedenkstätten*, the former concentration camps, or in education. Jews were, and remained, for GDR politicians something of a negligible quantity. East German Jews in the party apparatus who had management posts, such as Gerhart Eisler, Albert Norden, Alexander Abusch or Hermann Axen, often kept quiet about their Jewish origin. Otherwise this could have harmed their careers in the GDR.

At the beginning of the 1950s anti-Zionism was officially included in the East German party doctrine. Zionism was, according to the East German translation of Stalin's work, a 'reactionary nationalist current, which found support in the Jewish bourgeoisie, the intelligentsia and the backward layers of the Jewish working class. The Zionists attempted to isolate the Jewish working masses from the common struggle of the proletariat.'[2] But through such constructions it was possible for anti-Jewish sentiments to be kept alive.

The 1950s seemed to hold a new persecution of Jewish East Germans. The dying Stalin was afraid that he would be murdered by Jewish doctors. Erich Mielke, the head of the East German secret service, acted as a willing tool for Stalin and began to keep a check on whether somebody was Jewish or half-Jewish.[3]

Another reason for the revival of anti-Semitism in the GDR was the indictment of the leading Czechoslovak party official, Slansky. Slansky and his 'group' were accused in 1952 of a 'Zionist conspiracy'. On 20 December 1952 the Central Committee of the SED set out its 'lessons from the trial against the core of conspirators around Slansky'. These 'lessons' turned out to be an East German variant of the 'Protocols of Zion'. The original 'Protocols' are a falsification of history from Czarist Russia which were produced by a member of the secret service to create a pogrom mood against Jews. The statement by the Central Committee of the SED said, among other things:

> Sailing under a Jewish-Nationalist flag, camouflaged as a Zionist organisation, and as diplomats of the American vassal regime of Israel, these American agents plied their trade. It emerges unambiguously from the 'Morgenthau Acheson plan' which was unveiled during the trial in Prague that American imperialism organises and carries out

its espionage and sabotage activities with the help of Zionist organisations in the Socialist countries.

In the same resolution the German Communist, Paul Merker, was accused of being an agent of Zionism who acted 'in the same way as the criminals in Czechoslovakia'. Merker, who during his exile in Mexico from 1942 to 1946 took the fate of the Jews to heart, had demanded reparation payments from the German state for Jewish Germans. The German Democratic Republic neither acceded to this demand nor thanked him for his efforts. The resolution stated:

> It can no longer be doubted that Merker is an agent of the US financial oligarchy, whose demand for compensation for Jewish properties is designed only to infiltrate US financial capital into Germany. This is the real reason for his Zionism. ... He demands the displacement of German national wealth with the words: 'Compensation for the harm that has been done to Jewish citizens will be given both to those who return and to those who want to stay abroad.' Merker has illicitly transformed the maximum profits squeezed out of German and foreign workers by monopoly capitalists into alleged property of the Jewish people. In reality 'Aryanisation' of this capital merely transferred the profits of 'Jewish' monopoly capitalists to 'Aryan' monopoly capitalists.[4]

As a result of such proclamations, which aroused an anti-Jewish mood, many Jews fled the GDR.

The media further fanned the flames. When in November 1956 a Soviet military cemetery in Radeberg was daubed with *Sieg Heil* slogans, the *Sächsische Zeitung* immediately knew who the culprits were:

> The same powers who brutally attacked the land on the Nile and in Hungary lit the torch of counter-revolution. They are the same powers who still today in the countries controlled by them incite the Fascist rabble against Communist party offices and Soviet embassies, out of impotent fury at their defeat in the Hungarian People's Republic.[5]

These were crass words, which gave a very negative and partisan picture of Israel. The GDR recognised the State of Israel only in 1990. It is true that from 1988 onwards Erich Honecker did seek a *rapprochement* with a Jewish private organisation. He negotiated with it on a one-off 'symbolic' restitution payment of US$100 million. But the most important motive in this was probably that he wanted to make his first state visit to the USA as soon as possible. He could not disguise this by awarding the chairman of the World Jewish Congress, Edgar Bronfman, the decoration *Stern der Völkerfreundschaft in Gold*.

The image of Israel was also fairly negatively coloured in the upbringing and education of the East German young. Even in a 1985 textbook for history for the secondary schools it was stated: 'Another centre of gravity of the aggressive policies of imperialism in the 1960s was the Middle East. Via the aggressive policies of Israel, financed and directed by US imperialism, the intention was that on the southern flank of NATO a change in the balance of power in favour of imperialism should be forced.'[6] It was not surprising that this consistently one-sided, anti-Israeli picture promoted an anti-Jewish mood.

But in the GDR even clearer examples of anti-Semitism could be recorded. In 1974 the Jewish cemetery in Zittau was desecrated, as was the Jewish cemetery in Potsdam in 1975. In 1977 the cemetery of the Jewish community in Dresden was damaged.[7] Quite soon after the *Wende*, the grave of Bertolt Brecht was daubed with slogans like *Juden raus* and *Saujud*. However, there was no question of organised anti-Judaism in the GDR. And today only a very small minority of East Germans regard themselves as anti-Semitic. After the fall of the Wall there was sometimes in the former GDR, partly as a result of an inadequate confrontation with the Holocaust, a possible latent anti-Jewish mood. After this turning point, the attitude towards Jews also often remained ambivalent.

A few figures may make this clear. From a survey carried out by the American Jewish Committee on behalf of the united Germany, it emerged that 44 per cent of East Germans believed 'that it is time to put the memory of the Holocaust behind us'. In another survey of

1991, 51.1 per cent agreed with this. Almost 44 per cent of East Germans were against paying reparations to Jews after the reunification.[8] A more recent case of an anti-Jewish mood was the refusal of the East German village of Gollwitz in 1997 to accept Jewish immigrants from the former Soviet Union. At first the prime minister of Brandenburg, Manfred Stolpe, could appreciate this behaviour. The Brandenburg village of Gollwitz near Potsdam had only 400 inhabitants and the reluctance of the population had nothing to do with anti-Semitism, argued Stolpe. The *Süddeutsche Zeitung* saw this differently: 'Gollwitz', wrote the paper, 'is only a new example. The German capital is surrounded by a brown morass. Almost daily foreigners are attacked in Brandenburg and strangers are threatened. Anyone not speaking German is living dangerously. This is everyday life in Brandenburg.'[9] The chairman of the Jewish community in Berlin, Andreas Nachama, maintained that the hostility to Jews which had been regarded as overcome since 1945, had reached new and saddening heights.[10]

Anti-Semitism must not be underestimated. Not only because the memory of the victims of the Third Reich and their descendants is being debased, but also because often suppressed anti-Semitism could be transferred to other population groups. After the fall of the Wall in any case, this possibility seemed more than purely theoretical. Perhaps the one-sided and partisan way of dealing with the legacy of 'fascism' was also responsible for this.

7

'Our Goethe, Your Mengele', or Legitimising Anti-Fascism

The SED is continuing the work of the German Communist Party, and is fulfilling the legacy of the anti-Fascist resistance fighters. (From the party manifesto of the SED, 1976, p. 5).

THE history of the GDR can scarcely be understood without its 'anti-Fascist' base. 'Anti-Fascism' was one of the most important roots of East Germany's *raison d'être*. The concept of 'anti-Fascism' emphasised the struggle which German Communist Party members had carried on against National Socialism. The Communist Party members had after all made great sacrifices in their struggle with the Nazi regime. Immediately after 1945 the term 'anti-Fascism' was not yet tainted.[1] This concept was used by parliamentary parties in West Germany too. But in the GDR the legitimate aspects of 'anti-Fascism' soon disappeared into the background. 'Anti-Fascism' became a slogan with which the party and the state legitimised themselves, and it became watered down into an instrument of class struggle. This meant in the East German way of reasoning, for example, that history teaches us that the GDR is an admirable and necessary result of the struggle against National Socialism. Although less than 1 per cent of the East German population consisted of veteran 'anti-Fascist' resistance fighters, this group constituted the trend-setting and ideological elite. It was the same group that had very soon proclaimed themselves to be the 'victors of history'.

During a party conference at the Humboldt University in East

Berlin in 1986 I had my first opportunity to meet a typical old 'anti-Fascist' Communist Party member. The elderly grey-beard ascended the podium and thundered in a surprisingly loud voice in my direction: 'Christianity has had two thousand years to change the world! Now it's our turn!' The echoes of these words reverberated in my ears for a long time afterwards. The more so because the slogan 'Now it's our turn!' was used almost literally by many frustrated East Germans after reunification to give expression to their resentment at the injustices in the past and the present. For this old man and for many people of his generation the awareness of being one of the 'anti-Fascist victors' seemed to be a *raison d'être*. But the commemoration of the resistance against National Socialism soon became a ritual in the GDR, and this ceremonial also became a compulsory component of education.

This education was put into practice in a rigorous way. At school young children were almost forced to visit the torture chambers of the concentration camps. The compulsory meetings with Communist Party resistance fighters and the massive processions of the Junge Pioniere were also part of the 'anti-Fascist' ceremonial. In East German education and also in children's literature, 'anti-Fascism' was present. Here, the book *The Adventures of Werner Holt: a Novel of a Childhood*, by the author Dieter Noll, deserves some attention. This large volume is a treatise on a boy from the Hitler Youth who had to fight for the last two years of the war. This work was intended to contribute to a 'proletarian' and 'anti-Fascist' upbringing. However, for many people this compulsory school literature would have led to the opposite conclusion. Some people may have identified with the heroism of the Third Reich rather than with the grey routine of 'real socialism'. And some pupils may have asked themselves curiously at a young age what that Adolf Hitler really looked like. Photos of the Führer were not thought suitable in East German historical education.

The effect of this 'anti-Fascist' propaganda was probably partly counter-productive because it was obvious that one could resist the GDR by sabotaging its 'anti-Fascist' cult. For that reason some young

East Germans had, at an early age, half-consciously, half-unconsciously became latent anti-'anti-Fascists'. It is not impossible that the militant anti-'anti-Fascism' which manifested itself after the collapse of the Wall was partly a result of this. Closely connected with the 'anti-Fascist' struggle was the permanent eulogising of the Soviet Union. Indeed, the Soviet Union had liberated the German people from the Fascist yoke. But in East Germany this new freedom had turned into an ubiquitous dictatorship. 'Anti-Fascism' turned out to be mainly a gift of the victor.

The GDR presented itself from the very beginning as the only true 'anti-Fascist' state on German soil. Both the GDR and its population were declared officially the co-victors of the Second World War. In East Germany it was not so much a question of 'inability to mourn'[2] as the husband-and-wife writing team A. and M. Mitscherlich had once noted about the West German situation, but rather of an official ban on doing so. Upright East German anti-Fascists who, for example, worried about the increasing violence of right-wing young people, were sometimes spied on. The SED reasoning was quite simple: 'Anyone who worries about *that*, will also get involved in other social abuses,' a female staff member of Neues Forum once explained to me. There was in East Germany officially 'no' Fascism and one did not encounter the concept of National Socialism very often either. The Communist Party members usually spoke of 'Fascism' or 'German Fascism'. Reference to the term 'Socialism' might bring this component into discredit.

The essence of National Socialism had never been properly examined in the GDR because it was seen principally as an economic phenomenon. It was the Communist Party member Georgi Dimitroff who had defined National Socialism as 'Fascism' in 1935. 'Fascism', argued Dimitroff, was the 'openly terrorist dictatorship of the most reactionary, most chauvinistic, most imperialist elements of financial capital'.[3] This purely materialistic definition by the Comintern remained the official definition of National Socialism in the GDR until 1989. The East German Communist Party members believed that the economic organisation of a society, or its foundation, is decisive for the superstructure or the non-material aspects of that society. It started from the principle that National Socialism would disappear of its own accord when the economy was reorganised along Communist Party lines. But in so doing the East German Communist Party members largely neglected the non-material aspects of the National Socialist legacy. At the beginning the KPD had still been aware of the non-material consequences of the Third Reich. In particular, the elimination of the Nazi racial obsession had been an important agenda-point for German Communist Party members. As early as the appeal by the Central Committee of the KDP in 1945, the following provision was included: 'Equality before the law for all citizens without distinction of race, and the strictest penalties for all expressions of racial hatred.'[4]

On 1 July 1946 the Soviet zone of occupation issued a directive for the teaching of history. This laid down that one should make 'clear' to school children 'the causes of the most recent catastrophe which are rooted deeply in our history'. The first commandment for the teaching of history now became to keep this subject 'free of every distortion, falsification and particularly mystification of National Socialist historiography and racial ideology'.[5] This reasoning was an extension of the provisions of the Treaty of Potsdam. In this the Allies had declared that the NSDAP and its branches must be eliminated. In addition, there had to be guarantees 'that it would not be able to revive in any form; one must prevent any Nazi and militaristic action and propaganda'.

In the Soviet Zone of occupation and in the later GDR, war criminals were harshly treated in the first years after the Second World War. The Soviet military administration in Germany carefully kept to the provisions of the Treaty of Potsdam, which stated among other things:

> War criminals and those who took part in the planning or realisation of Nazi measures which resulted in outrages or war crimes, must be arrested and tried. Nazi leaders, influential Nazi supporters and the management of Nazi bodies and organisations and all other in-

dividuals who are dangerous to the occupation and its aims, must be arrested and interned. All members of the Nazi Party who took part in its activities in more than a nominal way and all other persons who are hostile to the occupation and its aims, must be removed from public and semi-public offices, and from responsible positions in important private corporations.[6]

In the 'anti-Fascist democratic revolution' and afterwards in the territory of the GDR up to 1965, 12,807 persons were sentenced for Nazi and war crimes. Of these, 118 people received death sentences, 231 were sentenced to life imprisonment, and 3,171 Germans were sentenced to more than ten years' imprisonment.[7] Up to the official end of de-Nazification on 10 March 1948, 520,734 former NSDAP members were removed from their jobs in East Germany.[8] These were impressive figures.

However, there was scarcely any question of official reflection on complicity, or a sense of sharing the guilt. Those responsible for the Third Reich were, according to the GDR authorities, exclusively in the Federal Republic. Now it was not difficult to point to the personnel continuities between Nazi Germany and the Federal Republic. Up to the summer of 1954 the German Bundestag issued a series of amnesty laws from which former Nazis could also benefit. Particularly famous were the so-called '131 people' who derived their name from Article 131 of the German Constitution passed in 1951. This Article made it possible *de facto* for many people who had been charged, including for example the bulk of former Gestapo staff, to become integrated into West German society again.[9] Hans Globke, the commentator of the racial laws of Nuremberg, and a Navy judge Hans Filbinger, for example, became secretary of state in the office of the Federal chancellor, and prime minister of Baden-Württemberg respectively. On this point the GDR continued to hold up a mirror to the face of Adenauer.

But on 12 May 1960 the German chancellor bounced this ball into the GDR's court in a painful way. The Adenauer government issued a bulletin with the title 'The man without conscience. Ulbricht as an unqualified judge – the red dictatorship simply took over from the brown one. A remarkable past.'[10] In this bulletin the Adenauer government pointed to ex-Nazis who had revived their careers in the GDR. This applied particularly to professions where there was a shortage of labour, but also the former National Socialist scientists and artists had found a safe haven in the GDR. It was, however, remarkable that some Communist Party members, including members of the Executive, had a dubious National Socialist past. The bulletin mentioned among others 56 former NSDAP members who sat in the East German *Volkskammer* elected on 16 November 1958.

The 'Research Committee of Independent Jurists' summarised in a publication the names of 220 former National Socialists who had a political or public position in the GDR. Among them were people who had become members of the NSDAP years before Hitler's assumption of power in 1933. This incidentally incomplete list contained the names of 15 vice-chancellors, two pro-vice chancellors, and 26 professors at universities and technical colleges. For example, the list mentioned Professor Herbert Kröger, who was then chancellor of the Walter Ulbricht Academy for Political and Legal Studies in Berlin-Babelsberg. In the Third Reich he had been a party member and at the same time *SS-Oberscharführer* in a part of Himmler's *SD-Hauptamt*. Both the president of the highest legal body in the GDR, Doctor Kurt Schumann, and the chairman of the Legal Department of the *Volkskammer,* Siegfried Dallmann, were former members of the NSDAP. An embarrassing case was that of Arno von Lenski. In the GDR he was a general and a delegate of the *Volkskammer*. In the Third Reich he acted as a co-judge of the infamous *Volksgerichtshof,* the highest judicial body of the National Socialists. Here he had put his signature many times to death sentences. Von Lenski, who was also a general under Hitler, was imprisoned by the Russians during the war. Subsequently he became a member of the Communist Party blanket organisation Nationalkomitee Freies Deutschland. Ulbricht conferred various high decorations on von Lenski, including the Medal for Fighters against Fascism 1933/45.

But according to the bulletin, former National Socialists were also represented in the diplomatic service and in the press. The leader of the press office of prime ministers, Kurt Blecha, joined the NSDAP in 1941. The deputy editor-in-chief of the central organ of the SED, *Neues Deutschland*, Dr Günter Kertzscher, had joined the NSDAP as early as 1937. The military and political commentator of East Berlin radio, Dr Egbert Freiherr von Frankenberg und Proschlitz, joined the NSDAP in 1931 and the SS in 1932. The former deputy editor-in-chief of *Neues Deutschland* and an envoy of the GDR, Gerhard Kegel, had been a member of the NSDAP since 1934. Doctor Siegfried Bock was a member of the Embassy Council and head of the Department of Legal Affairs and Treaty Matters at the Ministry of Foreign Affairs in the GDR. He was also the legal consultant of government allegations from the GDR during the Conference of Ministers of Foreign Affairs in Geneva in 1959. He had joined the NSDAP in 1944. The editor-in-chief of the magazine *Deutsche Außenpolitik*, Hans Walter Aust, joined the Nazi Party in 1933. Finally there was the case of Ernst Großmann, who was decorated as a 'hero' of labour in the GDR. Großmann had been a member of the Central Committee of the SED until 1959. In the Third Reich, as an *SS-Unterscharführer*, he worked as a guard at the concentration camp of Sachsenhausen.[11]

Ulbricht himself, the man to whom Adenauer's bulletin was devoted, was characterised very early by many Communist Party members, including the pre-war leader of the KPD, Ernst Thälmann, as an 'ice-cold apparatchik' and a 'man without conscience'. The statement by the Federal Government referred not without justification to Ulbricht's 'lack of character'. Ulbricht had emphatically defended the pact between Hitler and Stalin of 23 August 1939, until the outbreak of war between Germany and the Soviet Union. This treaty had driven many Communists to despair and sometimes even to suicide. In the Comintern newspaper *Die Welt* of 9 February 1940 he wrote from Stockholm in relation to this monstrous alliance: 'Many workers who want Socialism welcome the pact, particularly because it strengthens friendship with the great country of Socialism.'

On the other hand, Ulbricht saw the real enemy as Great Britain. In the same article he maintained:

> Both the German people, and peoples included in the German State (the occupied territories!) find themselves facing the question: not together with English major capital for the extension of war and a new Versailles, but together with the Soviet Union for peace, for national independence and the friendship of peoples! The working class, the peasants and the working intelligentsia of Germany, Austria, Czechoslovakia and Poland will be the strongest guarantee for the Soviet–German alliance and the frustration of the English plan.

The struggle against National Socialism should be stopped. The struggle was, as Ulbricht informed the KPD organisations in exile, against 'rapacious British imperialism'.[12]

From his exile in Moscow, Ulbricht had co-operated in the liquidation of rebellious Communists on the home front. He did this by passing circulars into the hands of Himmler's Gestapo. Ulbricht managed to discredit Communists who had fled to Moscow, so that they could be deported to Germany. The writer Margarete Neumann, one of the survivors of the concentration camp of Ravensbrück, was among those who met this fate. After the war she reported that German Communists, partly through Ulbricht's doing, were being murdered. The former editor of the *Rote Fahne*, and member of the Central Committee, Hugo Eberlein, confirmed that with the help of the Gosudarstvennoe Politiceskoe Upravlenie (GPU), Ulbricht rid himself of all party comrades who had called the pact between Stalin and Hitler a 'shameful betrayal of the international proletariat'.[13] Perhaps the memory of the monstrous alliance between Communist Party members and National Socialists was one of the reasons why the former National Socialists were able relatively simply to re–integrate into East German society. The list of ex-Nazis who occupied important posts in the GDR turned out in any case to be considerable.

The question arises of course why the Soviet Union tolerated these personnel continuities in the part of Germany occupied by it. Perhaps at the time Stalin's pronouncement prevailed: 'The Hitlers come and go, but the German people and the German State will continue to exist.'[14] In any case Stalin was under no illusions at all about the willingness of Germans to become Communists. In 1944 he said to the Polish prime minister, Stanislaw Mikolajczyk: 'Communism suits Germans like a saddle suits a cow.'[15]

Ulbricht had understood from early on that he needed a safety net for certain former National Socialist executives and workers. On 16 August 1947, in order not to lose people valuable to the production process, the Soviet authorities issued Order No. 201. This laid down that there should be a differentiation between 'Nazi activists' and 'former nominal members of the NSDAP'. After the official ending of de-Nazification on 10 March 1948, Ulbricht decided to give the former National Socialists who had been converted by decree their own political place in the GDR. To this end, on 16 June 1948, the National Demokratische Partei Deutschlands was founded. The East German *Wörterbuch der Geschichte* argued that in this party 'members of working classes allied with the proletariat' were organised. The NDPD emerged in the 'anti-Fascist democratic revolution as a petty-bourgeois democratic party' and 'developed into a social force in the socialist revolution in the GDR'.[16] These 'converted' Nazis 'drew the lessons from the past and broke consistently with Fascism and Imperialism', the historical dictionary went on. That, however, was far from always the case.

The former National Socialists made no secret of their German Nationalism, not even in the GDR. For example, in their manifesto of June 1951 they stated:

America contravened the Treaty of Potsdam and with malice afore-thought plunged us Germans into the greatest national crisis in our history ... but the American war must and will not take place! Germany must live! Therefore we National Democrats demand: Americans to America! Germany for the Germans. The Federal Republic is a child of national betrayal. ... Therefore we National Democrats demand: German unity over and above the government of national betrayal in Bonn, as a basis for peace, independence and prosperity for the whole of our German fatherland.[17]

The nationalism of the NDPD seems to exhibit a certain similarity to that of modern right-wing radicals. The NDPD paper was called *National-Zeitung*. The paper of Gerhard Frey, the founder of the right-wing radical Deutsche Volksunion in West Germany, has almost the same name (*Deutsche National-Zeitung*); and for both of them a right-wing authoritarian German nationalism seemed to be an important source of inspiration.[18]

In the GDR too the Cold War facilitated the integration of former National Socialists into society. The fact that these were fanatical German nationalists was no problem for Ulbricht. Because of the continuities in personnel between the Third Reich and the GDR, however, elements of National Socialist ideology were also preserved in the GDR. The effects of East German 'anti-Fascism' are difficult to quantify, and for many people the ideological charge in the SED would not have been uppermost. But 'anti-Fascism' in the GDR turned out to be mainly a 'foundation myth'. We shall examine in Chapter 8 the way 'anti-Fascism' was dealt with by using a practical example.

8

The *Ravensbrücker Ballade* and 'Anti-Fascism'

IN 1961, the year in which an 'anti-Fascist bulwark' was erected through Berlin, the East German writer Hedda Zinner wrote her play *Ravensbrücker Ballade*.[1] This play was a homage to the approximately 132,000 women prisoners who had been interned in the Ravensbrück concentration camp and its 70-plus satellite camps. According to estimates, the number of people who did not survive the terror of the principle of 'destruction through work' is between 50,000 and 92,000.[2] Zinner's play has a great measure of authenticity and tells a story of the rescue of the prisoner Wera. This Wera is able to escape death through the solidarity of the block elder, Maria, and others.[3]

The most remarkable thing about this play is that the situation in Ravensbrück is described in a well-balanced way. For example, there is talk of the tensions between the 'criminal' and 'political' prisoners. The play was praised in the GDR not only by the media but also by large sections of the public. Perhaps the painful recognition experienced by many survivors was an important reason for this positive appreciation. On the occasion of the 40th anniversary of the capitulation of the Third Reich in 1985 the play was to be adapted for East German television. Suddenly, however, an order was received from on high to abandon the production. What had happened since the first performance in 1961 to justify such a ban? It turned out that the president of the East German Committee of Anti-Fascist

Resistance Fighters, Otto Funke, had used his influence to halt the television adaptation. He felt that the role of the 'anti-social' elements and 'non-political' prisoners was over-emphasised. According to him the play also showed that a political prisoner gives way to SS pressure and betrays his colleagues, while an 'anti-social' prisoner behaves heroically. Finally, there was also a question of a too benevolent view of the SS. In vain Hedda Zinner argued that she had carried out thorough research and that glorification is the worst enemy of the truly heroic. It was all to no avail, because the ban stayed in place.

This censorship in 1985 of a play that had been so praised in 1961 indicates the evolution in the GDR from 'legitimate anti-Fascism' to 'legitimising anti-Fascism'. The Communist victims of the National Socialist terror had become, in the GDR, untouchable demi-gods, with the aim of legitimising the *raison d'être* of the SED and the GDR.

On the official side, the GDR made no efforts to deny this. On the contrary, on 24 August 1983 in a decree of the SED relating to the refitting of the *Mahn- und Gedenkstätten* of Buchenwald and Ravens-brück, it had been announced that:

> Honour is paid to the collaboration of former German women of Ravensbrück during the anti-Fascist democratic revolution, and in the construction of Socialism in the GDR, and their struggle for the preservation and protection of peace. The anti-Fascist basis of the GDR as a Socialist state of workers and peasants is emphasised.[4]

On one occasion during its regime, the SED paid the price for its political misuse of the concentration camps. During the revolt of 17 June 1953 rebellious East Germans also released condemned war criminals from jail. Among these, to the great indignation of the East German writer Bertolt Brecht, was Erna Dorn. After her release, this former commandant of the Ravensbrück concentration camp publicly 'made inflammatory speeches on the market square'.[5]

It also became apparent that the East German party dictatorship in fact was concerned with the concentration camps only in relationship to their *own* political doctrine. In September 1984, 20 lesbians planned to visit the former concentration camp at Ravensbrück. On their way there they were abused by employees of the East German secret service. ('You lot need a good f… ing'.) Subsequently they were jostled on their way from the station to the former concentration camp and bundled into lorries and arrested. The charge was 'unlawful assembly'. This one-sided approach by the GDR to National Socialism finally turned out to be counter-productive.

9

The GDR and the Legacy of German Political Lutheranism

IMMEDIATELY after 1945 Luther and Lutheranism were one of the 'intellectual roots of fascism' for many East German Communist Party members. They regarded the reformer as the 'gravedigger of German freedom', and the godfather of the infamous *Untertanen-gesinnung*, the 'orders-are-orders' mentality. For that matter such a view of Luther was not exclusive to East German historians and politicians. The German writer Thomas Mann, in his famous speech of 29 May 1945 in Washington, had also called Luther a 'massive embodiment of the essence of Germanness'. According to Mann, Luther was a 'hero of freedom', but 'in the German sense, because he had no awareness of freedom, that is, political freedom'.[1] In the same year the Swiss theologian Karl Barth suggested that a further development along the 'disastrous line' leading from Luther, Frederick the Great via Bismarck to Hitler should be made 'physically impossible'. Like other commentators he felt that there was a totalitarian thread running through German history. In his view one of the main protagonists in this totalitarian tradition was Martin Luther. He even regarded 'Hitlerism' as the 'present-day nightmare of the German pagans only Christianised in Lutheran form'.[2]

Was Luther really responsible for a 'line' which finally issued in Hitler's Thousand-Year Reich? And if so, which Luther, the theological one or the political one? It is indeed striking that all our autocratic, dictatorial and nationalist politicians in the Germany of the nineteenth and twentieth centuries have used Luther. In the nineteenth century it was the Luther Jubilee of 1883 that was one of the high points of German nationalism. A most important spokesman for this nationalist Luther interpretation was the historian Heinrich von Treitschke. In 1883 he wrote his treatise 'Luther and the German Nation' in the *Preußische Jahrbücher.* For Treitschke, Luther became the incarnation of the German soul and he argued:

> A foreigner may ask himself in despair how such marvellous contradictions could be united in a single soul, this violence of a crushing anger and this devout faith, such great wisdom and such child-like simplicity, such deep mysticism and so much *joie de vivre*, so much crude coarseness and so much gentle, sincere goodness. ... We Germans do not find this a mystery, we simply say: this is blood of our blood. From the deep eyes of this genuine German farmer's son flashed the old heroism of the Germanic people, which does not flee the world but tries to rule it through the power of the moral will.

According to this historian, with the help of Luther one could perfectly well exclude non-Germans: 'Wherever a German and a foreign national character conflicted with each other, Protestantism was always the safest guardian of our borders.'[3]

In the eyes of von Treitschke, the Jews in particular possessed a 'foreign' national character. In his article 'Our Prospects', published in November 1879 in the *Prussian Yearbooks*, he suggested in stylish academic language that 'the Jews are our misfortune'. In so doing he provoked the so-called anti-Semitism discussion. In a certain sense this historian made anti-Semitism respectable in Germany.[4] There was certainly a link between the racist anti-Judaism of the Luther admirer von Treitschke and Luther's theologically motivated anti-Judaism, to which the reformer had given malicious expression in his work 'On the Jews and Their Lies'.[5]

Luther was now proclaimed as a hero of the German nation and associated with Bismarck. The nationalists saw Luther not only as the embodiment of the unity of Wittenberg, Potsdam and Weimar; he was also now viewed as an important pioneer of the 'world empire of the German spirit' and promoted as the founder of the so-called 'cultural Protestantism'. Luther grew into the herald of anti-Catholic, anti-Socialist, anti-Slav, anti-Semitic and pro-Prussian Germany. He was not only at the foundation of 'German Christianity', but also became one of the axes of German nationalism, which soon degenerated into jingoism. National chauvinistic historians and politicians accentuated among other things Luther's national mission ('On the Christian Nobility of the German Nation in the Improvement of Christian Status', 1520), his creative linguistic powers, which were shown in his Bible translation, his blind faith in the authority of the State which was based on St Paul ('Be subject to the authorities which have you in their power') and his work ethic. Luther lived and worked, so they usually argued, mainly for his 'dear Germans'. The Reformer became the founder of the alliance between 'Throne and Altar'.[6]

During the First World War the 'political Luther' developed into an active supporter of German nationalism and militarism. Luther was associated with historical figures like General-Field Marshal Paul von Hindenburg.[7] This nationalist Luther formed the bridge over which the majority of Lutheran theologians in Germany marched towards National Socialism.[8] The political scientist Jürgen Falter argues in quite a loaded way that no other social factor had as much influence on the electoral successes of National Socialists as religion. In his view the Protestant camp was extremely receptive to the NSDAP.[9] But it is certainly true that during the elections in 1930, for example, the NSDAP made enormous advances, particularly in the Protestant agricultural areas.[10]

The fact that German nationalists in the nineteenth century and the National Socialists invoked Luther was in fact not that surprising. Luther formulated in a very radical way a view of life which was extremely obedient to authority, and for him authority resided exclusively with the Lutheran Prince on earth and with God in Heaven. A strict work ethic and other *ascetic* virtues of subjugation were for him of the greatest importance. Important virtues included obedience, order, punctuality and cleanliness. The Lutheran priests/princes should elevate these characteristics to 'State virtues', which were particularly popular in Prussia.

Luther's views on 'God-given authority' turned out to be suitable for all authoritarian political systems in Germany to support authority. Had not the Reformer argued:

> The Christian must allow himself to be duped and suppressed without the least resistance. Worldly matters do not concern him. He would rather allow robbery, theft, suppression, desecration, pennypinching, gluttony and rage to those who wish to pursue such things, as he is a martyr on earth. ... Wherever there is Christianity, blood sacrifices must be made, or they are not good Christians. They are not sheep for the meadow but for the slaughter; one always follows the other.[11]

At the time of the Peasant Wars Luther advised the authorities: 'The authorities should drive, beat, strangle, hang, burn, behead the common people and break them on the wheel, so that there is fear and that in that way the people are held in check.'[12]

Luther's intolerance, dogma of obedience, anti-Catholicism, anti-Judaism, his undisguised contempt for reason (he coined the phrase *Hure Vernunft* or 'that harlot Reason') and his plea for a strong work ethic were very easy for autocratic rulers to divert into political channels. In effect he was the founder of the alliance between 'throne and altar' in Germany, and the Lutheran nation became the sacred nation. It is not impossible that Luther, of course unintentionally and unconsciously, became the theological pioneer of the hostility between the West and the Protestant German territories. For him, Catholic Rome was the 'true Babylon' and he saw the Vatican as the 'synagogue of Satan'. This primarily theological contrast soon took a territorial form in Germany. In Luther's doctrine of the origins might be the source of the old animosity between the 'liberal' and 'decadent' Western *citoyen* and the 'disciplined' and the 'obedient' *Untertan*.

The National Socialists realised that at least. In the Third Reich too the reception of Luther was meant to fuse the Reformer with the State.[13] The National Socialists also made zealous use of Luther's work to fan hatred against the Jews.[14] Alfred Rosenberg, who was in such violent conflict with the theologian Karl Barth, regarded Luther's indignation, both as regards the 'national impulses' and the 'religious side', as a 'German protest of character'.[15] For him, Luther embodied the 'German Revolution'.[16] This 'German Revolution' formed and forms for militant nationalists the German reflection of the French Revolution. However, Luther's revolution proclaimed different values from those heralded in Paris on 14 July 1789.

Germany cannot, like France or England, pride itself on a tradition of successful revolutions. Revolutionary situations in German territories followed a set pattern, which allowed the reaction quickly to be victorious. This was different in countries like France or England. In England the Glorious Revolution of 1688 heralded the development of civil rights. The French Revolution of 1789 delivered France not only from feudalism but even today this revolution represents the principle of equality between people. In France the *citoyen* or citizen developed. In Germany the counterpart seemed to be more like an obedient subject.

This state of affairs came to an end in West Germany after the Second World War. In the GDR, however, the situation was different. Immediately after the war the Reformer was regarded as one of the most reactionary figures in German history, but the 'political Luther' was rediscovered at the beginning of the 1950s; this time in order to create the 'socialist personality' by means of Lutheran 'virtues'. Indeed, in Ulbricht's nationalism the 'political Luther' played an important role. The party leader realised that East Germans came from a culture in which Luther had occupied an important place. The old core areas of Lutheranism were in the territory of the German Democratic Republic. During the fifth party convention of the SED in July 1958 Ulbricht proclaimed his so-called 'Principles of Socialist Ethics and Morals'.[17] In this he appealed directly to the authoritarian aspects of political Lutheranism in Germany. The term 'commandments' was intended to emphasise the sacred and dogmatic character of these directives. The allusion to the Bible was not co-incidental. 'These moral laws, these commandments of the new

Socialist morality', argued Ulbricht, 'are a fixed constituent of our philosophy.' And he felt that 'only the person who commits himself actively to the triumph of socialism is acting in a moral and truly human way'. Here the distinction between 'Socialists' and 'dissenters' was established in a programmatic way. The world was divided into good and bad, black and white, 'socialist' and 'non-socialist', human and non-human. Within such a dualistic way of reasoning there is scarcely any room for tolerance and humanist consciousness. No one was more useful to Ulbricht in this than the 'political Luther'.

These Communist Party 'Ten Commandments' contain in a nutshell a number of characteristics of the whole of GDR society. With this political morality, Ulbricht tried to establish his 'community of socialist human beings'. Intolerance in respect of dissenters and the use of force against 'non-socialists' played an important part in this. For example, in a second commandment the Communist Party principle of 'legitimate force' was formulated: 'Thou shalt love thy fatherland and be always ready to commit thy strength and capacities to the defence of the workers-and-peasants-power.' The seventh commandment read: 'Thou shalt always strive for an improvement in your performance, be thrifty and establish the Socialist discipline of work.' Here one hears an echo of the Protestant work ethic. This 'Socialist work morality' was, according to Ulbricht, 'the core of all moral relationships in Socialist society'. In the eighth and ninth commandments the ascetic aspects of political Lutheranism come to the fore: 'Thou shalt bring up thy children in the spirit of peace and Socialism into multi-faceted, strong, firm characters and physically toughened human beings'; and 'Thou shalt live cleanly and decently and honour thy family.'

However, under Honecker, the Reformer was politically instrumentalised much more directly than had been the case in the Ulbricht era. In a certain way he even became 'synthesised' with the political system as had happened under Bismarck, Hindenburg and Hitler. At the beginning of the 1980s there was a renaissance in German-Prussian history in the GDR. Luther, Frederick II and Bismarck again became prominent historical personages. Some GDR historians – and one should not forget that history in the GDR was mainly political – pointed to the important role of Luther for the development of an individual GDR identity. The direct cause of this large-scale very positive re-evaluation of the Reformer was the Luther Jubilee in 1983. In 1980 an official Luther Committee was set up to prepare the festivities of the Luther Year in the GDR. The chairman was none other than party leader Erich Honecker. He proclaimed Luther as 'one of the greatest sons of the German people'.[18] This honorary title was also used literally for Karl Marx and one can scarcely overestimate the political importance of the rehabilitation of the Reformer. Probably the SED leaders were not completely aware of the consequences that this rehabilitation might have. Whether the GDR could obtain a greater national identity by means of Luther was doubtful. However, with the restoration of the Reformer in the GDR certain authoritarian aspects of German political Lutheranism were reinstated.

There were, besides the East Germans' striving for more national identity and delimitation from the Federal Republic, other good reasons for the renewed interest in Luther. The SED, for example, via the re-evaluation of Luther, was also trying to extend its influence over the Evangelische Kirche in Deutschland. The EKD was, within the GDR, the most important gathering place for voices critical of the system. The Lutheran Church had for many East Germans also evolved into a kind of link between the GDR and the Federal Republic. It is not impossible that many church-goers and preachers fantasised about reunification. This might help to explain the large proportion of vicars in the last cabinet of the GDR.

At least as much importance was given to Luther's striving to distinguish himself from 'feudal Catholicism'. 'Feudal Catholicism had orientated people towards idleness, laziness and begging,' argued Brigitte Bayer in 1983 during a broadcast on East German Schools Radio.[19] However this was also a swipe at Catholic Poland, where Solidarity was meanwhile celebrating its triumphs. The borders between the GDR and Poland were closed in 1981. The SED was particularly worried that the unrest in Poland might spread to the GDR. This locking out of Poland met with scarcely any resistance in East Germany. On the contrary, complaints about the 'lazy' and 'idle' Poles and the 'nuisance' experienced from their 'chronic hoarding' were heard constantly. Through the rehabilitation of Luther, which also implied anti-Catholicism, the East German government tried in a subtle way to increase the distance between East Germans and Poles.

Since 1980 Luther was idealised and honoured in the GDR. His life and work suddenly changed into an epic of heroism. Luther's militant anti-Judaism and his role during the Peasant Wars, which according to old Communist Party members had been a miserable one, became an insignificant historical footnote. The aims of Luther's 'revolutionary' adversary, Thomas Müntzer, who for decades had been a hero of the Communist Party, were now even sometimes dismissed as 'Utopian'.

'We must finally realise', argued the East German historian Gerhard Brendler, who wrote Honecker's speeches about Luther, 'that in our case Socialism is advancing in a Christian country.'[20]

It looked as though the Communist Party and sections of Lutheranism had to be synthesised. Not only because Lutheranism had historically developed in the territory of the GDR, but mainly because the Lutheran 'state virtues' again turned out to be of the greatest importance. In 1980 the GDR historian Hanke even formulated the Catalogue of Virtues which East German socialism needed: 'Order, punctuality, professional honour and bond with the organisation, precision and accuracy, honesty and solidarity with one's colleagues, cleanliness, culture in the village, house, farm and garden.' And further 'solidity, quality, the work ethic, professional honour and thrift', wrote Hanke.[21] These were the virtues not only of the East German brand of socialism but also of the *Untertan*.

Now the SED, just as it had done under Ulbricht, had also given its political view of the Reformer a sacred character. As is well known,

Luther had nailed his theses to the church door in Wittenberg. The Communist Party now proclaimed its own *Theses* on Luther. It is remarkable that the SED's *Theses on Martin Luther* do not say a word about Luther's tirades of hatred against the Jews and their consequences.[22] These *Theses* were, in their references to the development of German culture, fairly German-nationalist and Protestant in colour. They did not mention, for example, that from the Catholic side too large contributions had been made to the development of German culture.

The use of the 'political Luther' was not merely an East German matter. Karl Carstens, for example, argued that Luther in the present is a symbol of unity in a divided Germany: in both parts of Germany Protestants and Catholics, Christians and non-Christians celebrate Martin Luther's birthday.[23] And Chancellor Kohl cautiously pointed the way to the future of Germany by speaking of 'both parts of our fatherland' and by wishing that the people of the GDR and the Federal Republic of Germany will also be able to visit each other freely after the Luther Year. Luther is the Luther common to all Germans, his work is also important for politics.[24]

As chairman of the SPD, Willy Brandt too emphasised, for example, that Luther belongs to all Germans. His legacy cannot be divided into a Western and an Eastern part. According to Brandt Luther offers orientation, and is an example in an age when making sense of life is in crisis.[25] It is probably not sensible to yoke Luther to the chariot of political and social meaning. After all, a political appeal to Luther had generally not been a success in Germany; the more so because the 'political Luther' had often been at the centre of nationalist agitation and chauvinism. It is not a matter of the extent to which the historical personality or the theologian Luther is responsible for this. German political Lutheranism as a 'state religion' had always carried the values and 'virtues' in its banner, which seemed to play into the hands of nationalism, intolerance and violence. Germany's authoritarian, nationalist and conservative politicians always felt attracted to the Reformer. It is accordingly probably not a coincidence that right-wing radical spokesmen in Germany appeal to the 'political Luther'. In 1982, for example, the new-right historian Hellmut Diwald argued in his biography of Luther that Luther embodied 'the right of his whole people'. Luther had always assured people: I am 'born for my Germans and I serve them!' Alfred Rosenberg had already also appealed to this sentence.[26] Luther, according to Diwald,

> is not responsible for the first division of Germany, as has so often been argued. On the contrary, he is rather the person who shook the political awareness of Germans and their longing for freedom, and hence their solidarity, was awakened. His personal feelings break through most powerfully, when he suffers and he despairs of his country and his people.[27]

The leader of the right-wing radical Republikaner, Franz Schön-huber, referred to the Reformer. When in the summer of 1989 a priest refused to appear publicly with Schönhuber, he declared: 'I respect Luther, but not these internationalists. The reverend gentlemen are confusing the Sermon on the Mount with the Communist Manifesto. If in future they bite the hand that we are offering them, then we shall make the question of a church tax an item in our manifesto.'[28] The German right-wing extremist Manfred Roeder appealed even more clearly to the 'political Luther'. On 22 and 23 June 1996 he published in various regional newspapers in Hessen and Thuringia advertise-ments with the title 'Ninety-five Theses on the Occasion of Luther Year'. In them he rejected German *Alleinschuld* for the Second World War and opposed attempts to continue to impose a collective feeling of guilt on the German people for ever by means of a 'manipulation of history'.[29]

Unlike right-wing agitators, whose appeal to Luther is not particu-larly sophisticated, the GDR deployed the 'political Luther' in a more subtle way. However, both German right-wing radicals and East German party Communists used the Reformer to legitimise a political line which has not much in common with a Western democracy. In this respect they could also make a strong appeal to another legacy.

10

The GDR and the Legacy of Prussian Political Ideals

DURING and shortly after the Second World War the Allies agreed that Prussia represented a great threat. Prussia was associated by them with concepts such as 'fight-to-the-death' discipline, barrack despotism, militarism, expansionism and National Socialism. As early as November 1941 Churchill emphasised in a letter to Stalin: 'Of course the first task must be to prevent Germany, and particularly Prussia, attacking us a third time.' And at the Teheran Conference in 1943 the British prime minister declared: 'Prussia is, I want to stress that, the root of all evil in Germany.'[1] Churchill regarded Prussia as the seedbed of the eternal German traits. The other Allies seemed to be of the same opinion, because in 1947, by Decree No. 46 of the Allies, Prussia was abolished.

But not only the Allies: the German Communist Party had also initially had a decidedly negative opinion of Prussia. This state functioned for them as a poignant example, with which the 'better Germany' should contrast itself. Karl Liebknecht maintained as early as 1912: 'We cannot say with self-confidence like other people: I am a Prussian. When other people appeal to their nationality, it is because they feel themselves to be citizens. But when one speaks of Prussia one thinks of Prussian spiked helmets, of police and soldiers. ... That is the true nature of Prussia.'[2]

Despite its cultural legacy, Prussian history was indeed permeated with militarism and despotism. As far back as the eighteenth century, the Frenchman Mirabeau remarked of Prussia: 'This isn't a country with an army, but an army with a country.' And after the foundation of the Reich by Bismarck in 1871 this 'army with a country' dominated the whole of Germany. This preponderant Prussian influence was for that matter received in the rest of Germany with mixed feelings. In Bavaria, for example, people always kept the greatest possible distance between themselves and the 'bloody Prussians' in the north. Even after the foundation of the Reich, autonomy remained the main principle. And revolutionary social democracy spoke scathingly of a 'pan-Prussian and militaristic Reich'. However, the commentaries on the 'national mission of Prussia' within revolutionary circles was not wholly negative. Marx and Engels, for example, saw something positive in this 'German appeal of Prussia'. Their attitude towards Prussia and Bismarck was far from as one-sidedly negative as that of Karl Liebknecht. Engels went so far as to call the founder of the Reich admiringly 'friend Bismarck'. He did, it is true, consider the Prussification of Germany a great disadvantage, but he reproached Bismarck for not immediately annexing German-Austria after winning the war with Austria in 1866. Because now the result would be 'an immediate *increase in the Slav element* in Bohemia, Moravia and Karinthia'. And Engels was far from pleased with this 'Slav element'. He sighed: 'Unfortunately nothing can be done against the *two of them*.'[3]

In 1856 Marx stated that world history had never produced anything more 'foul' than Prussia. The reason for this harsh judgement was that Prussia 'had not subjugated a single powerful Slav nation' and 'in five hundred years, it did not even manage to obtain Pomerania until it was finally "exchanged". For that matter the Brandenburg Marches, when the Hohenzollerns took them over, never made any real *conquests* in the true sense of the word, with the exception of *Silesia* ...'. And he concludes his argument with the words: 'It is disgusting!'[4]

We must pause for a moment to consider this anti-Slav attitude of Marx and Engels. Anti-Slav sentiments were quite common in nineteenth-century Prussia. In itself that was odd because a large proportion of the inhabitants of Prussia were more Slav than German.

This had been the case since the time of the Great Elector and his son Frederick II. The core of the Prussian army consisted of non-Germans, including many Slavs. These were mainly Poles, Lithuanians, Kashubes, Wends, Pomeranians and Mazurs. There were many people of Slav origin not only in the rank and file but also in leading positions. At the Congress of Vienna, Prussia was designated as a 'Slav kingdom', and as late as 1830 Hegel still spoke of Brandenburg and Mecklenburg as being populated by 'Germanised Slavs'.[5]

What was the background to this anti-Slav attitude of Marx and Engels? At the time of the Industrial Revolution, the German bourgeoisie had had a great share in the definition of the concept of German. They believed they could raise their own profile through their anti-Slav attitude. As a result not only German nationalism but also German chauvinism emerged. This nationalist chauvinism is a product of Romanticism and a myth. In ethnic terms the Germans are a rather mixed nation, in which the Slav element is prominently represented. However, together with the wish of the bourgeoisie to found a national state, the need developed to define that state ethnically. This led to odd situations. The Prussian armies, which as has been said consisted in large measure of Slavs, were declared by the bourgeoisie to be *typically German*. Anti-Slav sentiments were obviously a good bonding element for this nationalist bourgeoisie. Marx and Engels may have been the designers of a new world, but they still had one foot in the tradition of German nationalism and Romanticism. The later German Communist Party was to adopt and use parts of both the nationalistic and the anti-Slav thinking of Marx and Engels.

At the end of the nineteenth century not only Jews, but also Slavs, and particularly Poles, were regarded as second-class citizens. Prussia had embraced Lutheranism at an early stage. There was a transition from the Lutheran virtues of obedience and discipline to militarism. The non-Lutheran Slavs, on the other hand, were generally regarded as inferior. The German empire regarded itself as a power that had to bring the Slav north-east into line. An example of this mentality was the Ostmarkenverein, founded in 1894. The object of this association was to Germanise the provinces that had been added to Prussia through the Polish partition, particularly Posen and West Prussia. One means they used to achieve this was German settlements. This missionary work was strongly supported by the Alldeutsche Verband founded in 1891. One of the principal manifesto points of this alliance was the elimination of 'foreign influences'. Most nineteenth-century German intellectuals shared these anti-Slav sentiments. As, for example, the sociologist Max Weber, who was a member of the Pan-German alliance, put it: 'It was we who humanised the Poles.'[6] Weber also made a plea for a 'German world power policy'. This corresponded with the political motto of the German empire: 'We Germans fear God and nothing else in the world.' And this Prussia, this old centre of the German empire, had always been an important axis of German identity both for German nationalists and for the National Socialists.

It was consequently not surprising that, immediately after the Second World War, an anti-Prussian iconoclastic fury raged in the part of Germany occupied by the Soviet Union. In East Germany the Berliner Schloß, the old residence of the Hohenzollerns, was blown up in 1950, and the street names were changed. Russian 'cultural officers' had the greatest difficulty in keeping this merciless settling of accounts with the Prussian past within bounds. For example, they were just able to prevent Christian Daniel Rauch's statue of Frederick II on the Unter den Linden Avenue from being melted down. Instead, the rider and horse disappeared into an out-of-the-way place near the palace of Sans-Souci in Potsdam. The Soviet Union knew all too well, from its own experience, that the cultural legacy of a country must not be literally destroyed, but ideologically reforged into an instrument of class struggle.

Ulbricht had learned these lessons of the Russian 'cultural commissars' well. He too realised that the GDR was largely within the former area of Prussia. Prussia was the most important state and it overshadowed the influence of Saxony, Sachsen-Anhalt, Mecklenburg and Thuringia. During Ulbricht's 'turn towards nationalism' in 1952 certain characters from Prussian history were consequently brought to the fore again. This applied to the Prussian military reformers Neidhardt von Gneisenau (1760–1831) and Gerhard von Scharnhorst (1755–1813), in the period of the Napoleonic Wars. Indeed, the highest military award that one could gain in the GDR was the Scharnhorst Order. But the nationalist *Turnvater*, Friedrich Ludwig Jahn (1778–1852: 'The purer the people the better; the more interbred the more criminal'), who was admired by the Nazis as a *Kämpfer gegen Ausländerei*, the nationalist philosopher Johann Gottlieb Fichte (1762–1814), and the political author and historian Ernst Moritz Arndt (1769–1860), were also praised. More remarkable than the rehabilitation of the Prussian reformers at the beginning of the 1950s was the partial rehabilitation of Fichte and Arndt. These 'best men of Prussia' were now opposed to the 'gang of traitors around Adenauer'. Ulbricht's historians thought it important to 'restore the great political and national (*vaterländisch*) importance of these men in their full glory in the Leninist Stalinist spirit, so they can be a luminous example for the struggle for the unity and independence of Germany for all honest and decent patriots'.[7] In his *Speeches to the German Nation*, Fichte had proclaimed that the Germans were an '*Urvolk*' and 'the epitome of a nation'. It was obvious that 'only the German … really has a nation and is entitled to have one' and that 'only he is capable of true and intellectual love of his nation'.[8] And Ernst Moritz Arndt tried to outdo this when he argued:

> I hate every amalgamation of peoples on earth because it is a means of watering down and hence a political and moral death of the various nations. It is precisely the Germans who have been wary of any merger of peoples, and hence have sacrificed the least of their natural originality. Much more than other peoples they have remained pure and have been able to develop from this purity their character and nature …[9]

Although on the one hand Ulbricht appealed to the Prussian and German basis of the GDR, on the other hand Prussia was painted in very negative terms, particularly in education. Despite or perhaps because of this *duality*, the negative picture of Prussia in education by no means always had the desired effect. The West German commentator Eckart Förtsch observed in 1981 that Prussia was positively evaluated by a large proportion of GDR schoolchildren in the 1950s and 1960s.[10]

However, it was not only elements of the political leadership or sections of school population, but also the East German historians who regularly expressed themselves in positive terms about Prussia. In 1965 the GDR historian Ernst Engelberg could no longer hide his admiration for the Prussia of history. So he maintained of the actions of the German soldiers in the Franco-Prussian War of 1870–71 that they fought against the French with 'death-defying bravura', 'self-sacrificing courage' and 'conscious discipline'.[11] The GDR historian Klaus Vetter also saw the positive sides of Prussian militarism. A propos of the collapse of the Prussian army in the face of the Napoleonic troops, he said in 1970 of the commanders that they

> surrendered to the enemy without a struggle. Only a few fortresses were illustrious exceptions, for example, Kosel in Silesia, Graudenz in West Prussia and Kolberg in Pomerania. The capitulation of the fortresses was quite consistent with the miserable chapter in Prussian history which had been heralded by the defeats at Jena and Auerstedt.[12]

The positive appreciation of parts of Prussian history by the East German elite was clearly unavoidable. The GDR could not simply continue to deny to its own population the Prussian part of its identity. The positive view of Prussia was, it is true, limited to aspects of Prussian history, but these were certainly publicly and continually highlighted. Suddenly the emphasis was on the fact that former despots like Frederick II and Bismarck, though unconsciously, had made a contribution to the pre-history of the GDR. The GDR now became aware of its national identity, which was largely Prussian. In 1980 the statue of Frederick the Great was brought back again from Sans-Souci and re-erected in East Berlin. This was done officially 'for cultural historical reasons to embellish the Lindenforum'. Wicked tongues in both East and West maintained, however, that he was now once more riding eastwards. But in any case Frederick II now regained the place he had lost during the Communist Party iconoclastic fury after 1945. Erich Honecker now even spoke of Frederick 'the Great'. Television series on the Prussian reformers appeared in which these military men were presented quite positively. And Bismarck too, the incarnation of the Prussian spirit and in fact of everything that the early GDR found despicable, was genuinely praised for his *foundation of the Reich*. With undisguised nationalism, the East German historian Ernst Engelberg argued in 1985 of the Franco-Prussian War of 1870–71: 'From a historical point of view France was in the wrong, because it was resisting the national movement towards the unity of Germany.'[13] Engelberg's biography of Bismarck could be obtained only as an exclusive *Bückwahre*, an under-the-counter product. This re-evaluation of Prussia seemed to further fantasies of reunification rather than keep them in check. Some West German politicians and commentators for that matter turned out to have been of that view for some considerable time.[14]

In 1987 I asked the East German historian Ingrid Mittenzwei, who was one of the architects of the new image of Frederick II, whether this revised view of the 'exploiters' might not lead to a changed view of the Third Reich. Because the *whole* of German history, including Prussia, was being paraded in the GDR to legitimise the State and the party, might not these re-evaluations – logically – also lead to the view that there were 'good sides' to the Third Reich? After all, the GDR had always described four people in German history as villains: Luther, Frederick II, Bismarck and Hitler. Three of them had been rehabilitated since the beginning of the 1980s. And what was the situation with number four? Were there positive sides to him too? After all, the GDR was a result of Hitler's Germany. But at the time she maintained:

Despite all his aggressive foreign policy and the stabilisation of existing relationships at home, a man like Frederick II smoothed the path for aspects of social progress (in the direction of a capitalist society), while a man like Hitler led the German people and many peoples in Europe into catastrophe. He, like other Fascist rulers, made absolutely no contribution to social progress.[15]

To answer the question whether this renaissance of Prussia might not have alarming consequences, Mittenzwei said:

> As far as Prussia is concerned, the first thing to notice is that this state no longer exists, so it can no longer present dangers for the present to which the historian reacts in a conscious or unconscious way. Secondly, in the GDR the social forces which had been decisive for the reactionary Prussian ideal and its aggressive foreign policy have lost all their support. Thirdly, there has been a period of intellectual reflection (in the schools too) on the reactionary aspects and consequences of Prussian policies.[16]

The eradication of the 'reactionary Prussian ideal' was an important part of the East German *raison d'être*. According to the GDR Communist Party, the reactionary Prussian ideal had been one of the roots of National Socialism. How had the founders of the GDR achieved their objective? First, by abolishing on paper the state of Prussia; secondly, by driving out the Junkers, the great landowners, and decreeing new property relationships; and finally, by informing young people about these acts. Reactionary Prussian ideals in their territorial and economic forms were abolished *by decree*. But this does not automatically mean the intellectual legacy of the reactionary Prussian ideal disappeared completely. We have seen that the GDR itself appealed to the Prussian 'virtues' in order to establish its dictatorship. And these Prussian 'virtues' have always been a good basis for totalitarian, anti-Slav and anti-Semitic sentiments and resentments. It was not only the legacy of the political Prussian ideal, which had not been fully come to terms with, that favoured these developments; there were also other social events that seemed to play into the hands of these trends.

III

The Right Wing of
the United Germany

11

An Anti-'Anti-Fascist'
Iconoclastic Fury?

THIS part of my book deals essentially with political developments in the former Federal Republic which, especially after the fall of the Wall, were to give fresh impetus to right-wing radicalism within Germany as it became unified.

In the GDR, some former concentration camps were set up as 'anti-Fascist museums' which were to serve the purpose of political education. One of these *Mahn- und Gedenkstätten* was the former concentration camp of Sachsenhausen. After the opening of the museum complex in 1961, all kinds of political mass demonstrations took place there. The oath-taking ceremony for the Nationale Volksarmee was conducted here, the Freie Deutsche Jugend made its political promises on this spot, and young East Germans were here installed as members of the Communist youth movement during the so-called *Jugendweihen*.

After the fall of the Wall it quickly became apparent that the 'anti-Fascist' message which was supposed to issue from the museum camp of Sachsenhausen had taken insufficient root. The railway yards from Berlin to Oranienburg were paved with the worst intentions. At almost every station, swastikas and countless insults to Jews and Russians were daubed on walls and benches. As the journey continued the stream of abuse only increased.

It was perfectly understandable that the German government should wish to take the reorganisation of these museum camps in

93

hand as quickly as possible. They had, after all, served mainly as a means of political indoctrination, and were not a contribution to an adequate confrontation with the National Socialist past. There were, nevertheless, a number of awkward aspects to this reorganisation arising from the position of Germans interned in the former concentration camps at the end of the Second World War.

Both the Treaty of Potsdam and the Allied Control Commission had determined that National Socialist functionaries must be interned. The Americans set up internment camps in, for example, the former concentration camps of Dachau and Neuengamme. In the Western occupation zones, 600,000 people were imprisoned from 1945 to 1948, 322,000 of them in the American zone alone.[1] In the part of Germany occupied by the Soviet Union, Germans also found their way to the former concentration camps. These were set up as so-called *Speziallager*. There were 13 of these camps in all in Soviet-occupied Germany, which administratively formed part of the Stalinist *Gulag* camps. The three best-known *Speziallager* in the Soviet zone of occupation were Buchenwald, Sachsenhausen and Bautzen. Not only National Socialists but also ordinary citizens, including (supposed) opponents of the East German regime were interned here.

In the former concentration camp of Sachsenhausen, from 1945 onwards, between 50,000 and 60,000 Germans were confined in the so-called *Speziallager No. 7*.[2] The *Speziallager* was located both within and outside the walls of the old concentration camp. According to rough estimates, between 15,000 and 30,000 people died from hunger, disease, cold, abuse and isolation between 1945 and 1950. Several thousand prisoners were deported to the Soviet Union, and many of them never returned. Shortly after the fall of the Wall, the mass graves of these prisoners were discovered at the edge of the camp.

In Sachsenhausen today this category of internees also receives proper attention. A special brochure published by the camp museum there is entitled 'Sachsenhausen 1936–1950. The History of a Camp'. The brochure states:

Sachsenhausen was in the first instance the scene of criminal activities by National Socialism and the SS but it is also a place where crimes were committed in the name of another ideology, with no less inexorable consequences. The creed of National Socialism and of Communism was the same: the opponent must be destroyed.[3]

Such conclusions seem to lead to an implicit equation of the victims of the period 1936–45 with those of 1945–50. This implicit equation is also apparent from another detail. *Within* the walls of the former concentration camp of Sachsenhausen since 1990 is an official memorial cross for the 'Victims of Stalinism 1945–1950'.

There was also a proposal in 1992 to commemorate the victims of the camp jointly in the camp museum. But this course of events provoked the criticism of Andreas Nachama. Nachama, who was the director of the exhibition Jüdische Lebenswelten in Berlin, maintained that the National Socialist element should alone be the theme of the museum. He found it 'intolerable' that the history of the *Speziallager* should be included in the exhibition on the camp site. In his opinion such an approach would play down the Nazi terror. However, the history of the *Speziallager* could be included as a short introduction into the pre- and post-history of Sachsenhausen. Today no one would demand of a united Germany that it should not commemorate the victims between 1945 and 1950. After all, many innocent people fell victim to the purges in East Germany even after 1945. But those interned in Sachsenhausen *during* and *after* the Second World War nevertheless represent completely different categories of victims, even if only because, after 1945, hundreds of SS guards were also interned in Sachsenhausen. If one were to lump all these prisoners together without comment, then one might indeed be playing down the essence of National Socialism.

However, not only the museums but also German justice appeared to equate National Socialism and the Communist Party of the GDR. In 1992 the first former East German judge of a *Speziallager* was sentenced and imprisoned in the so-called *Waldheim* trial. In 1950 this GDR jurist had been partly responsible for more than 20 death sentences. In 1990 the German public prosecutor also prosecuted two East Germans who on 4 June 1947 had murdered the *Oberstabsrichter* Erich Kallmerten in a prisoner-of-war internment camp in Lithuania. The National Socialist jurist was murdered because it appeared from his diary entries that he had pronounced hundreds of death sentences against deserters and partisans. This trial was all the more remarkable because after the Second World War judges with a severely compromised National Socialist past had been virtually untouchable.

The internment of the former head of state and party, Erich Honecker, was not regarded by everybody as a lawful act. This was, after all, an attack on the leader of the State which in 1978 had been recognised by 123 countries, a man who had been received as head of state in the Federal Republic as late as 1987. This legal procedure had a rather bitter aftertaste for some people, mainly because the vast majority of former National Socialists had got off scot free in West Germany, and had relaunched their careers there. The trial of Honecker awakened suggestions in many East Germans that might was obviously right and hence this was *Siegerjustiz*, a fact which, particularly in a time of social discontent, could have unpleasant consequences.

It is not beyond the realm of possibility that for some people 'confrontation' with the GDR past also meant confrontation with the National Socialist past. This tendency seemed to be encouraged by the often implicit equation of the GDR party Communism and National Socialism. And this, often implicit, equation might have been *partly* responsible for the fact that a social climate emerged in which the negative impact of National Socialism was played down. In this atmosphere anti-Semitic campaigns were not long in coming. The attack of 25 September 1992 on the Museum for Jewish Victims in Sachsenhausen can be understood in this broader social context. When the German foreign minister, Klaus Kinkel, visited Sachsenhausen after the attack, he threw more oil on the fire. He posed before the gutted ruins of the 'Jewish hut' and argued for a quick solution to the problem of asylum-seekers.

The former concentration camp of Ravensbrück had also been set up as an 'anti-Fascist' monument. But here too 'anti-Fascist' education had taken insufficient root. During a walk through one of the outer suburbs of Berlin at the beginning of 1991, I saw chalked on the walls slogans like: 'If you are hungry, if you are cold, go back to Ravensbrück.' In reply to my question why these texts were not being removed, an astonished passer-by said that these slogans had been there for a year, and walked on. As early as 1991 similar slogans had been daubed on the walls of the former camp at Ravensbrück by right-wing radicals. When a visitor from West Berlin who was present tried to stop them, he was beaten up.

In 1992 the Ravensbrück camp closed two rooms 'symbolically' to make it clear that various things were to be renovated. Many inhabitants of Fürstenberg, the locality close to the Ravensbrück concentration camp, had experienced the presence of the con-centration camp and, for a long time, that of the Red Army as a kind of 'second occupation force'. Subsequently, in 1991, plans quickly surfaced for the construction of a supermarket, a café and a car showroom in the immediate vicinity of the former camp. But to the displeasure of the inhabitants of Fürstenberg this led to protests at home and abroad which were aimed at preventing the building of the shops on this site. The general mood in Fürstenberg, however, seemed to be 'Let's get rid of it!' Given this attitude, it was not surprising that a fire bomb attack took place on this camp too.

The attacks in 1992 on former concentration camps in the new Federal territories reveal not only the failure of East German 'anti-Fascism', but also an increase in anti-Semitism. Right-wing radicals even delivered two pigs' heads to the site of the Jewish community centre in Erfurt in Thuringia. In a letter attached, they claimed: 'Pigs must die; Galinski [the former chairman of the Jewish Council] too. More Jews have to die.'[4] These outrages, with a strong anti-Semitic character, seemed to be encouraged by a social climate in which the legacy of the Third Reich was often played down.

But it was not only the policy of some German authorities that seemed to foster this trend. In 1992 many people believed that a line should finally be drawn under the National Socialist past. As early as 1990 the American Jewish Committee had established from surveys that over half of all Germans were in favour of suppressing the memory of the Holocaust.[5] According to a mid-1992 survey by the Emnid bureau, 62 per cent of those interviewed took the view that in future not so much attention should be given to the persecution of the Jews. *'A line should now finally be drawn under the past.'*[6] In Schwarz-heide in East Germany this was put literally into practice: the whole site of the former concentration camp was razed to the ground. This involved the devastation of the last concentration camp in Germany still largely in its original state.[7] Some East Germans may well have tolerated this because many of them would have particularly associated the Third Reich with the imposed 'anti-Fascism' of the GDR. However, a consequence of this was that both *legitimate* and *legitimising* anti-Fascism were *lumped together*. This tendency seemed to be more encouraged than inhibited by the reorganisation of the former concentration camps.

The often implicit equation of National Socialism and East German party Communism went beyond the reorganisation of the former concentration camps or legal practice to the renaming of East German streets and squares. It was the names of former Communist Party 'anti-Fascists' that suffered particularly. Together with them, the memory of Communist resistance to National Socialism also threatened to disappear.[8] In 1991 a street in Berlin which had been named after the Jewish doctor Georg Benjamin was re-designated. Johannes Becher also lost his Berlin street, which is now called Breite Straße. In Dresden the Bästleinstraße was given another name. Bernhard Bästlein was a Communist Party resistance fighter from Hamburg. This Reichstag member, executed in 1944, had to make way for the soprano Erna-Berger. In Leipzig, on the other hand, it was decided that street names commemorating Communist Party members executed by National Socialists must not be changed.

But it was not only the names of Communist Party resistance

fighters that disappeared from street signs. In Lübben in Brandenburg even the Heinrich Heine Straße was renamed. And in Ponitz in Thuringia the school named in honour of Hans and Sophie Scholl was given a new name. The memorial plaque on the school wall commemorating these students was removed in August 1991. These two German students, murdered by the Nazis, were the conscience of the small minority of young academics who had not committed themselves to the new masters under the National Socialist dictatorship. According to the headteacher of the school, these actions were the result of a decree by the Ministry of Education and Science. The department had determined that all the names of schools in Thuringia had to be changed. In Ponitz itself this measure met with resistance, which was not surprising. Local critics of the East German party dictatorship had for years taken their cue from Hans and Sophie Scholl in expressing their dislike of the regime. In many cases, it is true, the renaming of a street or square was desirable: a road which bore the name of the Stalinist Wilhelm Pieck pleased no one, but some Federal citizens wondered what the case was with names like Hindenburgdamm or Manfred von Richthofen Straße in West Berlin. They maintained that these had been militant exponents of German nationalism and militarism.

During this spring cleaning in the new Federal territories the statues were also removed. Socialist-realist art had once been designed to represent the socialist personality. Most East Germans were fed up with this. Nevertheless quite a lot of Berliners resisted the demolition of Lenin's statue. The opponents of the proposed demolition maintained that they were mostly concerned with the retention of a part of the GDR identity. After all, a whole generation had been shaped by it. Nevertheless, the German government ignored the reservations in a rather unsubtle way and removed the memorial. This course of events created bad blood.

In this rather tense atmosphere, which often showed the features of an anti-Communist cultural revolution, there were also plans to restore part of Hitler's bunker complex in Berlin. The bunker complex, which had been found near the Neue Reichskanzlei, was not the Führer Bunker but a shelter for the SS. The SS bunker could not be opened until March 1990 because this was in the 'death strip', the border area where the Wall had previously run. After the bunker had been opened the walls were promptly daubed with neo-Nazi graffiti. Nevertheless the director of the local archaeological service in Berlin, Alfred Kernd'l, wanted to convert this bunker complex into a museum. Moreover, both the parties of Bündnis 90 and the Greens supported Kernd'l's proposal. The Greens tried in this way to prevent a large-scale building project on this site. However, the Jewish community protested almost immediately against Kernd'l's plans. It maintained that this bunker would become a 'place of pilgrimage for old and new Nazis'. Plans to make this bunker open to the public seemed ill-judged in terms of the message this would give. Many right-wing youngsters in the new *Länder* would feel attracted to such a site. This would be most embarrassing, the more so because there are well-advanced plans to construct and erect a memorial for the murdered Jews of 17 countries in the immediate vicinity of the bunker.

Although there are similarities between National Socialism and party Communism, including its GDR variant, the differences between the GDR and the 'Thousand-Year Reich' are much greater and more fundamental. The GDR did not unleash a world war or pursue an imperialist war. There were no concentration camps there (as Chancellor Kohl believed), where millions of people were systematically murdered. Nor did the GDR force hundreds of thousands into slave labour and cause the deaths of many of them, whether or not through the principle of *Tot durch Arbeit*. When 'real Socialism' no longer existed, no Maidanek or Treblinka had to be liberated. No one in the GDR descended to the level of Hitler, Goebbels or Himmler. Putting National Socialism and GDR party socialism (implicitly) on a par reduces the impact of the Third Reich. Nevertheless German authorities seemed to want to suggest that both ideologies were equally contemptible. In this a number of West German conservative historians and politicians had already laid some groundwork.

12

The *Historikerstreit*: A Prefiguration of the Swing to the Right

The victors always write the history of the vanquished, survivors that of the dead. (Theodor Lessing, *Geschichte als Sinngebung des Sinnlosen*, 1927, p. 63)

NOT only did large sections of the German population feel that a line should be drawn underneath the Nazi past, but many conservative historians agreed with them. This view could also be read between the lines in a war of academics waged in the German media at the beginning of the 1980s. The official cause of this *Historikerstreit* was the question of whether or not the Third Reich was 'unique'. In itself this question was not new. As early as the Cold War period, National Socialism and party Communism were often lumped together in Western political theories. The equation of the two dictatorships culminated in the theory of totalitarianism. For adherents of this theory, both National Socialism and party Communism were branches of the same tree.

After this view had been forced more into the background in the 1960s, new life was breathed into it in the 1980s in the *Historikerstreit*. On the one hand, the 'uniqueness' of the Third Reich was a moral question, because German guilt for the Second World War was an issue. However, if Nazi Germany and the Stalinist Soviet Union were to be equally criminal, and Nazi Germany was therefore not really 'unique', this could imply that the Soviet Union might perhaps be a

101

little *more* guilty. After all, the Stalinist regime had existed *before* the emergence of the Third Reich, and Hitler and his like had made no secret of the fact that they feared the 'Red Menace'. On the other hand, this debate also had a current political dimension. Some conservative historians particularly seemed to realise that German reunification could be supported better by a German history that did not continually issue in 'Auschwitz'.

It was mainly the West German historian Ernst Nolte who expressed the need for such a history and also took the initiative in the debate. True, in an article in 1980 Nolte admitted that 'it would be a gross simplification if one were to see in the destructive urge of National Socialism nothing except a reaction to the destructive acts of Bolshevism.'[1] But, he maintained, 'this does not detract from the fact that the so-called destruction of the Jews in the Third Reich was a reaction or a distorted copy, and not an unprecedented or original act'.[2] If there was an element of uniqueness, then in his view this could be reduced to the 'technical procedure of gassing'.[3] Nolte reasoned consistently that it might be legitimate to argue that Hitler was entitled to intern German Jews as prisoners-of-war. Chaim Weizmann had after all announced in September 1939 that Jews all over the world would fight on the side of Britain.[4]

According to Nolte, in the dictatorial troika of National Socialism, Fascism and Marxism-Leninism, National Socialism was a *reaction* to Stalinism. Party Communism constituted the 'original' (in Nolte's words the 'prius'), and National Socialism was just a copy. For him, there was a causal connection or 'nexus' between the mass murders of the Russian revolution and Nazi Germany. 'Auschwitz', according to this reasoning, was a reaction borne of fear in the face of the destructive acts of the Russian revolution. In other words, Stalin and people like him were partly responsible for the creation of the Third Reich, and Auschwitz and the *Gulag* were for Nolte more or less equally criminal, apart, that is, from that 'technical procedure of gassing'.

There are similarities and differences between the two political systems. Let a number of similarities suffice: what for Lenin and

Stalin was 'class' for Nazis became 'race'.[5] What party Communists saw in 'capitalists', Hitler saw in 'Jewry'. For the party Communists, the New Man was the 'proletarian'. The Nazis got rid of the 'proletarian' in favour of the 'Aryan'. But the differences between National Socialism and party Communism are altogether weightier.

In National Socialism the principle of a biologically-motivated *inequality* of people was raised to the level of *dogma*. In party Communism – at least according to the manifestos – the crux was the principle of *equality*. National Socialism was by definition German nationalist. Party Communism, on the other hand, as regards its manifesto, is internationalist. In addition, the National Socialist mass destruction of people was carried out meticulously, dutifully, 'in an orderly fashion' and on an industrial basis.

The ideological motives behind this mass murder were a mixture of the rational and irrational. On the one hand, the peoples of the countries occupied by Germany were often demoted to the status of *Untermenschen* and deployed as work fodder for German industries. On the other hand, they were the victims of a unique racial delusion. Both the quantity and the quality of the organised mass murder by the National Socialists make the Third Reich, despite similarities with Stalin's Soviet Union, 'unique'. The more so as Hitler's assumption of power was authorised by an electorate.

Nolte's theses led to protests from many German historians and commentators. These Germans, among them the philosopher Jürgen Habermas, felt that certain conservatives were in the process of playing down the (road to) the Third Reich. It was seldom said aloud, but was not Hitler also the man who was the first to fight the 'Red Monster' from the East? Nolte 'lost' this war among academics. President von Weizsäcker pulled rank and declared the Third Reich to be unique. Nevertheless the reasonings of Nolte and others did have an effect on parts of the German population.

Reunification almost immediately heralded a new round in this debate. And now too some conservative historians, including Ernst Nolte, seemed to want to play down the essence and significance of the Third Reich. In his book *Nietzsche und der Nietzscheanismus* (1990) he returned to his thesis. Again the point of his argument was that National Socialism and party Communism were in fact closely related. Nolte interpreted Nietzsche's thoughts on his 'party of life' as a kind of philosophical design for Nazi genocide. Nietzsche, argued Nolte, had propagated a concept of a 'biological' and simultaneously 'historical-philosophical destruction'. This concept was partially linked to a 'social destruction' by a 'causal nexus'.[6]

Nolte claimed that Nietzsche postulated 'civil war unreservedly as a precondition' for the salvation of 'culture'. In short, Nietzsche had made an important contribution to the ideological basis for the extermination of many people by the Third Reich. True Nolte sees differences between Marx and Nietzsche, but for him both Marx and Nietzsche are the 'most important ideologues' of the European Civil War between 1917 and 1945.[7] Here too the message was clear: both Nietzsche and Marx, *National Socialism* and *party Communism* respectively, were in fact equally rotten. In his *Geschichtsdenken im 20 Jahrhundert (Historical Thought in the Twentieth Century)* (1991), Nolte went a little further. Though not directly in his words he follows the pattern indicated in a letter by Kurt Hiller and suggests that the gas chamber also had a defensive feature – with the aid of the gas chamber the 'soul' defended itself against the 'mind'.[8]

Another example of the equation of National Socialism and party Communism was given by the German publisher Wolf Jobst Siedler in his interview with the historian Arnulf Baring. In Baring's book *Deutschland was nun? (What Now, Germany?)* (1991), Siedler called National Socialism 'simply an authoritarian system' with an 'incredible criminal energy'.[9] Party Communism – obviously also in the GDR variant – was, however, given the label 'truly totalitarian system', certainly 'without great criminal energy', but 'socialism really leaves a desert behind it, admittedly without piles of corpses, but in a profoundly ravaged world'. In short, party Communism, even in its GDR version, was in fact *worse* than National Socialism. At least the Nazis left bourgeois institutions intact.[10]

Now the aim of these historians, as has been said, was not only to play down historical guilt as an end in itself. The second round of this *Historikerstreit* was, like the first one on the eve of the German reunification, determined by politics, because German history was also used as a vehicle for territorial questions. For example, Siedler argued: 'Of course we don't want to drive out the Poles, but I indeed believe that, Pomerania and Silesia and Bohemia-Moravia will one day again orientate themselves towards Germany.'[11] Poland, he speculated, might well ask for the stationing of German troops on its territory.[12]

Conservative historians like Ernst Nolte and Arnulf Baring seem to want to minimise the significance of the Third Reich. They are not the only ones. Many conservative politicians also gave evidence of their wish to draw a line under the Third Reich. As early as 1983 the CDU politician Alfred Dregger declared that the Germans 'must come out from the shadow of Hitler', and again become 'normal'.[13] On 25 January 1984 in the Israeli Knesset, Chancellor Kohl spoke of the 'blessing of a late birth'.[14] But the Austrian president Kurt Waldheim, who was criticised internationally because of his part in the war, was implicitly defended by the chancellor. Talking about his critics, Kohl pointed to the 'arrogance of those born later'. Kohl compared Gorbachev with Goebbels, and told the world that 'concentration camps' existed in the GDR. In 1985 he also received President Reagan in the cemetery in Bittburg where members of the SS were also buried. Such activities not only play down the nature of the Third Reich; it was also clear that German conservatives were from an early date taking account of the feelings of broad sections of the population and of nationalist commentators.

A most qualifying attitude was professed by so-called revisionist historians. Historical revisionists suggest or argue generally that the Third Reich was in fact a kind of protective dike against the Communist East. In other words, Nazi Germany was a monumental attempt to rescue the West. The whole of historical writing about the Second World War is in fact in the eyes of these revisionists one great falsification of history. They propagate, for example, a contemporary variant of the old *Kriegsschuldlüge* and the 'stab-in-the-back legend'. In the *Kriegsschuldlüge* German guilt about the outbreak of the First World War is dismissed as an Allied lie. The stab-in-the-back legend was a myth launched in 1919 by Paul von Hindenburg. This General-Field Marshal of imperial Germany maintained that Germany had lost the war because of its 'democratic' traitors. On the 'field of honour' Germany was undefeated. German nationalists attempted in those days to neutralise through such myths their rage and frustration at the loss of the First World War.

The German journalist Ralf Giordano once remarked of the stab-in-the-back legend that it constituted fertile soil for the development of 'nationalist and National Socialist lies about history'.[15] In his view it was clear from the denial of military defeat which was widespread among the population that there was a complete inability to take personal responsibility for the disasters of national history. After the fall of the Wall, the incapacity to face up to such responsibility seemed once more to be rather topical. Approximately 2.4 million East Germans had been members of the SED, or one of the parties in its block.[16] Again some of them refused to confront their own past. This often earned them the contempt of their children. Out of rage at the behaviour of their parents, some young people went to the extreme pole of the old ideology. But not only these young people; some ex-Communists also succumbed to right-wing authoritarian sentiments because they were furious at the old system. Right-wing radical groupings were able to function as a kind of psychological safety-net for these new pariahs. And there they were often cordially welcomed because, many right-wing radicals believed, were these new classless ones not also 'victims' of the (lost) Second World War?

According to the historical revisionists Germany has no responsibility for the outbreak of the Second World War. Listen, for example, to an original voice from the revisionist camp, Hellmut Diwald: 'The consciousness of guilt for the war (after 1945) is an example of a quite simply incomprehensible desire for self-recrimination. It is truly without equal in human history.'[17] Revisionists like the English historian David Irving not only deny the authenticity of the diaries of Anne Frank; they also deny – and this often goes hand in hand – the mass murders that took place in Auschwitz. According to them, this 'myth' was created only in order to discredit Germany for an unlimited period. The revisionists often appeal to the so-called 'Leuchter report'. Fred Leuchter, an expert in the field of gas chambers for American prisons, once took an illegal brick sample from the crematoriums at Auschwitz. From Leuchter's findings, which were recorded on video film, he argued that it showed that no gassings could have taken place. These, he argued, could not have been possible simply for technical reasons.

But no one expressed the revisionist point of view better than David Irving. According to Assheuer and Sarkowicz he declared to his opponents, 'I will enter the "gas chambers" of Auschwitz, and you and your friends may lob in Zyklon B in accordance with the well-known procedures and conditions. I guarantee that you won't be satisfied with the result!'[18] Now one could simply dismiss such views as pure nonsense, were it not that these ideas do nevertheless have a certain social influence. They make some people uncertain, the more so since Irving's books are published by the renowned German publisher Ullstein Verlag. Despite a ban on entering Germany, Irving was able to argue his case in Munich, Dresden, Leipzig, Gera, Stuttgart, Weinheim/Bergstraße and Oberhausen.[19] In June 1990 he travelled through the GDR, where he gave a dozen lectures under the title 'An Englishman Fights for the Honour of the Germans'. In these he argued that for decades the Allies had with the aid of 'forged documents' on Nazi atrocities, wanted to 'humiliate' the German people.[20]

Irving and those with similar views were also given indirect support by the previously-mentioned historian Ernst Nolte. Admittedly Nolte came out clearly against the 'Leuchter' report, but in 1990, in the right-wing radical magazine *Junge Freiheit*, he defended the revisionists implicitly by stating:

If revisionists and Leuchter among them have made it clear to the public that even 'Auschwitz' must be an object of scientific enquiry and controversy, then they should be given credit for this. Even if it finally turned out that the number of victims was even greater, and the procedures were even more horrific than has been assumed up till now.[21]

Besides Irving, the previously quoted historian Diwald is a well-known historical revisionist. In 1990 he published his book *Deutschland Einig Vaterland* (*Germany United Fatherland*). Diwald had maintained in 1978 in his *Geschichte der Deutschen* that only 7,000 people had died in Bergen-Belsen of contagious diseases and malnutrition.[22] The courts ordered him at the time to scrap these passages. Subsequently, the author did concede in his book *Deutschland Einig Vaterland* that there had been 'systematic' killing of Jews during the Third Reich, but he immediately qualified this. This 'simple observation', he maintained, 'is not adequate to the task of explaining the true course of events. Its meaning goes no further than, for example, the observation that in 1939 war broke out between Poland and Germany.'[23] No, Auschwitz was being abused by 'deliberately misleading and exaggerated statements', maintained Diwald, in order to discredit a whole people.

Caught up in these lines of reasoning, Diwald posited that in the summer of 1941 the Soviet Union was intending to attack Germany[24] and, *mirabile dictu*, Britain and France were supposed to have been intending to attack the Soviet Union at the end of June or the beginning of July 1940.[25] The book, which went into its third printing within six months, obviously nevertheless met a popular need. And that enthusiasm seemed to issue from the wish finally to draw a line under the Third Reich. As early as 1990 Diwald's conclusion had been that German unity would result in 'a radical and amazingly rapid change in the historical picture'.[26] Diwald's prediction proved correct.

Many German conservatives in the CDU and CSU accepted such opinions. The historian Hans Mommsen maintained as early as 1987 that, because of the 'liberal accommodation by the Federal government of extreme right-wing positions' and 'the offensive by neo-conservative commentators ... whose aim is to regenerate "normal" national consciousness', the 'dividing line between Neo-Nazi and neo-conservative positions ... has to a large extent disappeared'. 'The social tabooing of nationalist positions, together with their anti-Semitic and racist undertones, has as a result finally ceased to exist.'[27] In 1991 the political scientist Hans-Gerd Jaschke came to the conclusion that Diwald is formulating a perspective that has been adopted in the conservative political spectrum. According to Jaschke, this applied both to the *Frankfurter Allgemeine Zeitung*, particularly in the leading articles of Michael Stürmer, and to the *Republikaner*.[28] However, Diwald was not alone. He forms part of a movement which can be designated with the term 'the New Right' and which has a greater range of activity than one might suspect at first sight.

13

The New Right

> If the ... constitutional unity of Germany is achieved, then those
> political forces in the Federal Republic, which in spite of all critic-
> ism have always disapproved of the existence of an independent
> GDR nation, will have contributed to this [aim]. [These political
> forces] felt bound by the preamble to our constitution and have
> worked towards making it possible for the whole GERMAN NATION
> to achieve unity and freedom for Germany freely and autonom-
> ously.[1]

IN 1981 a report on the dissemination of right-wing extremist views
in society appeared in West Germany.[2] The conclusion of this *Sinus*
study was that over 13 per cent of the population of the former
Federal Republic had an extreme right-wing mentality. The survey
rightly warned against premature conclusions. But, in the view of
the researchers, it would be wrong to conclude that Fascism did not
change historically. It does not always have to be centrally organised,
and neither does it always look the same.

When it became known in 1997 that a problematic form of right-
wing radicalism exists in the German army, it was also clear that
extreme right-wing views were not a thing of the past. The immediate
cause was the news that one of Germany's most notorious neo-
Nazis, Manfred Roeder, had appeared as a guest speaker at the
German army's *Führungsakademie* in Hamburg on 24 January 1995.
Roeder, who is a convicted terrorist, had been able to give a talk at
this renowned academy on his projects for the re-Germanisation of
'North-east Prussia'.[3] In addition, it emerged that the German army

had given him the use of old equipment for his Deutsch-Russisches Gemeinschaftswerk, a radical right-wing organisation dedicated to the re-Germanisation of East Prussia.

The minister of defence, Volker Rühe, tried to dismiss the matter by stating that it was an 'isolated case' and spoke of 'media hysteria'. Chancellor Kohl immediately promised Rühe his full support and declared that he would not allow right-wing 'idiots and ideologues' to blacken the reputation of 'our sons' army'.[4] However, reports now appeared in the German press which gave an indication of the scale of radical right-wing attitudes in the army.[5] In 1995 there was a internal enquiry in the German army into the political views of soldiers. This showed that 21 per cent of would-be officers held nationalist conservative opinions. According to the survey, 55 per cent of the student intake of 1991–94 were right of centre.[6]

With some justification, the former secretary general of the CDU and present vice-chairman of the CDU/CSU parliamentary group, Heiner Geissler, observed in 1997 in an interview with *Südwestfunk* that the real problem was not so much Roeder's talk to the Bundeswehr, but 'a renaissance of *völkisch* [i.e., *Blut und Boden*] thinking in the last six or seven years'. According to Geissler, nationalism is socially '*à la mode* again'.[7]

Some of these right-wing extremist views are expressed by the New Right movement. The New Right is not a political party in the true sense of the word. It is rather an organisational and ideological social network which gained prominence particularly in the 1970s and 1980s. The ideas of the New Right can be traced back to Hegel and propagate reverence for the State, the nation and history. New Right views have great similarities with the ideas of the 'conservative revolution' in the Weimar Republic. Those former conservative-revolutionaries, like Arthur Moeller van den Bruck, Hans Freyer, Edgar Julius Jung and Ernst Jünger, turned out in practice to be direct precursors of National Socialism. Their 'counter-revolutionary' activity was directed at the time explicitly against the ideals of the French Revolution: freedom, equality and fraternity. According to the old conservative-revolutionaries, these were substitute values alien to the German State. For the conservative-revolutionaries the people, State and nation were more or less congruent concepts. They took their cue from imperial Germany and wanted to pick up the thread from before the (lost) First World War. Such nationalist and anti-Western sentiments and resentments played an important part in their thinking.

The New Right has largely adopted the political principles of these old conservatives. Here and there they add ideas which relate to present situations. The leitmotif of New Right aspirations is clearly expressed by New Right author Klaus Kunze:

> The most important is the breaking of the taboo. That is the first step on the road to the necessary re-evaluation of values. This begins with effective ridiculing of those parts of the opponent's 'ideology', which cannot be utilized and 'turned round', as, for example, the democratic principle can be.[8]

Important spokesmen of this grouping include the publicist Bernard Willms, Günter Maschke, and Hans-Dietrich Sander. They proclaim a 'national imperative' and do not regard the post-reunification German borders as definitive. This 'national imperative' is linked to a decidedly anti-Western attitude, in which the Second World War plays an important role. The latter is regarded in the words of the New Right publicist Hans-Dietrich Sander as part of a 'hundred-year war of the Western world against Germany'.[9] For that matter, as far as this anti-Western attitude was concerned, the New Right had a good sense of what was going on in broad strata of the German population. The German historian Baring made a catalogue as early as 1988 of many examples of a West German change of course. In his book *Unser neuer Größenwahn* he considered 'all those unspoken tendencies to detach ourselves from the West, the internal neutralising of the Federal Republic, with the links with the West remaining formally in place, but gradually being undermined'.[10] Baring pointed out at an early date that there would be a change of mood in West German society. The political leitmotif of influential parties in West Germany seemed to be the aspiration to achieve reunification. He even suggested that the German of the present day was beginning to look more like the pre-1945 Germany.[11]

Among other ways, the anti-Western attitude of the New Right expresses itself through a certain attachment to Russia and through anti-Americanism. There are various reasons for this. The New Right regards America as a society of 'traders' and such a community is totally opposed to the New Right view of the world. Central to this is a German *Volksgemeinschaft* geared to Prussian values. According to the researcher Margret Feit, the New Right opposes 'the levelling notion of equality' and propagates a 'society of achievement'. And yet they are not supporters of a free market economy on the Western model. On the contrary. The New Right regards liberalism as 'the cancer of our century and fundamentalism as the cure'.[12] The New Right maintains a view of an anti-Marxist *and an anti-capitalist* 'European socialism', which is to usher in a 'New Order'. And this 'New Order' is also to be spread within Europe, in order to achieve realisation in the 'European nation'.[13] The 'European nation' will eventually have to operate as a third power separate from the USA and Russia. According to its advocates, however, there is little doubt that Germany will dominate this 'European nation'.

But the New Right not only dislikes the fact that the Americans are 'traders'; in its anti-Americanism there is also disguised racism. For them, America is the perfect example of an immigrant society, and they are opposed to a 'multi-cultural' society. Usually the New Right's racism is not openly professed, but is cloaked in the observation that every race has a right to its own territory. For this reason the New Right propagates the concept of so-called 'ethno-pluralism'. In this 'ethno-pluralism', three large groups are distinguished, namely the Caucasian, the Negroid and the Mongol races. At the back of the idea is the view that a mixture of these races must be prevented and in practice a form of apartheid is advocated.[14] 'Ethno-pluralism' is an intellectual variant of the right-wing radical slogan 'Germany for the Germans'.

Furthermore, after the implosion of Communist Party rule in Europe, anti-Americanism offers a new vision of the enemy. According to its advocates, it is now about time the Americans were brought down a peg or two, not least because of their 're-education' of Germany after 1945, and the role they played in the division of Germany. In their view the German admission of guilt for the Second World War was dictated and they believe that a line should be drawn under the Third Reich once and for all.

Another prominent characteristic of the New Right is its anti-parliamentary attitude. For years it has opposed the 'waffle of the chattering classes'. It emphatically regards West German democracy and 'anti-Fascism' in the former GDR as a gift of the victors, mainly intended to humiliate the Germans. In the eyes of the New Right, liberal democracy is doomed to failure. The New Right periodical *Nation & Europa–Deutsche Monatshefte* expressed this clearly:

> There can be no doubt about it: the prevailing liberal-totalitarian system with its dream of a 'multi-cultural' society will fail. ... To the right a new generation is growing up which stands up for the nation; but no longer unconditionally supports this republic which increasingly harasses and persecutes them because of their beliefs.[15]

While the majority of Germans would certainly choose democracy as their form of government, such lines of reasoning could gain a certain degree of popular support as a result of strong attacks on politicians due partly to a number of corruption scandals and to a standstill in society. The more so since the Utopian thinkers of the New Right have long maintained that majorities are by definition incapable of leading the masses. The New Right will exploit the potential of democracy to the full, with the sole intention of abolishing it as quickly as possible. New Right authors have meanwhile left their publicity ghettos in order to join in the debate on power politics. Immediately after reunification it was mainly the right-wing radical Republikaner which sought to promote many of their ideas.

14

The Republikaner

THE Republikaner came into being on 26 November 1983 in the Bräupfanne café in Munich. The founders of the party were two dissident CSU members who felt that the CSU was no longer ideologically pure enough. The immediate reason for their break with Franz-Josef Strauß's Bavarian State Party was the DM 1 billion loan Strauß had granted to the GDR. This political manoeuvre went too far for a number of CSU members. One of the patriarchs of this right-wing radical association was the ex-SS man Franz Schönhuber. In his book *Ich war dabei*, published in 1981, he had depicted his membership of the *Waffen* SS in heroic terms. He soon became the public face of the Republikaner.

After some initial teething problems, the Republikaner scored their first great electoral successes in January 1989 during the so-called 'miracle of Berlin'. They took their place in the assembly there with 7.5 per cent of the votes.[1] In Berlin 14.3 per cent of 18- to 23-year-olds had voted for the Republikaner.[2] This breakthrough appeared to be partly a consequence of increasing racism and nationalism, particularly among the young. The Republikaner consequently did not hesitate to appeal directly to such sentiments. This was clear, for example, from a television election broadcast put out during their campaign on Sender Freies Berlin. This featured shots of foreigners and their children, with Ennio Moricone's 'Play Me the Song of Death' in the background.

The *whole* political establishment was outraged by this gross racism.

Both the left-wing Alternative Liste and the CDU protested. But the public prosecutor's office failed to pursue the indictment. A statement maintained that while the television broadcast was hostile to foreigners, there was no question of incitement to the persecution of any particular group in the population.[3] When Sender Freies Berlin decided under great pressure not to allow a second transmission, the Republikaner took it to court – and won.

On 18 January 1989 Schönhuber's party wanted to hold an election meeting in Berlin. Again this was opposed by a broad coalition. Tens of thousands of demonstrators tried to prevent the meeting. When the demonstrators reached the venue for the election meeting there was a very violent clash with the police. Several police officers and many demonstrators were injured. However, this secured a great deal of publicity for the Republikaner and their electoral successes increased still further. At the municipal council elections in Hessen on 12 March 1989 they took 10.5 per cent and 7.0 per cent of the vote in the two constituencies where they were represented.[4] But the Euro-elections of 18 June 1989 provided their greatest success.[5] The principal slogan of the Republikaner at these elections was: 'Europe Yes – this EC No'. Schönhuber's view of Europe is quite clear from his book *Ich war dabei*:

> Did not I share Europe's common destiny while I was in the *Waffen SS*? Did not the French feel themselves not only French, the Dutch not only Dutch, the Belgians not only Belgian, but especially as Europeans? They not only fought for this ideal, they died for it. The survivors paid the price in various prisons and internment camps, in some cases in barbaric conditions. They were also shot for it. But had they not also tried to stem the Soviet tide?[6]

Obviously the Republikaner regarded the Third Reich as 'Europe's common destiny' which was to 'stem the Soviet tide'. Despite such statements, more than two million Germans voted for this right-wing radical party in the European elections on 18 June 1989. That was 7.1 per cent of votes cast, which gave them six seats in the Strasburg parliament.[7] This good fortune gave Schönhuber and his party DM

16.1 million in election funds, and with this money it was possible to conduct an effective propaganda campaign. After the Republikaner had gained their first election victories, a section of right-wing radicals switched to this party. In 1989 the Republikaner scored still more successes. On 1 October 1989 they took 7.4 per cent of the votes in the municipal council elections in Nordrhein-Westfalen. They now had seven representatives on Cologne's municipal council.[8]

However, this right-wing radical upsurge was halted by German reunification. After all, one of their most important demands had been met. The ensuing crisis was aggravated by the official ban on the Republikaner by the East German authorities. On 5 February 1990 they were not allowed to take part in the first and last free elections for the GDR *Volkskammer*. This was not surprising, since Republikaner and neo-Nazis often seemed to be a single entity. The slogans 'Hitler Lives!' and 'We're There – REP (*Republikaner*)' occasionally appeared together.[9] Despite the ban by the East German authorities, the Republikaner enjoyed reasonable freedom in the GDR. Schönhuber was counting on the support of many *Wiedervereinigungs-verlierer* and assumed that there was an 'enormous potential pool' of sympathisers. After German reunification they were again admitted as a political party in the new Federal states, and this also meant a triumph for the New Right.

After the entry of the Republikaner into the European Parliament, the established political parties were well and truly alarmed. People began taking a keen interest in Schönhuber's party and the people who voted for it, and targeted surveys were carried out. What exactly was the kind of social reservoir Schönhuber was able to tap into? According to Claus Leggewie, a political science professor at the University of Gießen, the average Republikaner voter was male.[10] From a sociological point of view he was a 'man without habits'. On one occasion he assumed the shape of a frustrated young manual worker, on another he was a resentful elderly man from the *Hitler-jugend* generation, or else he was a former assistant anti-aircraft gunner. He also turned up as a man on unemployment benefit, or again in the shape of a dentist in dire straits, fighting the 'socialist' reform of the health-care sector.[11]

It is not easy to draw up a profile of the Republikaner voter. One can, however, say that the Republikaner form a small right-wing populist party, which appeals mainly to three target groups:

- shopkeepers, who in their view are the victims of exploitation by marginal groups;
- farmers, who must self-sufficiently 'ensure the safety of our food and protect us from political dependency and blackmail';
- and the police, who are included among the social professions.[12]

The programme of the Republikaner bears the clear stamp of the New Right. The authors Assheuer and Sarkowicz describe the party programme of the Republikaner as 'a mixture of nationalist pathos, trashy historical apologetics, resentment against foreigners and the petty-bourgeois need for certainty'.[13] The only thing that these voters appear to have in common is a diffuse nationalism and xenophobia. Like the old national-revolutionaries at the time of the Weimar Republic, the Republikaner preach a form of German nationalism with a *völkisch* or ethnic tinge; they are aiming for a modernised German *Volksgemeinschaft*. According to this concept, the German nation is not defined socially or pluralistically, but constitutes a community characterised by *Deutschtum* (German-ness). At a Republikaner Party rally, for example, Schönhuber gave his view of the racial attack in Hoyerswerda in East Germany: 'Hoyerswerda is the sole responsibility of the complacent and lazy politicians in Bonn who have pursued *Entdeutschung* [destruction of the German character].'[14]

One practice of the Republikaner is to offer nationalist solutions to social problems. In this Schönhuber went much further than other 'right-wing' German conservatives, since he wanted to implement *real* radical changes in Germany. At the political *Aschermittwoch* gathering of the Republikaner in Cham on 28 February 1990, Schönhuber proclaimed himself the 'Renewer of Germany'. He demanded the conclusion of a peace treaty and the immediate withdrawal of foreign troops from Germany. He fiercely opposed statements agreeing to the surrender of former German territories. Not *de jure,* but *de facto* the Republikaner pursue 'pan-German' aims. This applies not only to the *Ostgebiete* and Kaliningrad. According to Michael Schomers, even parts of Italy (South Tyrol), France (Alsace-Lorraine), Belgium and Denmark are candidates for restitution.[15] The Republikaner will probably try to win back voters with these demands, in addition to their xenophobic manifesto points.

The journalist Michael Schomers worked undercover with the Republikaner for a while. He argued that underlying the practice of many Republikaner officials is a 'Fascist elitist theory'. According to Schomers, unequal rights are derived from the premise that 'all men are unequal'.[16] Schomers is not alone in making these assertions. Alexandra Kliche once had a management position with the Republikaner. In her book *Nichts wie weg!* (*Get Out of Here!*) she confirms Schomers's conclusions. She maintained that brawls and swearing-matches, intrigues, obscenities, slander, misappropriation of funds, spying, lust for money and power were the order of the day with the Republikaner. The infiltration of the party by 'Nazis', 'neo-Nazis' or 'Fascists' finally led to her leaving Schönhuber's party. She also called the Republikaner a 'crazy mixture', in which 'no one can any longer distinguish the conservatives from the right-wing extremists. In this way right-wing extremism is gaining legitimacy. Or rather, it has already gained legitimacy.'[17]

The party of Schönhuber – who, as it happens, left the party himself in 1994 to be able devote himself to the unity of the European right – is at present for tactical reasons keeping its distance from right-wing radicals and extremists. This ostensibly moderate course was already apparent from the party manifesto approved at a conference in Rosenheim on 13–14 January 1990. But this declaration, whose authors included the New Right historian Hellmut Diwald, is actually a camouflaged mixture of national-revolutionary ingredients. The changes are mainly semantic in nature, as can be shown by a number of utterances by leading Republikaner figures.

On 31 July 1996 the chairman of the Berlin-Charlottenburg regional section stated on his section's information line: 'We Republikaner have the obligation to make the German will to survive credible to the world and to prove in the face of history that Germany is not waddling to its multi-criminal, multi-cultural and Maastricht-inspired doom.'[18] In an election address on 10 March 1996 for the municipal council elections in Bavaria, the then deputy federation chairman Otmar Wallner inveighed against the supposed 'extermination of the German people'. In addition he demanded a 'homogeneous nation', thus excluding minorities from German society: 'We Republikaner want to maintain the Germans as a homogeneous people. We do not want a multi-cultural society or a Balkanisation of our fatherland. The extermination (*Endlösung*) of the German people through national suicide must be stopped.' In a pamphlet published by the Mark constituency, the deputy-chairman of the Republikaner in the state of Nordrhein-Westfalen, Reinhard Wnendt, wrote: 'We Germans are becoming a minority in our own country! ... Anyone trivialising the problems arising from mass immigration is deliberately contributing to the subversion of our people (*Umvolkung*)!'[19]

The Republikaner also attack the *Umerziehung*, the re-education and reorientation of the Germans by the Allies at the end of the Second World War. Right-wing radicals and extremists regard this *Umerziehung* as imposed and illegal, and are consequently questioning the legitimacy of the liberal-democratic constitution. In their view this *Umerziehung* must be superseded by a *Nationalerziehung* or national education. In a pamphlet issued by the Thuringia state association, *Grundsätze 01/96* (*Principles 01/96*), the Republikaner maintain:

> The failures from the Weimar republic and those re-educated by the Allies – the parties of dissolution, the CDU alias the centre, the SPD, the FDP alias the Deutsche Staats Partei, and the PDS alias the KPD/SED – are pursuing the unconstitutional dissolution of the Federal Republic and are creating a monstrous multi-cultural state without a German identity and without the German Mark. [They] tolerate all kinds of gangs: mafiosi, Triads, anarchists, dropouts, squatters, etc.

With a mentality that stems from their re-education, they tolerate organised crime like that in the USA. ... The abolition of Prussian values as a result of re-education by re-educated politicians ... has led to the nepotistic republic on the Rhine with values like greed, the provision of special privileges and corruption in public institutions resulting in losses that run into billions.[20]

On the one hand, they feel obliged to present an 'acceptable' manifesto. At the same time, however, they must more or less 'hide' this official programme from their own voters. Despite the apparently 'moderate' line of the party, a ban on this political group is not beyond the realm of possibility. The grounds for this would go beyond manifesto pamphlets. The party press, its propaganda and its chosen means of agitation, as well as the speeches of party officials, indicate whether a political party is democratic or not, and in the case of the Republikaner that is open to doubt.

According to the German internal security service, there were indications as early as 1996 that the Republikaner were turning against the democratic order. However these indications, according to the German authorities, tended to decrease. This is due in no small measure to the role of the new party chairman Dr Rolf Schlierer, who was re-elected chairman at the National Party Assembly on 4–6 October 1996. Schlierer makes sure that the government has as little hold on the party as possible. He does this partly by distancing himself from right-wing extremist groups. Moreover, the Republikaner have the image of a serious party and present themselves as a democratic alternative for potential conservative and National-Liberal voters and sympathisers. They obviously do this with some success.

In 1996 the Republikaner participated in the parliamentary elections in the Federal states of Baden Württemberg and Rheinland-Pfalz and in the municipal elections in Bavaria and Niedersachsen. After their electoral losses in 1994 and 1995, they now scored a success. In the elections for the parliament of Baden Württemberg on 24 March 1996 the Republikaner took 9.1 per cent of the votes

and 14 seats (1992: 10.9 per cent = 15 seats). As a result they succeeded for the first time in being re-elected to the parliament of a
Federal state. In the elections for the parliament of Rheinland-Pfalz
on 24 March 1996 the percentage of votes cast for the Republikaner
increased to 3.5 per cent. (1991: 2 per cent). At the municipal elections
in Niedersachsen on 15 September 1996 they gained 31 seats (1991:
21 seats). The number of votes cast for the Republikaner in the
Bavarian municipal elections on 10 March 1996, on the other hand,
fell to 1.8 per cent (1990: 5.3 per cent). In the municipalities not
included in a *Landkreis* (rural district) and in the district assemblies
they gained a total of only 72 seats (1990: 254).[21]

After the electoral successes in Baden-Würtemberg and in
Rheinland-Pfalz in 1996 the Republikaner obtained approximately DM
4.5 million from state funds – the party was preparing for the
Bundestag elections in 1998. According to the security service of
Nordrhein-Westfalen, the Republikaner will try particularly to exploit
the high level of unemployment and social deprivation in Germany. In
May 1997 the minister of foreign affairs, Franz-Josef Kniola, therefore
warned expressly against an underestimation of the Republikaner. In
his opinion this party represented 'a much greater danger' than one
might suspect from press reports. Under their new leadership the
Republikaner, in Kniola's view, are, without taking a high profile in
public, obviously pursuing the goal of 'sneaking across the five per
cent threshold'.[22]

These developments are not 'typically' German and probably not
essentially different from similar developments elsewhere in Europe.
It is more worrying that some of the Republikaners' manifesto points
seem to be influencing the Conservative political establishment in
Germany. In a certain sense the Republikaner are situated between
the Conservative parties and the right-wing radicals. For some German
conservative politicians they are a barometer of what is happening in
certain sections of 'the people'. The conservative parties take up
manifesto points from the Republikaner, adapt them and subsequently
present them in an 'acceptable' way. This became clear during the

Historikerstreit, but the reluctance of Helmut Kohl in 1990 to recognise the Western frontier with Poland, or the 'asylum debate' in 1991–92 also show the influence of the Republikaner.

It is not impossible that the conservative parties felt that in this way they could neutralise the influence of the New Right. In itself a similar endeavour is not new. There is a rumour for example that, as early as 1968 at a meeting of the CSU in Bad Reichenhall, Franz-Josef Strauß is supposed to have said: 'One must use the national forces, however reactionary they are. That's what De Gaulle did. Subsequently it's always possible to ditch them in an elegant way.'[23] It is, however, debatable whether right-wing radicals will allow themselves to be used as 'convenient stooges' by the conservative political establishment or by anybody else.[24]

The echoes of Schönhuber first became audible during the so-called *Historikerstreit*. The Republikaner had campaigned for years for taking German culture 'out of the criminal sphere'. The Republikaner go much further, and one can even pinpoint anti-Semitic undertones. That there are anti-Semitic patterns of thought in the party is shown, for example, by the pamphlet *Grundsätze 01/96*, which was published by the Thuringia state section: 'We are not anti-Semites, but we don't want a Canossa republic. As German patriots we reserve the right to speak out against Jewish slanders and Jewish patronising behaviour. There must be an end to the Jewish indoctrination of the Germans intended to exploit their sense of guilt.'[25] And here too they are touching a sensitive chord in German society which deserves some attention.

15

Anti-Semitism

THE West German government and the political parties have always taken the phenomenon of anti-Semitism very seriously. Since the Second World War German society has tried honestly to exterminate anti-Semitism root and branch. Consequently, no single politician or party wishes to attract the charge of being anti-Semitic; and any accusations in that direction are almost always immediately and correctly dismissed. Yet in 1992 so many offences with an anti-Semitic character took place in the united Germany that the World Jewish Congress contemplated the introduction of penalties against Germany.

It does indeed look as if Germany is still struggling with an anti-Semitic legacy. According to a 1992 survey by the weekly *Der Spiegel*, 32 per cent of Germans believed that Jews themselves were partly responsible when they were 'hated and persecuted'; 42 per cent maintained that the Nazi regime had both good and bad sides;[1] 75 per cent of West Germans questioned were also against paying Jews compensation after reunification – in East Germany that percentage was almost 44 per cent.[2]

In December 1997, Ignaz Bubis, the president of the Jewish community in Germany, stated:

Anti-Semitism is still not a thing of the past in Germany. On the contrary: after a declining tendency in the last two years we can in fact record in the last six months a further increase in anti-Semitic and xenophobic acts of violence, although not to the same extent as in the period from 1992 to 1994.[3]

Anti-Semitic attitudes in the population as a whole have not increased. It would be better to admit these were always quite widespread. However, what has changed is the fact that anti-Semitism has become more overt. As the distance from the end of the Second World War increases, many more people who in secret always had anti-Semitic ideas are daring to admit it. Another new feature is the continuing trend to the right in German universities – anti-Semitism and xenophobia in circles of so-called intellectuals who were supposedly left-wing. It is a matter of importance to monitor this development closely.[4]

As the distance from the Second World War increases, the tendency among certain intellectuals to relativise the impact of the Third Reich becomes stronger. When in October 1998 the well-known German author Martin Walser received the respected 'peace prize of the German book trade' he said in his word of thanks in Frankfurt's Paulskirche that no serious person could deny Auschwitz or its consequences. However, at the same time he deplored the 'permanent presentation of our shame' and warned against using Auschwitz as a 'moral club' (*Moralkeule*). According to Walser, the Germans were a 'normal people' now.

Part of this normalcy, however, is an increasing number of anti-Semitic incidents. On 28 October 1998, for example, unknown persons rushed a pig through East Berlin's Alexanderplatz with the Star of David and the name 'Bubis' painted on it. This incident was neither mentioned in police reports nor made public – allegedly to avoid copy-cat crimes. In the same month an explosive device was set off at the grave of Heinz Galinski, former chairman of the Jewish community. In December 1998 Julius Schoeps, director of the Moses Mendelssohn Centre for European Jewish Studies in Potsdam, stated that 'every week now in Germany seventeen Jewish cemeteries are being violated'.[5]

Neither the former GDR nor West Germany has been able to banish anti-Semitism completely from society. According to a report of the co-ordinating council of associations for Christian–Jewish collaboration, almost 160 Jewish cemeteries were desecrated between

1948 and 1957. Up to the end of January 1960 almost another 700 anti-Semitic incidents were recorded.[6] It is uncertain to what extent the East German secret service had a hand in this. But it is certain that the Ministerium für Staatssicherheit staged anti-Semitic incidents in order to discredit West Germany. Nevertheless Konrad Adenauer thought the scope of these incidents so alarming that he felt obliged to reassure his Jewish citizens in a television broadcast on 16 January 1960.

According to the German journalist Ralph Giordano the suppression of the National Socialist past played, and continues to play, an important role in the xenophobic and anti-Semitic violence which has taken place in Germany since reunification. Giordano was speaking with reference to the undigested Nazi past of a *zweite Schuld* or renewed culpability. De-Nazification, the cleansing of German society of former National Socialists, had, generally speaking, been inadequate in West Germany. The National Socialist social elites continued to exist in the Federal Republic to a great extent. Only a handful of former Nazis were convicted. Those who were punished were mostly punished for their *criminal* acts. The *political* and *moral* guilt was however often underexposed.

Fortunately, the majority of young West Germans and the West German intelligentsia concerned themselves actively with the criminal nature of the Third Reich. This led at the end of the 1970s to a so-called *Hitlerwelle*. Despite this wave of interest in the Third Reich, Christian Zentner observed in 1975 in a publication intended for wide circulation:

> As young people we were the first who were addressed by the failed encounter with the past. We were to be democratically re-educated. Parents, teachers, politicians, commentators all failed in the same way. Passionate and hypocritical condemnation, well-intentioned and blind apologetics, cowardly and helpless suppression still characterise the situation. The older generation is still struggling with guilt and responsibility, apology and recognition. ... One needs to understand why even today one hears people cry for 'Adolf' when, in taxis and pubs they are talking about crimes, long-haired hippies and oil sheiks.[7]

The mid-1970s saw the appearance of many publications dealing with the Third Reich. This was not only to satisfy popular 'scientific' curiosity. German young people were now posing the question 'What did you do during the War?' to their parents' generation. This interest in Nazi Germany sometimes went hand in hand with deeply masochistic side swipes, and overkill in terms of often gruesome information. It is not impossible that this also, unintentionally and unconsciously, contributed to keeping anti-Jewish sentiments and resentments alive.

An often inadequate coming to terms with National Socialism was perhaps also apparent in the attitude to political conflicts in the Middle East. In the student riots of the 1960s, radical left-wing and anti-American German students chanted 'Kill the Jews, make the Middle East red!'[8] The Yom Kippur War of 1973 and the policies of Menachem Begin towards the Palestinians also seemed to result in a latent anti-Semitism in Germany; also among sections of the political left. When in the summer of 1982 Israeli troops invaded Lebanon, the Social Democratic magazine *Vorwärts* spoke of the 'end of the taboo period', because 'after the Lebanon campaign we Germans dare for the first time in decades to express a critical view of Israel'.[9] It may be argued that this 'taboo period' was ended too prematurely. After all, during the 1990 Gulf War the reaction of the political establishment and sections of the West German population could be called quite simply unhappy. Iraq attacked Israel and threatened it with gas missiles which had partly been supplied by German companies. Thousands of Germans took to the streets to demonstrate for a ceasefire. Such an action was unrealistic and, in Israel, in any case met fierce criticism. The visit of Foreign Minister Genscher did little to change this.

Anti-Semitism also still occasionally lurks in the German language. The Berlin scholar Wolfgang Benz argued that Nazi jargon such as *arisch*, *ausmerzen* ('scrap', literally 'exterminate'), *Endlösung* and *Sonderbehandlung*, continues to be used without any reflection.[10] This applies equally to the highest political levels. In 1989 Chancellor Kohl visited

the former concentration camp of Auschwitz. Because this was initially scheduled on a Saturday some Jews protested because it was
after all the Sabbath. Kohl's government spokesman, Hans Klein,
stated subsequently that he had not wished to insult *internationales
Judentum*. However, the term *internationales Judentum* retains the
language of the Third Reich when it was used by the Nazis to indicate
a 'Jewish world conspiracy'. It is not surprising that such usage at
government level finds imitators in the street. For example, in 1990,
in the Hermann Maternstraße in East Berlin there were posters up for
a few days with the slogan: 'Defend yourself against *internationales
Judentum*'. It can be argued that such slogans kept alive an 'anti-
Semitism without Jews', whereby the psychological mechanisms which
underlie the hatred of the Jews could be transferred to other population groups. Some Turks living in Germany appear to be of this
opinion when, after arson attacks on their compatriots, they cried in
dismay and rage in front of the cameras 'We are not Jews!' The
atmosphere between Germans and non-Germans had certainly not
improved since German reunification. This was partly due to the way
in which many German politicians had dealt with the problems
relating to asylum-seekers.

16

The 'Debate on Asylum-seekers' and the Influence of the New Right

In the same way as we lack political talent, we lack psychological in-sight. Because both are the same thing: empathy. (Walther Rathenau, 'Konnten wir Frieden schließen – als es Zeit war?', 15 January 1920, in: *Was wird werden?*, p. 15)

ALMOST immediately after the fall of the Iron Curtain Germany again became a 'front-line state'. This time the 'menace' was a potential immigration from the East; the threat seemed to consist of large numbers of migrants from Central and Eastern Europe. Almost half the refugees heading for Western Europe sought sanctuary in the Federal Republic.[1] The reception of such a large quantity of people was bound to cause problems. These are not only of a technical and organisational nature; the integration of these people into German society is a difficult matter. At the moment the inconvenience which this migration movement entails is largely borne by the united Germany. Under the Schengen Agreement it was determined that Germany would have to carry out the role of 'policeman'. The agreement stipulated that border controls were to be dismantled between the countries that were signatories to this agreement. On the outer borders, however, more strict inspections are planned and these inspections fall largely on the shoulders of Germany.

For Germany to bear the main responsibility for these streams of migrants would not be tolerable. After all, since the end of the Second

129

World War the whole of Western Europe has hoped for the disappearance of Communist Party rule in Central and Eastern Europe. And all Western European democracies have continually pointed to the lack of freedom in which those Europeans had to live. Now that this Western European dream has come true, that must mean a *common* political and social responsibility for the consequences. This is an essential premise for any discussion of the problems arising from the large numer of asylum-seekers.

German asylum law, which was embedded in the constitution after the Second World War, was a very generous arrangement: whoever asked for asylum was granted it. This hospitality was not surprising. The founders of the German constitution after all had themselves been refugees for long enough, and in particular these exiles realised only too well how valuable the right of asylum is. But changed circumstances require new solutions. It is therefore not surprising that Article 16 of the German constitution ('political refugees have the right to asylum') was amended on 1 July 1993. This change was, however, very rigorously implemented. *De jure* the right to political asylum remains in place, but *de facto* it appears to have been virtually abolished. Refugees who enter Germany via so-called 'safe third-party states' can no longer apply for asylum. The list of these safe *Drittstaaten* automatically includes all EU countries, Poland, Sweden, Switzerland, Austria and the Czech Republic. These are all countries via which one can reach the Federal Republic overland. Additional safe lands of origin include: Bulgaria, Finland, Gambia, Ghana, Norway, Romania, Sweden, Senegal, the Slovak Republic and Hungary. Anyone attempting to enter the country from a safe land of origin by aeroplane is first accommodated at the airport and then deported.

Deportation via a safe land of origin cannot be contested by the administrative courts. Asylum-seekers can appeal against this only from abroad. Only those who can prove that they do not originate from a safe country, and have not entered Germany via a safe neighbouring country, are included in the procedure. The vast majority of asylum-seekers will not meet these conditions. This policy is having an effect. In 1997 76.2 per cent fewer asylum-seekers came to Germany compared with 1992. Only 4.9 per cent of them were recognised by the government (in 1996: 7.4 per cent).[2] It must be emphasised that this change has come about with the support of the EU countries. In this matter the German government is both an interested party and the implementer.

The debate on an amendment to the right of asylum took place long before the fall of the Wall. That is at a time when there was still scarcely any question of large movements of immigrants. It was mainly the German conservatives who, from the beginning of the 1980s onwards, did not let an election go by without making the right to asylum and the 'flood of foreigners' an election slogan.

In 1983 the UN Commissioner for Refugees spoke of 'unique measures to deter asylum-seekers in the Federal Republic'.[3] In 1984 the German bishop Franz Hengsbach argued that the treatment of asylum-seekers 'was disgraceful for a civilised nation'.[4] Since 1973 refugees were gathered and accommodated in so-called *Sammellager*. Slowly but surely they all received the same food and were forbidden to work. Social provisions were also reduced to a minimum, and their freedom of movement was limited.[5] An integration of foreigners into German society was not promoted by this policy.

After the collapse of the Wall a latent xenophobia among sections of the German population turned into an open hatred of foreigners. Not only nationalist agitators but also most political parties indulged in invective against asylum-seekers in particular. In 1991 and 1992 slogans such as 'We are not an immigrant country', 'flood of asylum-seekers', '*Asylantenschwemme*', 'pseudo-asylum-seekers', and 'inundation' were the order of the day. These slogans were partly responsible for activating the latent racism in society. Extremely negative references to asylum-seekers gradually became part of the normal vocabulary of many German politicians. Right-wing radical groups used largely the same jargon; they simply went much further. For them it was only a short step from 'inundation' to *Überfremdung* – a word that has in the meantime also become an election slogan of the CSU.

It was mainly the Republikaner who formulated views which were current among many people in German society. It emerged from a survey by the West German bureau Emnid, published by the weekly *Der Spiegel* in 1991, that 34 per cent of those questioned had some sympathy for the emergence of right-wing radical tendencies as a reaction to the number of 'foreigners'.[6]

This was not a development which had begun only after the fall of the Wall. As early as 1987, the researcher Wilhelm Heitmeyer from Bielefeld had come to the conclusion that 43.5 per cent of 16- and 17-year-olds appeared to agree with the right-wing radical slogan 'Germany for the Germans'.[7] For a long time such tendencies, which were expressed, for example, in computer games with names like 'Kohl Dictator' and the 'anti-Turk game', were not taken seriously by the German authorities. But during the so-called 'asylum debate' in 1991 and 1992 it became increasingly clear that the German conservative parties, particularly the CDU and the CSU, had recognised this worrying trend among the population, and were trying in their own way to neutralise these developments.

Some right-wing radical slogans became *salonfähig*, that is socially acceptable, for them, as is shown by a number of examples. The Bavarian CSU politician, Edmund Stoiber, who in 1993 was elected as prime minister of Bavaria, talked of the threatened miscegenation (*Durchmischung* and *Durchrassung*) of the German people. The jurist Manfred Ritter (CSU) compared refugees to a 'swarm of locusts, which wherever it alights leaves a desert behind it'. The CDU mayor of Lebach in the Saarland, Nikolaus Jung, maintained: 'The town will not allow gypsies to dance here.' And the local politician Wilhelm Schmans from Jesteburg said unashamedly: 'That rabble must go.'[8] In October 1991 the prime minister of Mecklenburg-Vorpommern, Alfred Gomolka, even challenged the 'multi-cultural society', and argued in favour of 'a nationalistic creed'.[9] The barrage of abuse against foreigners still continues: in April 1997 the CSU member of the Bundestag, Erich Riedl, declared when appearing in a beer tent that the Balkan peoples grow up 'with a knife' from birth and 'still have a knife on them in the cemetery … '.[10] The CDU politician Otto Hauser, who was appointed as government spokesman by Kohl in 1998, rebuked the minister of education and cultural affairs, Annette Schavan, because she had allowed a teacher from Afghanistan to wear a headscarf: 'If you allow that woman to wear the Islamic headscarf while she carries out her duties as an official, I suppose tomorrow you will have to allow the wearing of a red star or neo-fascist symbols.'[11]

This list of examples can be extended almost indefinitely. Many conservatives had no qualms about using the problems relating to asylum-seekers for electoral purposes. For example, on 18 September 1991 the secretary-general of the CDU, Volker Rühe, proclaimed in *Bild Zeitung*: 'If the SPD makes trouble during the interview with the Chancellor on 27 September, from that day on every asylum-seeker will be an SPD asylum-seeker.'[12]

A policy directed against asylum-seekers, however, was not by now an exclusive province of the Conservative parties. Even before the 1991 elections the SPD mayor of Bremen closed the door on asylum-seekers from certain countries. In the same year the Social-Democrat mayor and corporation of Höhenkirchen-Siegertsbrunn rejected the building of accommodation for 200 asylum-seekers. Formally he appealed to a zoning plan. He regarded this as the 'only chance' of preventing the construction. The SPD mayor of Datteln, Horst Niggemeier, joked on 18 September 1991 with reference to receiving asylum-seekers: 'We are so full, that we couldn't even offer an African ant asylum.'[13] At the beginning of 1993, under pressure from its rank and file, the SPD too finally voted in favour of an amendment of the Asylum Act. In protest at this, the German writer Günter Grass left the SPD.

Both the street-fighters and the New Right commentators could feel strengthened by the amendment of the Asylum Act. It was mostly the German conservatives who were doing their utmost to keep right-wing voters within their own ranks. Within the CDU it was mainly the National-Conservative Deutschland Forum which campaigned against asylum-seekers. At the end of 1992 a spokesman from this grouping, Rudolf Krause, took the initiative of publishing a memorandum on German national questions. In this Krause talked of the 'West German media landscape that is one-sidedly left-wing and makes a mockery of German honour'. In the media, in Krause's view, 'criminal asylum fraudsters were given more attention, understanding and cordiality than our own German *Volksgenossen*'. According to Krause, foreigners who had committed criminal acts should not be allowed to 'have a lazy life in welfare prisons'. Instead this East German CDU politician demanded 'hard work in the service of the German community, such as building roads'.[14] In the first instance the Christian Democrats scarcely protested against these statements. They seemed to be frightened of losing voters on their right wing. Only after long-term criticism did the party decide to take measures against Krause, and to suspend him because of his right-wing radical views. Krause subsequently went over to the Republikaner in Sachsen-Anhalt.

The German conservatives had seen such developments coming – and reacted in their own way. As early as October 1991 the Vereinigung der Verfolgten des Naziregimes submitted an indictment against the Braunschweig CDU to the public prosecutor.[15] The reason for this was that during the elections for municipal councils in Niedersachsen the Christian Democrats had distributed a leaflet, insulting in its contents. In it 95 per cent of all asylum-seekers arriving in Germany were branded as 'pseudo asylum-seekers'. The Christian Democrat mayor, Rudi Steinbacher, maintained: 'They simply come to us and try to gain by deceit the status of asylum-seeker.' He described the gypsies as 'Sinti and Roma' who liked travelling around and talked of 'the man from West Africa who wants to make money by selling drugs in our country'.[16] Reports of the persecution of the Roma in Romania were not mentioned by these politicians. Since the fall of Ceaucescu the gypsies' villages have often been burned to the ground. Statements like those of Steinbacher are all the more pernicious because the Roma and Sinti are among the groups of victims of the Third Reich.

The label 'pseudo asylum-seekers' was also used by some politicians to make a distinction between the various groups of refugees. This emerged, for example, from a remark of the Berlin senator for Internal Affairs, Dieter Heckelmann. In August 1992, this CDU politician maintained that 'pseudo asylum-seekers' were threatening the reception of victims of the Yugoslav civil war. At a press briefing Heckelmann wondered how long the politicians 'would wait to get the Germans to accept the daily spectacle of the swelling stream of asylum-seekers'.[17] Heckelmann was able to rely on wide social support for his statements. The sympathy among the German population for Bosnian or Croat refugees appeared to be greater than, for example, that for Romanies.

Nor were the 'ethnic Germans' from Eastern Europe designated as 'pseudo asylum-seekers'. These 'ethnic Germans' are the descendants of German ancestors who often emigrated long ago and frequently no longer speak the German language. Nevertheless they are able to claim rights as Germans. For them, both German politicians and the media used the word *Aussiedler*, which means something like evacuees. For others, particularly southern migrants and refugees, however, the term *Asylant* was used. The designation *Asylant* seemed to be intended to distinguish the groups of migrants 'linguistically'. However this word has a pejorative undertone and in German suggests the words *Simulant* (faker) and *Querulant* (trouble-maker). Not only at the grass roots but also in the political arena, a racist mood began to be discernible increasingly clearly. The delegate for foreigners in the Berlin Senate, Barbara John, asserted in 1992 that people in Germany were still pursuing 'a bit of apartheid'. This despite the international treaty of 1966 for the removal of every form of racial discrimination which Germany had signed in 1969.[18]

In 1991 and 1992 large sections of the media also created an anti-asylum-seeker mood. The German scholars Andreas Quinkert and Siegfried Jäger felt that, with a few exceptions, all organs of the press were opposed to the Asylum Act and the asylum-seekers, with the *Bild Zeitung* at their head. At a time of increasing racist violence this, the largest paper in Germany, put up hoardings with texts like 'Asylum-Seekers in the Area. Who is Supposed to Pay for Them?' These were the same slogans that the right-wing street terrorists used. All refugee organisations agreed that the 'asylum debate' has contributed to the increase of racist violence in Germany. The head of studies of the Tutzing Evangelical Academy, Jürgen Micksch, went so far as to maintain that this asylum debate has done 'deep damage' among the German population.[19]

A policy focusing on integration between Germans and foreigners was not really being promoted by the German conservatives. A spokesperson for the German Ministry of Foreign Affairs maintained in an annual report of 1991 that 'political common sense' requires a 'cautious implementation of immigration':

> When the traditions [*sic*] of a people do not accept movements of immigration, it may lead to uncontrollable reactions to 'alien elements'. Such peoples, of which the densely-populated German-speaking areas are part, can tolerate only a certain proportion of foreigners. If this is exceeded, the nationalist forces are the beneficiaries. In the case of such a development the right of asylum, which is so important for persecuted people from other countries, may suffer.[20]

Obviously these authorities worked on the principle that one simply had to accept unpleasant 'traditions' from German history. Such views seemed to suggest that there was little understanding of xenophobia on the official side. It would have been much better if the German authorities had pursued from an early date a policy which was explicitly geared towards the integration of foreigners into German democracy.

An essential question is who is actually a German and who is not. The German conservatives still want foreigners to obtain German nationality under the provisions of an antiquated law. In its main outlines this law dates from the regime of Kaiser Wilhelm II, namely from 22 July 1913. One becomes German by descent from a German father, or by illegitimate birth from a German mother. One can always become German if a German father recognises the child. Another possibility is a declaration by a foreign woman that she wants to become a German citizen when she marries a German. Finally there is the possibility of naturalisation. Anyone born in Germany of a German mother in a married relationship with a father of *another* nationality is not automatically a German, even though he has – often with his whole family – lived all his life in Germany. He has the same responsibilities as every other German, such as the payment of taxes, but he remains a foreigner and will continue to have to apply for a residence and work permit. This person does not have the *right* to German citizenship. The authorities which have to decide this question are allowed to do so 'as they see fit', as the old law puts it.[21] However if he does obtain German citizenship, then he must give up his other nationality because dual nationality is not allowed.

Such an arrangement causes great inconvenience, particularly for the 2.2 million Turks living in Germany. Turkish inhabitants, for example, get into problems in relation to their hereditary rights in Turkey if they give up their Turkish nationality. Not only is the number of foreigners being artificially increased by such a procedure, it is also a negatively discriminatory practice which makes it difficult to integrate into German society. Since the end of 1992 and, in particular, after the murder of five Turks in Solingen in Germany in 1993, initiatives have been developed in Germany which are intended to make it possible for foreigners to obtain dual nationality. It is after all not fair to expect, for example, Turks living in Germany to be prepared to give up their Turkish nationality and hence one of their identities. However, all initiatives in this direction have almost always originated from the SPD and Bündnis 90/The Greens, and were firmly dismissed by the CDU/CSU.[22] Of Turks living in Germany at the end of 1997, approximately 125,000 held a German passport.[23] The chairman of the Turkish community in Germany, Hakki Keskin, accused Chancellor Kohl in particular of reinforcing the prejudices against the Turkish community.[24]

On the legal level a fair amount needed to be done, all the more so because 60,000 'foreigners' are born in Germany each year.[25] In

spite of already announced proposals from the Social Democrats and
the Greens to change German citizenship laws, many Germans still
have hesitations about integration and no longer appear to be aiming
it. In 1997 the leading left-liberal German weekly, *Der Spiegel*, for
example, stated bluntly that 'the integration of foreigners has failed'.
On the front page of the magazine entitled 'Dangerously foreign' a
shouting woman waving a red flag is depicted; to the left young
Muslim girls are reading the Koran, while to the right young boys
are showing their knives and other weapons.[26] Anetta Kahane, who
in 1997 headed the regional offices for matters relating to foreigners
in the former GDR, maintained that this *Spiegel* article 'poured oil on
the flames of the generally racist (*völkisch*) mood in the East [ex-
GDR]'.[27] Leading Social Democrat Gerhard Schröder has adopted
many conservative slogans concerning the 'criminal behaviour' of
foreigners, and in the start-up phase of the elections of 1998 was
disseminating them on a regular basis. Schröder was criticised by the
syndicate 'Asylum in the Church' for 'indirect arson'.[28] Cornelia
Schmalz-Jackobsen, who is the Federal delegate for questions concerning foreigners, argued that it is only a short step from the powerful
statements of Schröder to a general campaign of slander against
foreigners.[29]

A restriction of the right to political asylum is unlikely to solve the
problems relating to the integration of foreigners into German society.
The fact is that economic and political refugees will still try to get
into Germany, and if these asylum-seekers are officially 'criminalised'
by the German authorities, violence against them might even increase.
Germany also requires an immigration act which can control migration correctly. However, neither the Schröder government nor the
conservatives are inclined to introduce such a law. Many, particularly
conservative, German politicians still deny that Germany should be
given the status of a country receiving immigrants. Such a view is,
however, not realistic. The fact is that Germany *is* an immigration
country. A modern history of German territories is in fact one great
history of (im)migration. Since 1945 alone, 15 million refugees

migrated from the former *Ostgebiete* and the Eastern European states to the three Western Allied occupation zones. There they integrated fairly well into German society and made a great contribution to the reconstruction of the country.

There are not only ethical and political but also economic arguments for a positive attitude towards foreigners. The economic *Wirtschaftswunder* which Germany experienced in the 1950s and 1960s was partly made possible by foreign workers. In 1955 they came from Italy, in 1960 from Greece and Spain, in 1963 from Morocco, in 1964 from Turkey and Portugal, in 1965 from Tunisia and finally in 1968 from Yugoslavia. But these *Gastarbeiter* not only had a great economic significance in the past; even today they are of great importance to the proper functioning of the German economy.

Despite the increasing xenophobia, the *enfant terrible* of the CDU, Heiner Geißler, persisted in his demand for 'multi-cultural cohabitation'. As early as 1991 the deputy chairman of the CDU maintained:

> The Swabians, the Hessians, the people from Baden and the Pfalz who emigrated to America 150 years ago did not do so because of the statue of liberty – that did not yet exist – but because they were perishing and starving here. They were economic asylum-seekers. In world history people have always left a place where they had nothing to eat, and made for the spot where there was something to eat. ... Those who do not understand the moral categories should at least understand the material consequences.[30]

Geißler's criticism was mainly directed at his party's coalition partner the CSU, which seems to be eager to neutralise the influence and ideas of both the Republikaner and Gerhard Frey's Deutsche Volksunion. In 1998 he frankly stated: 'The CSU argues highly irrationally. And everything irrational is grist to the mill of the right-wing extremists.'[31] This appears to be no overstatement. In 1998 the CSU planned to deport parents of 'foreign' children found guilty of a crime. This is not only the exact opposite of integration but is tantamount to a new form of *Sippenhaft*.[32]

Again in 1999 the German conservatives demonstrated an inclination to approach questions relating to 'foreigners' in a rather irrational way. Shortly after the change of power in Bonn, the new minister of the interior, Otto Schily, put forward his plans to make it easier for aliens to become German citizens. The gist of his proposal was that foreigners, among whom are many people of Turkish origin, should be allowed to have dual nationality to facilitate their integration into society. However, under the direction of the Bavarian prime minister, Edmund Stoiber, and the new chairman of the CDU, Wolfgang Schäuble, the conservatives immediately organised a massive petition against this proposition of the Schröder government. Within three weeks, in Bavaria, Hesse and Berlin alone, almost one million people signed this petition to show their dissatisfaction with Schily's plans. This campaign, which was strongly supported by former chancellor Helmut Kohl, also contributed in a large measure to the conservative victory in the state elections in Hesse on 7 February 1999.

It appears that the CDU and the CSU will fight tooth and nail to prevent 'foreigners' from having double citizenship and to avoid creating 'Schily-Germans'. However, it is patently obvious that they are applying double standards, since they take for granted the fact that *Volksdeutsche* from Central and Eastern Europe can possess two passports. This is very remarkable, the more so since these *Volksdeutsche*, whose ancestors left Germany centuries ago, have usually never been in Germany and often no longer speak German.

The conservatives' concept of 'German' is defined by an 'ethnic' view, which also finds substantial support outside the conservative electorate. After it became clear that the campaign against dual citizenship for 'foreigners' had been a great success, Edmund Stoiber commented on this victory with a quotation from Martin Luther: '*wir müssen dem Volk aufs Maul schauen*', that is 'we have to listen to what people really say'. Although he added that one should not 'curry favour with' the people, it was quite clear that Stoiber, Schäuble and many fellow members of the CDU/CSU go along with widespread xenophobic sentiments among the population.[33]

Not surprisingly such politics activate a racist undercurrent in

German society which further influences the SPD. Under pressure from their rank and file, the Social Democrats collaborated in 1993 in the indirect abolition of the right of asylum. After the successful campaign against dual nationality by the CDU/CSU in 1999, the SPD was again roped in and plans for *unlimited* dual citizenship were abandoned.

Germany has a rich tradition in relation to the assimilation of people. Nevertheless in 1992 many Germans appeared to agree with the slogan 'Germany for the Germans'.[34] After the fatal arson attack on a Turkish family in Mölln in West Germany such numbers fortunately drastically reduced. If one were to adopt the cry of 'Germany for the Germans', even only in part, then great social upheaval would loom on the horizon. It was high time to remove the issue of 'asylum-seekers' and 'foreigners' from the maze of party politics. To that extent it was right that an Asylum Act came into being. But in its present form this legislation makes it virtually impossible for asylum-seekers to enter Germany. And it is highly questionable whether the new procedure will solve the problems regarding the integration of foreigners in any real sense. An immigration act is particularly necessary. In addition German society, just like that of other European countries, will have to cultivate a disciplined rationale and a humane awareness with regard to the question of 'asylum-seekers'.

Such an awareness seemed, after the fall of the Wall, to be absent mainly among a number of conservative politicians. The Nobel Prize winner for peace, Elie Wiesel, maintained as early as 1991 that 'he had not heard any opinion from Kohl that was clear and humane enough to weaken the hatred against foreigners'.[35] Wiesel's assessment turned out to be correct, because at the funeral of the five Turks murdered in Solingen, Kohl again did not make an *acte de présence*. Was he perhaps afraid of frightening off voters on the right wing of the political spectrum or in his own ranks? But a 'swing to the right' in the population, however, cannot be corrected by a swing to the right at the top level of politics.

It was not only the relationship between Germans, asylum-seekers and Turks that had come under great pressure in united Germany. Other 'foreigners' had also had a hard time of it. There was a particular resentment of Poles which was fuelled not only by the legacy of the past, but also by contemporary politics.

17

Poland, the New Right, German Conservatives and 'Ordinary Germans'

AFTER 1945 Germany lost its *Ostgebiete*, Pomerania, Silesia and East Prussia, almost completely to Poland; only the northern part of East Prussia went to the Soviet Union and the Memel area to Lithuania. Politicians and commentators of the New Right wish to have these former German territories back. They do not recognise the present border with Poland. For them, this is a kind of 'demarcation line' which has to disappear as soon as possible. Johanna Grund, a member of the Republikaner with a seat in the European Parliament, gave clear expression to this aspiration. After the fall of the Wall she campaigned against the 'scrupulous willingness to give things up' in a contribution to the right-wing radical magazine, *Europa vorn*. She proposed the immediate foundation of the states of Pomerania and Silesia within the territory of the GDR. Greifswald and Görlitz should be the provisional capitals.[1] Such proposals may be no more than the fantastic dreams of right-wing Utopians. But the agitation and the propaganda connected with them make clever use of resentments against Poland, which are resistant to the effects of time in both the old and the new Federal Republic.

Even in the former GDR, many East Germans were not very well disposed to the Poles. The East German party dictatorship had not been able to prevent this. On the contrary, the political relationship between the GDR and Poland tended to be cool, sometimes even

143

hostile. The leadership of the East German state did not seem to be able to forget that there were former German territories in Poland. As late as 14 September 1946, the then second chairman of the SED, Max Fechner, stated in the SED newspaper *Neues Deutschland* with regard to the Oder–Neiße border: 'As to the Eastern frontier, I wish to state that the SED will oppose any reduction of German territory. The Eastern frontier is only a provisional one and can be finalised only at a peace conference and with the co-operation of all the major victors.' However, as a result of the intervention of Moscow, the border was shortly afterwards recognised without any kind of protest as a 'peace frontier'.[2] But the memory of the violent ousting of the Germans by Poland after 1945 placed a heavy burden on the imposed friendship between the two Socialist countries. In order to camouflage such, mostly latent resentments, the border with the Eastern neighbour was therefore described as the 'Oder–Neiße peace frontier'.

This 'peace frontier', however, was opened only in 1970. The East German–Polish relationship often turned out in actual practice to be a Cold Peace. After the political difficulties in Poland in 1980–81 the GDR again sealed off its border with its Eastern neighbours. Most GDR citizens thought it was just as well that this 'peace frontier' was again closed. For example, they had little understanding of the passion shown by many Poles for shopping in East German shops. Moreover, the Poles were constantly accused of laziness. And that was an accusation which weighed quite heavily in the GDR. Nevertheless the frontier with Poland was not resealed out of economic considerations. The direct reason for it was the campaigns of the Polish trade union Solidarity. It was important in the GDR to prevent 'Polish' situations developing at home.

At the beginning of the 1980s the revolution in Poland was even warded off with the help of German history. The rehabilitation at the beginning of the 1980s of the Reformer Martin Luther was *also* used as a means of differentiating Germany from Catholic Poland. But Prussian history was also forged into a political tool. In so doing the SED was not only letting West Germans know that there was such a thing as a separate East German national identity. The Poles were also reminded that there was a great difference between Prussia / Germany on the one hand, and Poland on the other side of the frontier. The remarkable restoration in the GDR of historical figures such as Frederick II and Bismarck, who had played an important role in Prussian-German history, raised quite a few eyebrows in Warsaw. That was not surprising because the East German renaissance of interest in Germany / Prussia tended to be conservative and national-istically coloured. Polish historians quite frankly disapproved of this renaissance of Prussia. Some even tried to put the brakes on the East German Prussian revival after 1980. This was, for example, confirmed by one of the directors of Frederick II's former palace and castle complex in Potsdam. The director of Sans-Souci stated in 1979 that 'Polish comrades' were trying in a 'impudent and presumptuous way' to interfere in the interpretation of GDR history.[3]

Every positive re-evaluation of Prussian history did indeed appear to be pernicious to Poland. Partly because of the German *Ostgebiete* lost after 1945, it was not simply a matter of German-Prussian culture, but also raised political and territorial questions. There was in fact a semi-official border dispute between the two countries. Since 1985 the GDR and Poland had been arguing about the territory in the curve of Pomerania north of Swinemünde and Szczecin. The former German Stettin and its western hinterland were, according to the Treaty of Potsdam in 1945, not to come under Polish administration. Only in September 1945 was an area of 800 square kilometres with half a million German inhabitants annexed. This was indeed counter to agreements, and as a result Berlin was cut off from its port of Szczecin.

Not only the top ranks of the GDR, but also the Polish *nomen-klatura* regularly let it be known that the basis of confidence between the two Eastern bloc partners was fairly precarious. Polish politicians, for example, were constantly alert to inter-German *tête-à-têtes*. The thought of German reunification was hard to swallow for most Polish politicians. Almost immediately after Erich Honecker had paid his state visit to the West German Chancellor Helmut Kohl in 1987, General Jaruzelski appeared in East Berlin. He wanted to know what the two German statesmen had discussed. Any inter-German rendez-vous was regarded by Poland with suspicion.

After the fall of the Wall it became clear that the latent German–Polish animosity in the top echelons was also felt among the population. There were regular incidents between East Germans and Poles. For example, at the beginning of 1990, on the initiative of the then East German *Runder Tisch*, the border between Poland and the GDR at Frankfurt-an-der-Oder was opened for a few hours. The formalities for entering the GDR were dropped. But what was sup-posed to be a contribution to easing the relationship between the two neighbours turned into a fiasco. Since it was a Sunday the shops were closed. Nevertheless many Poles went to the only shop in the town which was open on that day and bought virtually its whole stock. This enraged some inhabitants of Frankfurt and the day ended with a Polish–German skirmish.

The purchasing behaviour of Poles in GDR shops had been a thorn in the flesh of most East Germans for a long time. But, given the pathetic economic situation in Poland, this conduct of many Poles was understandable. The new East German premier, Hans Modrow, however, showed little understanding for these Poles. He announced almost immediately that goods could be sold only to people in posses-sion of an East German passport. For some shopkeepers the Poles were explicitly *unerwünscht*. The East German press went a step further and talked of a mass 'invasion' of Poles coming to buy up everything in the GDR.

But after the Deutschmark had been introduced into East Germany in 1990, the roles were reversed. Now many East Germans did their shopping with the recently acquired Deutschmark in Poland, some-times for next to nothing, a rather dubious practice in view of the economic crisis in Poland and the experiences which the East Germans had suffered for years with illegal money changers. It was as though some East Germans were taking it out on Poland after the *Währungs-*

union. After the initial euphoria many new Federal citizens soon began to feel like second-class citizens. These new underdogs looked in turn rather smugly at Poland or Germans who had come under Polish influence, whom they demoted to third-class citizens. They had obviously forgotten that it was the Poles who were the first to have opposed Communist Party rule, *en masse* and successfully, a success of which the GDR had also reaped the benefits.

After the collapse of the Wall, however, the number of anti-Polish incidents rapidly increased in East Germany. When Germany won the football World Cup in 1990, there were violent mass clashes with Polish citizens in Berlin. Hundreds of young people, sometimes sporting Nazi symbols, attacked Poles, or destroyed their possessions. The abolition of compulsory visas for Poles on 8 April 1991 did not appear to improve the relationship between the two countries, because there was immediately a new wave of anti-Polish violence. In Frankfurt-an-der-Oder a number of right-wing extremists waited to receive Poles with stones and abuse. As a result of this reception many Poles were very reluctant to enter the new Federal states. Attacks on Polish citizens became so violent that the Polish minister of foreign affairs, Krzysztof Skubiszewski, felt obliged to make an official statement on it. In Warsaw he criticised the 'eruption of feelings in Germany against foreigners aimed particularly against Poles'. 'Such actions', said the minister, 'should not be allowed to exist.'[4] German antipathy to Poles is not usually expressed in such a rabid way. But the relationship remains problematic. In November 1997 the Deutsch–Polnische Gesellschaft maintained in a statement that German public opinion regarding Poland had reached an all-time low.[5]

In West Germany too there was resentment against Poles. This was partly the result of the loss of the *Ostgebiete*. The *Heimatvertriebenen* particularly, many of whom had gone to live in West Germany after 1945, often looked back on the past with bitterness. With the emergence of the Cold War and the partition of Germany, however, the majority of the problems seemed to have been solved for good. Germany was divided into three sections: West Germany, the GDR and the *Ostgebiete*. Nevertheless the official West German aim remained to reacquire both the GDR and the territories in the East. It was predominantly the German conservatives in the CDU/ CSU who committed themselves to this; although this aim was projected into a distant future. With the reunification of the two German states, this important part of conservative aspirations was finally realised. But the resentments against Poland had not completely disappeared.

After the fall of the Wall Chancellor Kohl invited the Poles to apologise for the suffering inflicted on Germans by Poland. After the Second World War millions of Germans had been driven from the former *Ostgebiete* in a violent way. In 1945 – and in some cases even later – many Poles had vented their fury on the German population. Poland, however, refused to apologise. Many Poles will not deny that there were atrocities committed against Germans after 1945. It would not therefore be surprising if some Polish politician wished to apologise for this *à titre personnel*. But an *official* apology such as Chancellor Kohl and the conservatives proposed, was quite inappropriate. After all, Germany had invaded Poland and not the other way round. Kohl left the *pre-history* of the atrocities committed by Poles against Germans almost completely out of account.

Many of the over 14 million refugees in the Federal Republic have not given up their wish for the territories in the East to be returned. So also does a section of the conservative political establishment. In this they can appeal to the German constitution. The German constitution emphatically states that until a peace treaty was concluded German unity has to be realised within the frontiers of 31 December 1937. Such a peace treaty has not yet been signed. Furthermore, the constitutional court ruled in 1973 that any German occupant within these borders is and remains a German. Together with the Bavarian CSU politician Franz-Josef Strauß, the *Vertriebenen* were able to move the German court in Karlsruhe to maintain this *Schutzpflicht*. Two years later the same constitutional court ruled that all persons who in 1944–45 had German citizenship would retain, this as would their descendants, despite their Polish citizenship.[6] This situation remains unchanged until now.

Even the 'polonised Germans' in Poland come under the 'duty to protect'. Germany still promotes the interests of this group of people and their descendants. These 'polonised Germans' are mostly alienated from Germany and often no longer speak German. Nevertheless they can relatively easily apply for German citizenship. Through the *Schutzpflicht*, *Deutschtum* is also preserved in Poland. Some Poles have appealed with the help of obsolete assessment criteria to the 'duty to protect' and their status as Germans. The West Berlin historian Wolfgang Wippermann argued in an interview in 1993 that in the Berlin Document Centre, there were lists drawn up by National Socialists of Poles who according to the Nazis were *eindeutschungsfähig*, in other words were 'Germanic' enough to pass as Germans. This group and the category of Poles who fought in the German army – including the SS – are according to this scheme still German. This also applies to their descendants. The consequence of this definition of the concept of German was that some Poles tried to prove that their parents or grandparents had been collaborators in the war. In this way they would be able to gain admission to Germany as Germans, or acquire German status in Poland.

So, in the context of the *Schutzpflicht*, Germany still has an identity within the borders of 31 December 1937. This situation fuels fantasies about the recovery of the *Ostgebiete*, and applies not only to members of the *Bund der Vertriebenen*. In a certain sense the *Schutzpflicht* also represents a 'cause for agitation' for the New Right. This could have been prevented if, at the end of the Second World War, Germany had ceded the Eastern territories to Poland as a kind of reparation. However, that would have been possible only if the German conservatives, such as the former Social Democrat Chancellor Willie Brandt, had made a solemn admission of guilt. That, however, never happened. On the contrary, during his visit to Poland in 1989 Chancellor Kohl went so far as to maintain that Polish forced labourers from the war should not receive reparations.

An unsolicited positive settlement of this question would have
secured much goodwill for Germany in Poland. A material recognition of the misery inflicted on the latter country during the war
would also have been in a certain sense an acceptance of non-material
responsibilities. Instead of that Chancellor Kohl seemed for a long
time to cling to his plan of visiting the Annaberg in Upper Silesia
where the German *Freikorps Oberland* defeated the Poles in 1921.
Only after ten days could the chancellor be persuaded to abandon his
intention.

The territorial recognition of the Polish Western frontier was also
a long time in coming. In the first instance Chancellor Kohl had
quite simply bluntly refused to recognise the Western Polish frontier.
In this matter too he allowed himself to be influenced by the Republikaner. In 1990 he allegedly stated to the American ambassador that
he was trying to avoid a fixing of the frontier in order to 'force the
Republikaner below five per cent'.[7] But perhaps other motives were
also involved. On 2 October 1976 Kohl declared in a *Vertriebenen*
publication, the *Ostpreußenblatt*, that, for the CDU, the Federal Republic is only a part of Germany and that until there is a peace
treaty, Germany continues to have an identity within its frontiers of
1937. That, argued the chancellor, included the *Vertreibungsgebiete* of
East Prussia, Pomerania and Silesia.[8]

A number of West German politicians perhaps sensed at the time
that a vague frontier with Poland would also help to blur other
borders in Western Europe. That is exactly what the New Right is
hoping for. The aim of the Allies is the recognition of legal frontiers,
but in that case, argued revisionists, is the Treaty of Munich of 1938
so legal? Britian and France recognised the integration of the Sudeten-
land officially and before the outbreak of the Second World War.
What is the situation with the 1955 ban on Austria uniting with
Germany? This *diktat* was imposed by the Soviet Union, and that
country no longer even exists. Is this situation therefore still valid?

Such lines of reasoning have an immediate effect in conservative
circles. In July 1997 the Bavarian minister of internal affairs, Günther

Beckstein, appealed to Eastern neighbours of the Federal Republic, before joining the European Union, to give the *Vertriebene* the opportunity of returning home. For 100,000 Silesians the minister also maintained that the Silesians of Poland should be given the right to return to their *angestammte Heimat* (ethnic home). According to Beckstein, the integration of Central and Eastern European states is not only a matter of economic data, but also of 'the historic fact of expulsion'.[9]

This is playing into the hands of revisionism by the CDU and particularly by its sister party the CSU. The final recognition of the Polish Western frontier was also the result of political pressure from the Allies, which, from a psychological point of view, was regrettable. Since the end of the Second World War Germany has always maintained that a recognition of the frontiers was dependent on the signing of a peace treaty. However, when Germany was given the opportunity, it refused to sign such an agreement because, according to the politicians, this was ancient history.

Not without some justice right-wing radicals can maintain that a *final* recognition of frontiers was always made dependent on a *peace treaty* – and such an agreement was never made. What, for example, would the international community do if 'polonised Germans' (Germans forcibly turned into Polish citizens by the Polish authorities) wanted to set up a (con)federation with Germany with the support of Poland; or if they wanted to declare an 'independent' state? At the moment such a scenario is not on the political agenda, but such a situation is not completely hypothetical. The more so because the 'duty to protect' still applies to this population group. Chancellor Kohl also emphasised this. He maintained to the Poles that, before signing a border treaty, he first wanted to protect the 'cultural' rights of the 'polonised Germans' in Poland. It looks as if a German financial injection into the community of 'polonised Germans' will result in their feeling even more links with the new Germany.

Despite the admiration that many Poles harbour for the united Germany, many of them were initially frightened of a new German

Drang nach Osten. In 1990 68 per cent of Poles believed that the relationship with a united Germany would get worse.[10] In the mean-time in Germany voices were being heard which betrayed a fairly low opinion of the Polish feeling for national identity. 'If we allow the Poles to have their way,' maintained the conservative German historian Arnulf Baring in 1991, 'a large majority of them would probably join the Federal Republic.'[11] The Polish–German Treaty was finally ratified on 17 June 1991. The Bavarian CSU had tried to torpedo the treaty with a seven-point plan. The Christian Socialists argued for a *Nachbesserung*, relating to the position of the German minority in Poland. But a confidential meeting with the foreign minister, Genscher, prevented the matter being pushed to the limit. The official political formula reads at the moment that the desire is to achieve 'the opening of the border through recognition of the border'. The Treaty of Friendship that was concluded for a period of ten years between German Chancellor Kohl and Polish Prime Minister Bielecki could not really dispel anxiety among Poles. For example, an official supplement to the Treaty states emphatically that 'this Treaty does not engage in questions concerning nationality and property'.[12] The 'polonised Germans' in Silesia obviously heartily welcomed these clauses, to which scarcely any attention was given in the press. They regarded themselves as Germans and hoped that one day the balance of power in property would turn in their favour. Perhaps their wishes will be realised when Poland joins the European Union and Silesia is declared a 'Euro region'. In that event the Polish Germans in this former German territory will undoubtedly be able to count on the full support of Germany.

As regards the recognition of the Western Polish frontier, the conservative political establishment took account of the Republikaner.[13] Chancellor Kohl put it into words: if the conservative parties do not take this course, the Republikaner will benefit. But not only right-wing radicals see the Polish Western frontier as a 'demarcation' line. In 1991, according to Assheuer and Sarkowicz, 9 per cent of the East German population were against the final recognition of the

Oder–Neiße border.[14] In absolute terms this is, it is true, a very low score but this question could become more important in future in the event of an economic downturn in East Germany and an increase in social conflicts.

Even after the signing of the Polish–German Treaty the German conservatives gave evidence of a policy in respect of Poland that showed very little empathy. In August 1991, for example, Frederick II and his father the 'Soldier King' were solemnly reburied in Potsdam. But it was precisely these two rulers who had so strongly embodied Prussian militarism. It was not accidental that Voltaire at an early stage voiced his reservations about Frederick II, who not only turned his country into a great military barracks, but also conquered Silesia. In view of this historical background it is not surprising that his reburial left a nasty aftertaste for many Poles. The former Silesia is, after all, situated in Poland.[15]

For the revisionists also, this interment cast a shadow over Silesia. They want Silesia back not only for historical or economic reasons. They argue that a renewed German Silesia and Pomerania could also serve as a kind of 'buffer' against the (threat of) population migrations from Central and Eastern Europe. While in 1990 the conservatives promised the electorate in the former GDR 'blossoming landscapes', the New Right were among the first to see the immediate consequences of the disappearance of the Iron Curtain. As early as June 1990 the right-wing radical newspaper *Nation Europa* wrote under the heading 'News from the *Überfremdungs*-Front': 'Our struggle has found a new front. Daily foreigners stream into the east of our fatherland. At the moment these are in the first instance gypsies from Romania. We must not allow the territory of the GDR, which up to now has been kept free of foreigners, to become *überfremdet*.'[16]

The illegal border crossings on the East German frontier indeed caused a great problem after the Wall came down. In 1991 and 1992 the number of asylum-seekers constantly increased. These border crossings took place, for example, in the East German towns of Schwedt, Kietz, Frankfurt-an-der-Oder, Guben, Forst and Görlitz. The police, whose job it was to prevent them, were supported by soldiers from the *Bundesgrenzschutz*. These servants of the law, however, were, on their own evidence, also supported by the East German population. They reported illegal border crossings after the fall of the Wall almost as regularly as during the SED regime. Not only right-wing extremists but also perfectly ordinary citizens had formed groups which rounded up the refugees, who were mostly Romanies. Subsequently the police would arrive and these citizens would in turn be escorted by the police vans. The German government has meanwhile employed a number of these vigilante organisations officially as border guards.

A not inconsiderable section of the East German population from the border area reacted in a hostile way to refugees after the collapse of the Wall, and this was not prevented by the German authorities. For example, in 1997 taxi drivers in Zittau and other border towns with Poland and the Czech Republic were advised by their trade unions, including the Dresden Industrie und Handelskammer, to pay attention in the case of foreigners to the physical appearance of their passengers. The government supports this policy. If the passenger turns out to be an illegal immigrant, then the driver is charged with smuggling refugees. A result of this regulation is that foreigners are often refused a taxi and many taxi drivers have already received heavy sentences.[17] It was consequently no accident that the Deutsche Volksunion of the right-wing extremist Gerhard Frey quickly scored a success in Guben in East Germany.[18]

The fury of the East Germans, moreover, was directed not only at asylum-seekers. They were often just as angry with the Polish border guards, since the latter allowed themselves to be quite easily bribed by refugees. This shows what short memories some East Germans had. In 1989 many of them swam across the Oder and the Neiße, albeit in the opposite direction, and applied for political asylum in Poland in large numbers. Their wishes, however, were granted, and they were able to count on the sympathy of the whole world.

18

Weimar Revisited?

ON 26 April 1998 Gerhard Frey's right-wing extremist Deutsche Volks-union gained a sensational electoral victory in the East German state of Sachsen-Anhalt, gaining 12.9 per cent of the vote. It now became necessary for the Social Democrats and conservatives to begin talks on forming a coalition. When these failed the Social Democrat Reinhard Höppner was elected as prime minister with the support of the Communist Partei des Demokratischen Sozialismus (PDS). Immediately the CSU declared this to be the 'dirtiest election in a German parliament since 1933', and Kohl's newly appointed government spokesman, the CDU politician Otto Hauser, argued: 'This is much the same as if the National Socialists after the war had participated in government under another name.'[1]

However, the German conservatives were not the only ones to draw an analogy with the Weimar Republic. Shortly after the fall of the Wall the former East German television ideologist, Eduard von Schnitzler, stated that the party Communists' struggle would simply continue. All that had changed, according to this SED commentator, were some social circumstances. He seemed to be entirely uncon-cerned about a favourable result for the Communist Party. According to von Schnitzler, it was clear at an early stage that great similarities would emerge between the united Germany and the Weimar Re-public. The conservatives, he reasoned, may have been those who put the nails in the coffin of the GDR, but they would eventually become its executors. The whole process according to him was mainly the result of the increasing class oppositions in united Germany.

155

Von Schnitzler based his opinion on experience under the Weimar Republic. At that time the National Socialists and the German Communist Party were both able to develop because of the economic crisis and great class oppositions. Widespread anger at the Treaty of Versailles, poverty, unemployment, inflation and paralysis in political life were the order of the day in the first democracy on German soil. The proletarian masses were the foundation on which both the NSDAP and the KPD developed. The National Socialists had tried to abolish socio-economic contrasts by camouflaging them with the aid of nationalism; in other words, by making the *unemployed* German at least an unemployed *German*, and preferably of course a *working German*.

The Communist Party, however, soon saw what the result of this National Socialist policy would be. In the Weimar Republic they proclaimed themselves as the *only true* 'anti-Fascists' and presented themselves as the true and actual alternative to National Socialism. For them the party Communist Karl Liebknecht had provided the social blueprint for a better Germany, that is a classless society in a Soviet-style republic. Karl Liebknecht's motto was 'the enemy is in our own country', and the opponents were the German nationalists and reactionaries. According to the Communist Party, Liebknecht's failed November Revolution of 1918 still had to be carried through. Meanwhile the German Republic was polarising increasingly into left and right. One could also say: on the left the idea flourished of a soviet-style republic supported by the 'Fellows without a Fatherland'; on the right the renewed aim of a pan-German unity developed, which defined itself 'ethnically', that is based on *Deutschtum*. The Weimar conflict between the political left and right has in fact never been resolved, but was territorially fixed in 1945.

To summarise, a number of points strike one. First, the basis on which both the Communist Party and the National Socialists fought was economic misery. This misery went hand in hand with great class differences. Secondly, the Communist Party regarded themselves as the only reliable 'anti-Fascists' in Germany. In terms of numbers this view may have some justification. Thirdly, the Weimar Republic was torn by a battle between the 'Fellows without a Fatherland' and German nationalists.

But can this situation be equated with the situation in which the reunited Germany currently finds itself? If one compares these aspects of the Weimar Republic with those of Germany after reunification, we are indeed struck by a number of *tendencies* which are not dissimiliar to the Weimar Republic. Yet the differences between Weimar and Berlin are greater than the similarities. Take first the point about the economy and socio-economic oppositions. The *real* unemployment figures in the new Federal states are today in places higher than at the time of the Weimar Republic. That in itself does not have to be of overriding importance because at present there is good welfare provision. There is now a reasonably efficient safety-net for people who have got into material difficulties. Despite the high real unemployment figures, no one has to stand for hours in a queue in order to hand over his or her dole slip. However, it is not clear whether it will be possible to maintain social peace in the future. In 1997, according to the Economist Intelligence Unit, Germany was the most expensive country in the world for entrepreneurs. This was due mainly to high wages and taxes.[2] In order to make Germany more attractive to entrepreneurs and to promote economic growth, steps will have to be taken which will probably involve employees gradually earning less. Moreover, economies in welfare provisions are unavoidable.

The German conservatives seemed to be aware of the consequences of such an unpleasant policy and accordingly refused to take steps in that direction. And yet the solving of this *Reformstau* or reform log-jam in society, which urgently needs reforms in the future, is unavoidable. Whether this will also lead to an increase in the number of jobs remains to be seen. After all, there is no obligation on entrepreneurs to invest their profits in Germany. Neighbouring countries like Poland and the Czech Republic are much more attractive in this respect. Economies and cuts in wages would, however, certainly jeopardise social harmony in Germany. This applies particularly to the new Federal states, which are still in a serious economic crisis and where many are forced to rely on welfare provisions or subsidised jobs.

In this crisis not only right-wing radical but also left-wing radical parties are appearing, for example the PDS. This party regards itself as the continuation of the German workers' movement and as the successor to the SED. Its policy is totally focused on righting the socio-economic injustices in the five new Federal *Länder*. And the PDS was able to score early successes because initially it had more sympathisers than had been suspected. At the municipal council elections in Berlin on 24 May 1992, the PDS, for example, gained 30 per cent of votes in the eastern part of the city.[3]

In 1998 in the new *Länder* almost 200 mayors and nearly 1,300 representatives in the local political councils came from the PDS. In the parliamentary elections on 27 September 1998 the PDS gained 5.1 per cent of the vote. Translated into seats according to the rules of proportional representation in Germany this meant that the party had 36 representatives in the Bundestag, of whom four had been directly elected. Interestingly enough, all four came from Berlin.[4] In spite of their electoral successes one cannot speak of virulent left-wing radicalism in the new Federal states. At the end of 1996 the PDS still had only 110,000 members, of whom only 2,500 were in the old Federal territories. According to party chairman, Bisky, approximately 90 per cent of PDS members are former SED members.[5]

However, according to a study by researchers from Berlin, the PDS, despite its limited number of members, will in the medium term remain a constant factor in German politics. This is due partly to its character as the *Heimatpartei* of the East German view of life.[6] This sounds rather more innocent than it is in reality. The attitude of the PDS to parliamentary democracy is ambivalent. At the party conference in Magdeburg on 27 and 28 January 1996, party chairman Bisky maintained that one must not play the opponents' political game:

Taking back a little bit here or there, accommodating a little there, here making a little compromise, there a greater concession. The strategy is clear: if we became just the same as they are, then we would be toothless and soon become part of the system and super-fluous. For that reason too: let us defend our programme!⁷

In November 1996 Bisky again declared emphatically: 'Nothing, absolutely nothing has changed about the fact of us, as a socialist party, opposing the authority of the present situation and so being in the classical broad sense of the word a (social) opposition.'⁸ In the Weimar Republic, it was not only the right-wing radicals but also the German Communist Party who were very negative towards the political system. But the economic situation in which Germany finds itself today is less dramatic than in the Weimar Republic, which was indeed torn apart by class opposition. Only time will tell if this is to remain the case.

A second tendency which seemed reminiscent of Weimar was the greater political value given to the concept of 'anti-Fascism'. After the *Wende* 'anti-Fascism' threatened to become the best life insurance for the Communist Party. And again legitimate and legitimising aspects went hand in hand. At the end of 1989 a large Soviet Russian monument in East Berlin was daubed on by right-wing extremists. The SED–PDS immediately organised a national demonstration as a 'unified front against the threat from the right'. This was attended by 200,000 people. The German government took insufficient measures at the time against right-wing radicalism, which was spreading more and more widely in the new Federal territories. And for various reasons that was an unfavourable development. Not only because of the many outrages against 'foreigners', but also because it looked for a moment as if the PDS might begin to 'monopolise' the active struggle against right-wing extremism. Such a situation would not only provide this party with more members, but it would also play into the hands of those seeking to polarise 'left' and 'right'. But the combating of right-wing extremist violence is the task of democratic authorities. By the end of 1992, after maintaining a hesitant attitude for two years, the German authorities appeared to have understood this to some extent, largely under pressure from many concerned citizens.

Despite a diffused nostalgia for the GDR among some East Germans, one can conclude that the struggle between the 'Fellows without a Fatherland', and 'nationalists' has for the time being been settled in the favour of the latter. In this regard the Weimar conflict has been resolved to the satisfaction of most Germans. Despite great problems relating to the integration of East and West Germans, the majority of the German population support reunification. But this triumph of the 'national option' has unfortunately also led to some people drifting into nationalist waters. The violence against foreigners which still continues cannot be seen separately from the nationalist *revival* which the German conservatives have been proclaiming since the 1980s. This was apparent for example in the policies towards Poland and during the asylum debate. In the *Historikerstreit* too, some Conservative historians and politicians had shown that they were ready to draw a line under the National Socialist past. But this was also grist to the mill of the New Right.

The Italian sociologist V. Pareto argued that the art of government lies in taking advantage of sentiments:

> ... not wasting one's energy in futile efforts to destroy them; very frequently the sole effect of the latter course is to strengthen them. The person capable of freeing himself from the blind domination of his own sentiments will be able to utilise the sentiments of other people for his own ends ... this may be said in general of the relation between ruler and ruled. The statesman who is of greatest service to himself and to his party is the man without prejudice who knows how to profit by the prejudices of others.[9]

The German conservatives, led by Chancellor Kohl, seem to have taken this message particularly to heart. They, but also the Social Democrats, who often follow on the heels of the conservatives in many respects, have tried to neutralise the 'pull to the right' among the population by a 'pull to the right' in their own policies. Perhaps that was also one of the reasons why the German authorities acted only at a very late stage and very tentatively against right-wing radicals. Some critics of this course of affairs saw in that a particular similarity with the Weimar Republic. They maintained that this awakened memories of the tacit coalitions between the *Reichswehr* in the Weimar Republic and the Nazi street-fighters.

Nationalist views, which were professed particularly by German conservatives, have *partly* contributed to the creation of a social climate in which right-wing radicals felt they could campaign ruthlessly against foreigners and other 'aliens'. This mood was further strengthened by the unresolved legacy of many right-wing authoritarian views preserved in the GDR which matched New Right views proclaimed in West Germany. Certainly, right-wing violence in Germany issues from the fringes of German society, but the epicentre of this aggression seems to be located at the heart of that society. Contemporary problems do not make the reunited Germany into a modern 'Weimar', but there are signs that must give cause for concern.

Notes

Preface

1. According to a survey by Eurostat, the European Union's bureau for statistics, published at the end of 1997, one-third of the citizens of the EU regarded themselves as very or quite racist. Most xenophobic were Belgium and France, where approximately half of all citizens regarded themselves as racist. At 34 per cent Germany is in the middle of the table. Sixty-five per cent of EU citizens believed that their country could not cope with any more immigrants. In Great Britain this is as high as 85 per cent, in Belgium 82 per cent and in Germany 79 per cent. Nevertheless 82 per cent of those surveyed believed that democracy is basically the best system ('Jeder dritte EU-Bürger nennt sich rassistisch', *Süddeutsche Zeitung* (*SZ*), 20/21 December 1997).

2. 'EU soll Rassismus bekämpfen', *SZ*, 9 April 1997. In the context of the European Year against Racism in 1997, the EU established in Vienna the 'European Office for the Observation of Xenophobia and Racism'. One of the tasks of this office is the development of a European Information Network about Racism and Xenophobia (RAXEN). According to decree no. 1035/97 of the EU, the main tasks of this office will be the gathering, storing and analysing of information and the offering of advice. However, the office is not allowed to comment on EU affairs, or on internal or legal affairs of its member states. Prantl, H., 'Eine Art Frühwarnsystem', *SZ*, 26/27 September 1998.

Introduction

1. In a letter to me of 4 June 1993 the World Jewish Congress states that it was requested by various congregations affiliated to it to institute a boycott against Germany. The final decision, in which punitive measures were dispensed with, was taken after a discussion between the executive of the WJC and Ignatz Bubis, the chairman of the Central Council of Jews in Germany. See *WJC Report*, March/April 1993, XVII, 3. See also the report of the UN Committee against Racial Discrimination of 2–20 August 1993, which includes criticism of the situation in Germany.

2. Verbeeck, G., *Geschiedschrijving en politieke cultuur*, p. 162.

1. German Partition

1. Venohr, W., *Die roten Preußen. Aufstieg und Fall der DDR*, p. 39.

2. Ibid., p. 65.

3. Ibid., p. 146.

4. Weber, H., *Die DDR, 1945–1986*, p. 30.

5. Marx, K., 'Brief an Ruge', from *Deutsch–Französische Jahrbücher, Marx Engels Werke (MEW)*, Vol. 1, 1983, p. 337.

6. Weber, H., *Die DDR, 1945–1986*, p. 40.

7. *Neues Deutschland*, 14 April 1963, p. 3. Quoted in: Weber, H., *Ulbricht fälscht Geschichte*, p. 118.

8. Ulbricht, W., *Zur Geschichte der neuesten Zeit*, pp. 100, 101.

9. Norden, A., *Um die Nation. Beiträge zu Deutschlands Lebensfrage*, p. 208.

10. Protokoll der Verhandlungen der II. Parteikonferenz der Sozialistischen Einheitspartei Deutschlands, Berlin (E), 1952, p. 122, in: Neuhäußer-Wespy, U., 'Von der Urgesellschaft bis zur SED. Anmerkungen zur "Nationalgeschichte der DDR"', p. 145.

11. Quoted in Brinks, J. H., *Die DDR-Geschlichtswissenschaft*, p. 122.

12. Ibid., p. 127.

13. Ibid., p. 156.

14. Thälmann, E., *Geschichte und Politik, Artikel und Reden. 1925 bis 1933*, Berlin (E), 1973, p. 5. Quoted in Hörnig, H., 'Sozialismus und ideologischer Kampf', p. 675.

15. Brinks, J. H., *Die DDR-Geschichtswissenschaft*, Chapter 6.

16. Ibid., p. 193.

2. The Two-tier Society

1. 'Zwei Klassen im einig Vaterland', *Der Spiegel*, 38, 17 September 1990, pp. 28–33, here: p. 33.

2. Kocka, J., 'Geteilte Erinnerungen. Zweierlei Geschichtsbewußtsein im vereinten Deutschland', p. 108.

3. Funke, H., *'Jetzt sind wir dran'*, p. 57.

4. 'Immer die Schwächste Stelle', *Der Spiegel*, 25, 1992, pp. 112–21, here: p. 118.

5. Funke, H., *'Jetzt sind wir dran'*, p. 57. For example the McKinsey Report states that of the 9.7 million jobs in the former GDR only between 4.5 and 5.1 million are left. Ibid., p. 68.

6. 'Arbeitslosigkeit in Deutschland auf Rekordstand', *SZ*, 10/11 January 1998.

7. 'Abbau von Arbeitsplätzen im Westen fast beendet'. *SZ*, 6 November 1997.

8. The privatisation of the East German economy by the *Treuhand* and its

successor the BvS (Bundesanstalt für vereinigungsbedingte Sonderausgaben) cost the German government a total of DM 250 billion. ('Ost-Wirtschaft kostet DM 250 Millarden', *SZ*, 25 November 1997).

9. Herles, W., *Nationalrausch. Szenen aus dem gesamtdeutschen Machtkampf*, Munich, 1990.

10. Ibid., p. 246.

11. Dreher, Klaus, *Helmut Kohl. Leben mit Macht*, esp. pp. 483–506.

12. 'Staatsverschuldung erreicht Rekordniveau', *SZ*, 23 December 1997.

13. Maaz, H. J., *Der Gefühlsstau*, p. 137.

14. Ibid., p. 96.

15. The nadir was a pamphlet which was distributed on the former inter-German border in the Thuringia area. In it East Germans were insulted and described as lazy and disorganised. ('It's not for you lot to demand anything, you should keep your mouths shut'.) 'Flugblatt löst Empörung aus', *SZ*, 9 July 1997.

16. Mitscherlich, A. and M., *Die Unfähigkeit zu trauern*, p. 64.

17. Wahljahr '94. Kandidaten – Zahlen – Hintergründe. *Spiegel Spezial*, 1, pp. 59, 60.

18. Noelle-Neumann, E., 'Eine Generation, zwei Gesellschaften', *Frankfurter Allgemeine Zeitung* (*FAZ*), 16 April 1997, p. 5. Quoted in: Kocka, J., 'Geteilte Erinnerungen. Zweierlei Geschichtsbewußtsein im vereinten Deutschland', p. 109.

19. Engelberg, E., *Lehrbuch der deutschen Geschichte*, p. xvi.

20. Gessenhart, W., 'Das Freund-Feind-Denken der Neuen Rechten', in: Butterwegge, C. and Isola, H., *Rechtsextremismus im vereinten Deutschland*, p. 66.

3. Xenophobia and Right-wing Radical Tendencies among Young People in East Germany

1. Alwin Ziel, the Social-Democrat minister for internal affairs of Brandenburg, stated in March 1997 that the number of right-wing extremist acts of violence was again increasing in Brandenburg. In 1996, 517 offences were recorded, in 1995 there had been 444. However, he quite rightly stated that the incredibly blatant nature of the offences was more alarming than the increase itself. 'Mehr rechte Gewalttaten in Brandenburg', *SZ*, 22/23 March 1997.

2. 'Zahl der rechtsextremen Taten 1997 höher als 1996', *SZ*, 2 December 1997. Also: Funke, H., 'Demokratieaufbau Ost', p. 650. According to the federal agency for internal security, in 1997 62.1 per cent of 2,400 right-wing extremists known to the authorities were resident in the territory of the former GDR. Of Germany's 7,400 violent skinheads, 46.6 per cent lived in the Eastern part of Germany. 'Rechtsextrem ist "in" im Osten. Zwei Drittel aller Neonazis leben in den neuen Bundesländern', *SZ*, 26 August 1998.

3. 'Jeder zehnte Jugendliche für Rechtsradikale', *SZ*, 10/11 June, 1998. In its 'Social report' for the year 1998, the research institute for the social sciences in Berlin-Brandenburg stated that four-fifths of East Germans held the opinion that

too many foreigners were resident in Germany and that their number should be decreased in the coming years. 'Studie "Sozialreport 1998", Ostdeutsche über Einheit enttäuscht', *SZ*, 4 September 1998.

4. Funke, H., *'Jetzt sind wir dran'*, p. 131.

5. Ibid., pp. 134, 135.

6. Butterwegge, C., 'Rechsextremismus vor und nach der wiedervereinigung Grundlagen-Gefahren-Gegenstrategien', in Butterwegge, C. and Isola, H., *Rechtsextremismus im vereinten Deutschland*, p. 20.

7. Schröder, B., *Rechte Kerle*, p. 11.

8. *Verfassungsschutzbericht 1996.*

9. 'Höchststand rechter Delikte seit der Einheit. BKA registriert fast 12,000 fremdenfeindliche und rechtsextreme Straftaten', *Der Tagesspiegel*, 20 April 1998.

10. On 6 May the Federal Agency for Internal Security confirmed that extreme right crime soared to the highest level since unification in 1990. Violence by this group rocketed by 27 per cent. 'Verfassungsschutzbericht für das vergangene Jahr. Wachsende Gewalt von rechts. Zahl der Straftaten erreicht Höchststand', *SZ*, 7 May 1998. Sometimes the German authorities deliberately keep silent about right-wing offences. In 1998 Brandenburg's Ministry of the Interior, for example, instructed the police to keep silent about right-wing graffiti in former concentration camps. According to the ministry in Potsdam, such news coverage would only incite copycat offences. 'Nazi-Schmierereien sollen verschwiegen werden', *SZ*, 25/26 July, 1998.

11. 'Jugend Ost. Nach dem Mord an einem Punk', *Der Spiegel*, no. 8, 1997, pp. 78–9, here: p. 79.

12. Farin, K., and Seidel-Pielen, E., *Rechtsruck*, p. 86.

13. On the attitude of German police and officials towards foreigners, see also Amnesty International, *Jahresbericht 1995*, Fischer, Frankfurt am Main, August 1995, pp. 163–6 and 'Bundesrepublik Deutschland. Vorwürfe über Mißhandlungen an Ausländern – aktuelle Entwicklungen seit Veröffentlichung des Berichts vom Mai 1995', *Jahresbericht 1996*, pp. 177–80; *Jahresbericht 1997*, pp. 176–80. Also: *'Germany for Germans'. Xenophobia and Racist Violence in Germany*, Human Rights Watch, Helsinki/New York, April 1995.

14. Since in Germany the war flag of the German Reich, also called the *Reichskriegsflagge*, is also a recognised symbol of neo-Nazism, in 1993 the Ministry of Defence tabled a plan to ban the use of this flag in military barracks. However in 1997 the German minister of defence, Volker Rühe, refused to ratify this decision. 'Rühe steht zur Reichskriegsflagge', *SZ*, 19 December 1997.

15. Schröder, B., *Rechte Kerle*, p. 117.

16. This number also includes 16,000 members of the *Republikaner*. The German security service, however, states emphatically that not all members of the *Republikaner* pursue or support right-wing extremist aims. *Verfassungsschutzbericht 1996.*

17. *Verfassungsschutzbericht 1996.*

18. 'Neue "Kameraden" aus dem alten Sumpf', *SZ*, 2 December 1997.

19. 'Die Eierschalen der Subkultur sind weitgehend abgeworfen'. Interview by Eberhard Seidel-Pielen with Bernd Wagner, in: Butterwegge, C. and Isola, H., *Rechtsextremismus im vereinten Deutschland*, p. 167.

20. 'Auch mal irren', *Der Spiegel*, no. 31, 27 July 1992, p. 51. In 1997, according to the internal security services, there was in the whole of Germany a hard core of 6,500 right-wing extremists and skinheads prepared to use violence. 'Schwerin meldet Zunahme rechtsextremer Gewalttaten', *SZ*, 23 October 1997.

21. 'Radikal gegen rechts: die Neonazi-Jäger von Sachsen', *Der Stern*, 1997, no. 52, pp. 62–70, here: p. 68.

22. '"National befreite Zonen"', *Der Spiegel*, no. 13, 1998, pp. 52–70, here: p. 60.

23. *Verfassungsschutzbericht 1996.*

24. 'Skinheads formieren sich', *SZ*, 2/3 October 1997.

25. 'Razzia bei rechtsextremen "Tonträger-piraten"', *SZ*, 22 October 1997.

26. 'Die Sau von nebenan', *SZ*, 30 July 1997.

27. '12 doitsche Stimmungslieder', *SZ*, 16 July 1997.

28. '"National befreite Zonen"', *Der Spiegel*, no. 13, 1998, p. 60.

29. See also a short survey in: 'Das Vierte Reich heißt Cyberspace', *SZ*, 11 November 1997.

30. '"National befreite Zonen"', *Der Spiegel*, no. 13, 1998, p. 53.

31. 'Wasser auf die Mühlen der völkischen Stimmung', *SZ*, 15 April 1997.

32. Stöss, R., *Die Republikaner*, pp. 81–2.

33. West, Rebecca, *The Meaning of Treason*, pp. 127–8.

34. Heitmeyer, W., 'Einig Vaterland – einig Rechtsextremismus?', in: Butterwegge, C. and Isola, H., *Rechtsextremismus im vereinten Deutschland*, p. 121.

35. 'Bürgermeister wollte Radikale schützen', *SZ*, 8 July 1997.

36. Farin, K. and Seidel-Pielen, E., *Rechtsruck*, p. 82.

37. 'Vorläufiges amtliches Endergebnis', *SZ*, 28 April 1998.

38. 'Das Kreuz der Zornigen', *SZ*, 28 April 1998. Frey may have been too enthusiastic. In the parliamentary elections in Saxony-Anhalt, which were held a few months later on 27 September 1998, the DVU got only 3.2 per cent of the vote. In the state elections in the Eastern state of Mecklenburg-Vorpommern which were held on the same day, the DVU got only 2.9 per cent of the vote and did not reach its goal of entering the state parliament. But the DVU and the NPD together got 4 per cent of the vote, the NPD taking 1.1 per cent. In the new *Länder* as a whole the right-wing parties got 5 per cent of the vote, which means they attracted twice the proportion of voters as in the West. 'Landtagswahl 1998 Mecklenburg-Vorpommern. Vorläufiges amtliches Endergebnis', *SZ*, 29 September 1998; '"Donnerschlag" der rechtsextremen DVU blieb aus. SPD hält sich noch alles offen', *SZ*, 29 September 1998; 'Öfter mal was Neues. Ostwähler entscheiden spontan', *SZ*, 29 September 1998.

39. 'DVU stellt Alterspräsident', *SZ*, 28 April 1998.

4. National-revolutionary Sentiments in the Former GDR?

1. '"Verstummen und wegblicken". Hermlin vergleicht Herbst 1991 mit Beginn der Nazi-Ära', *Frankfurter Rundschau*, 5 October 1991.

2. See *Texte zur inneren Sicherheit*, p. 86. When Hitler in 1933 became chancellor of a 'cabinet of national concentration', many SA members regarded this as a betrayal of the Nazi movement, for which some of them never forgave him. At the time they also expressed their disapproval in a stinging parody of the *Horst Wessel Lied*, virtual hymn of the SA. The first stanza of the original song runs as follows:

'Die Fahne hoch! Die Reihen dicht geschlossen!
SA marschiert mit ruhig festem Schritt,
Kameraden, die Rotfront und Reaktion erschossen,
Marschieren im Geist in unsern Reihen mit.'

(Raise high the flag,
The ranks are closed and tight,
Storm Troopers march,
With firm and steady step.
Souls of the comrades
Shot by Reds and Countermight
Are in our ranks
And march along in step) (Translation by Frank Petersohn)

The parody goes:

'Die Preise hoch, Kartelle fest geschlossen.
Das Kapital marschiert mit festem Tritt
Die Börsianer werden bald Parteigenossen
und kommandieren frech in unsern Reihen mit.'

(Raise high the prizes,
The cartels are closed and tight.
The capital marches,
With a firm step.
The brokers will soon be party members
and cheekily joint command in our ranks)

Quotation of the German parody in: Putlitz zu, Wolfgang, *In Rok tussen de Bruinhemden. Herinneringen van een Duits Diplomaat*, The Hague, 1964, p. 100.

3. Mohler, A., *Die konservative Revolution in Deutschland 1918–1932*, pp. 4, 5.

4. Strasser, G., *Kampf um Deutschland*, p. 347.

5. Gunther, John, *Inside Europe*, p. 66.

6. Heiber, H., *Die Republik von Weimar*, p. 246.

7. *Wörterbuch der Geschichte, L–Z*, p. 744.

8. *Wörterbuch der Geschichte, A–K*, p. 294. The GDR has always turned nominal

members of the Nazi Party into victims. In a so-called *Braunbuch*, which contained the names of many former Nazis who made a career in Western Germany, the unnamed East German authors claimed that: 'Of course the *Braunbuch* does not contain names of nominal members of the NSDAP. The GDR has consistently distinguished between the millions of former members of Nazi organisations who were misled and deceived themselves, and that dreadful group of wire-pullers, initiators and profiteers from Nazi crimes. We would not dream of reproaching anyone for his or her past – least of all after twenty years – who once made a political mistake and has long since realized his error and pursued a new path.' In: *Nationalrat der Nationalen Front des Demokratischen Deutschland. Dokumentationszentrum der Staatlichen Archivverwaltung der DDR. Braunbuch. Kriegs- und Naziverbrecher in der Bundesrepublik. Staat. Wirtschaft. Armee. Verwaltung. Justiz. Wissenschaft*, Berlin (E), 1965, p. 10.

9. Viereck, P., *Metapolitics. The Roots of the Nazi Mind*, pp. vii, viii and ix. Hitler quotation from: Rauschning, H., *The Voice of Destruction*, p. 131. Viereck was not the only author who held this view. Already at the end of the war the sociologist Howard Becker, who was also a member of the Office of Strategic Services of the USA, argued that 'if and when the Nazi belief is cast aside it may well be replaced by espousal of a Germanized Communism, differing in important respects from the present Russian variety, that will retain fundamental elements of Hitlerian dogma'. Becker, Howard, *German Youth: Bond or Free*, pp. 224, 225.

10. Hitler, A., *Mein Kampf*, p. 557.

11. *Die rote Fahne* of 26 June 1923, in: Weber, H., *Der Deutsche Kommunismus. Dokumente*, pp. 143, 146.

12. Buber-Neumann, M., *Der kommunistische Untergrund. Ein Beitrag zur Geschichte der kommunstischen Geheimarbeit*, pp. 38, 39.

13. See Röhl, K. R., *Nähe zum Gegner. Kommunisten und Nationalsozialisten im Berliner BVG-Streik von 1932*, Frankfurt am Main / New York, 1994.

14. See *Texte zur inneren Sicherheit*, p. 96.

15. 'Rechtsradikale: Die neue Gefahr aus Sachsen. Rotbraun ist die Haselnuß', *SZ*, 5 March 1998.

16. Schröder, B., *Rechte Kerle*, p. 162. In 1992 Thomas Assheuer and Hans Sarkowicz felt that the significance of right-wing radical parties in the ex-GDR may be negligible, but that that reveals little about the real political views which are found among the population (Assheuer, T. and Sarkowicz, H., *Rechtsradikale in Deutschland*, p. 134). The East German psychiatrist and commentator Hans-Joachim Maaz did not exclude the possibility that these attitudes would be translated into politics. According to him, there are really only two possibilities. Either, argues Maaz, the GDR population will have to control itself and work towards reconstruction for a new generation, or people will look for hate figures and the 'desire for a "strong man"' will grow. The threat has already been defined' (Maaz, H.-J., *Das gestürzte Volk oder die unglückliche Einheit*, pp. 155, 156).

5. Imposition of the Party Line and the Militarisation of East Germany

1. From the appeal of the Central Committee of the Kommunistische Partei Deutschlands of 11 June 1945, in: *Geschichte Lehrbuch für Klasse* 10, p. 55.

2. From a party directive of 1977 on the occasion of the forthcoming 30th anniversary of the GDR, *Neues Deutschland*, 18 November 1977, p. 1, in: Meier, H. and Schmidt, W., 'Tradition und sozialistisches Bewußtsein', p. 1225.

3. Leonhard, W., *Die Revolution entläßt ihre Kinder*, p. 294.

4. *NVA-Kalender* 1987, pp. 116, 117.

5. Klemperer, V., *LTI*, Leipzig, 1982.

6. It is more likely that the Freie Deutsche Jugend followed the example of the Freideutsche Jugend of the German empire. The nature worship of this youth movement, slogans like 'Heil' or the ramrod arm salute which the *Wandervögel* (Roamers) reintroduced into German life, were adopted by the National Socialists. See Becker, Howard, *German Youth: Bond or Free*, London, 1946.

7. Gerard, James W., *Face to Face with Kaiserism*, pp. 263, 270.

8. Some statistics: the MfS kept personal files on six million people, four million in the GDR and two million in the old Federal Republic. There was a total of 180 kilometres of dossier material: 100 kilometres is found in the Central Archive in the Normannenstraße in Berlin; 80 kilometres is stored in secondary depots. The Central Archive was protected like a bunker. The F16 register alone, which contains the actual names of all screened citizens, is a kilometre and a half long. In Berlin there are at least 18 kilometres of personal files, of which 7 kilometres consist of judicial papers. There are also 11 kilometres of 'operative documents', that is, dossiers on the immediate surveillance of a person. A special 700-metre card index system was compiled. The whole is sub-divided into 122,000 bundles of files, 1,600 bundles of registration cards, 755 packs of forms, 13 tons of blank forms and 158 filing boxes. And in another 936 sacks is partially destroyed material; 1,000 packages and 122 boxes are as yet unopened, etc. The cataloguing of the material is far from complete. See Gauck, J., *Die Stasi-Akten*, pp. 11, 12.

9. The German scholar Norbert Madloch established that as early as the end of the 1970s there were 'Fascho' groups in the NVA and units of the police. Funke, H., *'Jetzt sind wir dran'*, p. 126.

10. Siegler, B., *Auferstanden aus Ruincn*, pp. 84–9.

11. The former editor Konstantin Münz, who worked at the radio station 'Die Stimme der DDR', maintains that the political background of right-wing extremist crimes was largely ignored and hence the contacts between right-wing extremists were trivialised. In: Siegler, B. *Auferstanden aus Ruinen*, pp. 77, 78.

6. The Language of the Third Reich and Anti-Semitism in the GDR

1. Simon Wiesenthal was kind enough to hand this documentation over to me: 'Die Gleiche Sprache: Erst für Hitler – Jetzt für Ulbricht. Pressekonferenz von Simon Wiesenthal am 6 September 1968 in Wien. Eine Dokumentation der Deutschland-Berichte', Jüdisches Dokumentationszentrum, Simon Wiesenthal Centre, Vienna.

2. Stalin, J., *Werke*, Vol. 2, p. 364.

3. Siegler, B., *Auferstanden aus Ruinen*, p. 122.

4. 'Lehren aus dem Prozeß gegen das Verschwörerzentrum Slansky',   pp. 51, 55, 56.

5. Assheuer, T. and Sarcowicz, H., *Rechtsradikale in Deutschland*, p. 120.

6. *Geschichte Lehrbuch für Klasse* 10, p. 196.

7. Assheuer, T. and Sarkowicz, H., *Rechtsradikale in Deutschland*, p. 121.

8. Funke, H., *'Jetzt sind wir dran'*, p. 121.

9. 'Stolpe und der braune Sumpf', *SZ*, 8 October 1997.

10. 'Juden kommen nicht nach Gollwitz', *SZ*, 30 September 1997.

7. 'Our Goethe, Your Mengele', or Legitimising Anti-Fascism

1. *Texte zur inneren Sicherheit*, p. 120.

2. Mitscherlich, A. and M., *Die Unfähigkeit zu trauern*, Munich, 1988.

3. *Wörterbuch der Geschichte, A-K*, p. 290. This definition was first formulated at the XIIIth Plenary Assembly of the Executive in 1933 and later, in 1935, at the VIIth World Congress of the Comintern.

4. From the appeal of the Central Committee of the KPD of 11 June 1945, in: *Geschichte Lehrbuch für Klasse* 10, p. 55.

5. *Lehrpläne für die Grund- und Oberschulen in der Sowjetischen Besatzungszone Deutschlands. Geschichte*, 1 July 1946, Berlin, pp. 3, 4.

6. Das Potsdamer Abkommen, 2 August 1945, Anhang. In: Ulbricht, W., *Zur Geschichte der Neuesten Zeit. Die Niederlange Hitlerdeutschlands und die Schaffung der antifaschistisch-demokratischen Ordnung*, pp. 385–405, here: pp. 390, 391.

7. Wippermann, W., *Antifaschismus in der DDR*, p. 2.

8. Siegler, B., *Auferstanden aus Ruinen*, p. 102.

9. Frei, Norbert, *Vergangenheitspolitik. Die Anfänge der Bundesrepublik und die NS-Vergangenheit*, pp. 19, 20.

10. '"Mann ohne Gewissen". Ulbricht als unbefugter Richter – Die rote Diktatur löste nur die braune ab. Eine bemerkenswerte Vergangenheit'. According to Markus Wolf, who headed the East German counter-intelligence for many

years, Gerhard Kegel, who was mentioned in this bulletin, was a Communist mole who had worked for the Soviet military intelligence before the war. See Wolf, Markus, *Spionagechef im geheimen Krieg. Erinnerungen*, p. 81, 254.

11. The so-called *Braunbuch DDR* by Olaf Kappelt also appeared in 1981. This contains a list of 900 former National Socialists who re-launched their careers in the GDR. Kappelt, O., *Braunbuch DDR. Nazis in der DDR*, Berlin, 1981, 424 pages.

12. Quotation in: Adenauer Bulletin. See also: Ulbricht, Walter, 'Hilferding über den "Sinn des Krieges"', *Die Welt*, Zeitschrift für Politik, Wirtschaft und Arbeiterbewegung, Stockholm, no. 6, 9 February 1940, pp. 135–7, in: Weber, Hermann, *Der deutsche Kommunismus. Dokumente*, here: 'Walter Ulbricht zum Stalin-Hitler-Pakt', pp. 364–7, esp. pp. 366 and 367.

13. Quotations from the Adenauer government's list.

14. Stalin, J. W., *Über den Kampf um den Frieden*, Dietz Verlag, Berlin, 1954, p. 243; quoted in: Ulbricht, Walter, *Zur Geschichte der neuesten Zeit. Die Niederlage Hitlerdeutschlands und die Schaffung der antifaschistisch-demokratischen Ordnung*, p. 59.

15. Mikolajczyk, S., *The Rape of Poland. Pattern of Soviet Aggression*, Westport, CT, 1948; here: Dutch translation by Otto G. Peyl, *Verkracht volk. In de greep van Soviet Rusland*, Bilthoven, 1949, p. 105.

16. *Wörterbuch der Geschichte, L–Z*, p. 726. The National Democrats also enjoyed their role as *passive victims* of National Socialism. In a paper presented at a party rally, Siegfried Dallmann, for example, argued with much self-adulation that: 'It is doubtless an outstanding mark of the greatness of the spiritual revolution that we have achieved, if today people from the middle classes and the intelligentsia, who in the past, to their own detriment, only too often persevered in nationalist and chauvinist lines of thought, and who let themselves be reduced to mere tools of a matching policy, now, step by step, grow into the world of ideas of socialist internationalism and co-produce this socialist internationalism.' Dallmann, Siegfried, 'Im Bewußtsein der Übereinstimmung mit den wahrhaft nationalen Traditionen unseres Volkes leisten wir unseren Beitrag zur nationalen Mission der DDR', pp. 68, 69.

17. Assheuer, T. and Sarkowicz, H., *Rechtsradikale in Deutschland*, p. 112.

18. On 20 March 1969 the Federal government submitted a petition to the constitutional court to abolish Frey's right to freedom of expression, and particularly that of press freedom. It was the intention that his publishing house should cease to exist. However, the court in Karlsruhe ruled against the petition. In 1971 Frey founded the right-wing radical *Deutsche Volksunion* (see *Texte zur inneren Sicherheit*, pp. 125–6). According to the German security services, this wealthy publisher from Munich produces right-wing radical newspapers in a run of more than 110,000 copies. Frey himself maintains the figure is 600,000 (See Stöss, R., *Die 'Republikaner'*, p. 33). Frey's Deutsche Volksunion, DVU-Liste D, gained 6.2 per cent of votes at the elections in Bremen on 29 September 1991. As a result this party was represented by six members in parliament. Assheuer, T. and Sarkowicz, H., *Rechtsradikale in Deutschland*, p. 40. Frey and his friends achieved this great success with slogans such as 'Homes, not Asylum-Seekers'.

8. The *Ravensbrücker Ballade* and 'Anti-Fascism'

1. Jarmatz, K., *Ravensbrücker Ballade oder Faschismusbewältigung in der DDR*, Berlin, 1992.

2. Faulenbach, B. et al., *Empfehlungen zur Neukonzeption der Brandenburgischen Gedenkstätten*, p. 39.

3. In a review of the play Henryk Keisch wrote on 10 October 1961: 'Those who help save her, save themselves, even if they lose their own lives.' See Jarmatz, K., *Ravensbrücker Ballade oder Faschismusbewältigung in der DDR*, p. 56. This fundamental statement of anti-Fascist self-sacrifice recurs often in anti-Fascist literature. The Stalin Prize winner, Ilya Ehrenburg, for example, has his heroine Agnès say during an interrogation by the Germans: 'Today I've understood everything. If one man dies, he saves somebody, he's certain to save somebody. ... The people. ... My people.' Ehrenburg, Ilya, *The Fall of Paris*, p. 375.

4. Ibid., p. 67.

5. Siegler, B., *Auferstanden aus Ruinen*, p. 96.

9. The GDR and the Legacy of German Political Lutheranism

1. Mann, T., Deutschland und die Deutschen, in: Mann, Thomas, *Reden und Aufsätze*, part 2, pp. 313–35, here: esp. pp. 319–21.

2. Barth, K., Ein Brief nach Frankreich (1939), pp. 113–14.

3. Treitschke, H. von, 'Luther und die deutsche Nation', p. 484.

4. Although von Treitschke speaks out about any vulgar outbreaks of anti-Jewish feelings, he still considered this attitude to be a 'natural reaction of the Germanic "Volksgefühl"' (i.e. healthy national feeling) against a foreign element which occupies 'too great a space in our life'. A notorious quotation from the article 'Our Prospects' reads as follows: 'Even in the most educated circles, among men who would repudiate with horror any thought of religious intolerance or national arrogance, the unanimous view is: the Jews are our misfortune!' Treitschke, H. von, 'Unsere Aussichten', p. 575.

5. In this treatise Luther gave his 'faithful advice' to the Christians, in particular in regard to the authorities. His seven-point programme begins as follows:

> Firstly, let their synagogues and schools be set on fire, what does not burn shall be covered and buried in earth, so that no man forever more shall see a stone or cinder of it. And this will be to the glory of our Lord and Christendom in order that God will see that we are Christians ... furthermore let their houses be broken and destroyed in the same way. For they are doing indoors the same as they are doing in their schools. For doing this one can put them under a roof or in a stable, just like the gypsies so that they will know that they are not masters in our country ... etc.

Luther, M., 'Von den Juden und Ihren Lügen' (1543), here particularly: pp. 522–6; quoted here p. 523. This is not the place to discuss Luther's theologically motivated anti-Judaism in detail. But this treatise does not stand alone. As early as 1538 Luther had written the treatise 'Against the Sabbathans' ('Wider die Sabbater') at the request of Count Schlick zu Falkenau. In 1543, in addition to the essay 'On the Jews and Their Lies' ('Von den Juden und Ihren Lügen'), the two treatises, 'On Shem Hamphoras and the Descent of Christ' ('Vom Schem Hamphoras und dem Geschlecht Christi') and 'On the Last Words of David' ('Von den letzten Worten Davids') were published, both written in the same tone. Even a few days before his death, during the last sermon he gave in Eisleben, Luther delivered his 'Admonition against the Jews' ('Eine Vermahnung wider die Juden'). See also Stöhr, M., 'Martin Luther und die Juden', in: Kremers, H. (ed.), *Die Juden und Martin Luther – Martin Luther und die Juden. Geschichte, Wirkungsgeschichte, Herausforderung*, pp. 89–108, here: pp. 98–9. While it is true that anti-Semitism was part of the general intellectual baggage of the intellectual establishment at the time, Luther expressed his anti-Judaism in a particularly aggressive way. Luther's anti-Judaism is given a certain extra value because it forms part of a complex of demands, almost all of which are aimed at the violent suppression of opponents.

6. Not only von Treitschke, but other historians too, in some cases even before the unification of 1871, described and interpreted Luther in a nationalist way. Some book titles may provide evidence for this: in 1862 Adolph Schottmüller's book, *Luther – ein Deutsches Heldenleben*, was published in Berlin; H. Eilsberger wrote *Luther als ein Deutscher*, Berlin, 1868; and Hermann Hoffmeister, *Luther und Bismarck als Grundpfeiler unserer Nationalgröße. Parallele zur Erweckung der Vaterlandsliebe und Pflege des Deutschtums*, reached its 4th edition by 1884.

7. Again some titles may substantiate this. Between 1912 and 1918 the following books were published: Müller, R. O., *Unser Luther. Ein Lebensbild als Vorbild für unser Volk*, Dresden, 1912; Friedrich, G., *Luther und Hindenburg*, Gotha, 1915; Hackmeister, K., 'Luther und das Vaterland', *Protestantische Monatshefte*, 1915; Fuchs, E., *Luthers deutsche Sendung*, Tübingen, 1917; Etzin, Franz, *Luther als Erzieher zum Deutschtum*, 1917; and Lenz, M., *Luther und der Deutsche Geist*, Hamburg, 1917.

8. For that matter, this also applied to the Roman Catholic Church in Germany. The Concordat between the Vatican and the National Socialists may be regarded as well known. The German journalist Ralph Giordano speaks with some justice of 'an official church which makes a mockery of the Christian principles of both confessions'. Giordano, R., *Wenn Hitler den Krieg gewonnen hätte. Die Pläne der Nazis nach dem Endsieg*, p. 76.

9. Falter, J. W., *Hitlers Wähler*, esp. pp. 169–93.

10. Heiber, H., *Die Republik von Weimar*, p. 226.

11. Martin Luther, *Sämtliche Werke*, Part 2, Vol. 24, Erlangen, 1830, here: pp. 270–1, 273, 282, 469; quoted from: Bebel, A., 'Glossen zu Yves Guyots und Sigismund Lacroix' Schrift "Die wahre Gestalt des Christentums"', in: Bebel, A., *Ausgewählte Reden und Schriften*, p. 469.

12. Ibid., p. 469.

13. Some book titles: Fronemann, W., *Der deutsche Luther*, Leipzig, 1933; Lerche, Otto, *Martin Luther, deutscher Kämpfer*, Berlin, Deutscher Luthertag, 1933; Berger, E. A., *Luther als deutscher Prophet*, Leipzig, 1933; Leisegang, H., *Luther als deutscher Christ*, Berlin, 1934; Witte, J., *Martin Luther als rechter Christ und echter Deutscher*, Berlin, 1934; Hashagen, L., *Martin Luther und die deutsche Reformation, mit der Wittenberger Rede des Reichsinnenministers W. Frick*, Hamburg, 1934.

14. See for example, Vogelsang, E., *Luthers Kampf gegen die Juden*, Tübingen, 1933; Linden, Walther, *Luthers Kampfschriften gegen das Judentum*, Berlin, 1935; Meyer, G. A. W., *Die Schicksalsfrage der Menschheit: Judentum – Altes Testament (Mit Luthers Schrift 'Von den Juden und ihren Lügen')*, Leipzig, 1933 (Arbeitsgemeinschaft nationalsozialistischer evangelischer Geistlicher).

15. Rosenberg, A., *Protestantische Rompilger. Der Verrat an Luther und der Mythus des 20 Jahrhunderts*, p. 17.

16. Ibid., p. 85.

17. Ulbricht, W., 'Grundsätze der sozialistischen Ethik und Moral', which were also known as the 'Ten Commandments of Socialist Morals'.

18. Honecker, E., 'Unsere Zeit verlangt Parteinahme für Fortschritt, Vernunft und Menschlichkeit', p. 11.

19. Bayer, B., 'Wider die Monopolia', here: esp. p. 7.

20. From an interview with Gerhard Brendler in *Die Zeit*, 1 April 1983; quoted in: Kuhrt, E. and Löwis, H. von, *Griff nach der deutschen Geschichte. Erbeaneignung und Traditionspflege in der DDR*, p. 118.

21. Hanke, H., Zur Rolle von Traditionen in Lebensweise und Kultur, here: esp. pp. 44–5, 47.

22. On the contrary, the *Theses* are anxious to integrate Luther into the 'anti-Fascist' tradition. The fourteenth *Thesis* states: 'Fascism wanted to integrate Luther into its traditions whilst submitting Lutheranism to control of a Fascist "Reichskirche". Against this attempt Martin Niemöller, Dietrich Bonhoeffer, Karl Barth and other followers of the "Confessing Church" organised both *the legacy of the Reformation* [my italics, JHB] and the humanistic cultural tradition on behalf of the anti-Facist struggle. 'Theses on Martin Luther', p. 891. Referring to Pastor Niemöller, not only was he a submarine commander in the First World War, but also, at the outbreak of the Second World War, he earnestly asked Hitler's permission to be allowed once more to fight for Germany. He was refused, not because his nationalism was suspect, but because he insisted that the Nazis would have no right to appoint his successor or in any other way to interfere with strictly religious matters. See Becker, Howard, *German Youth: Bond or Free*, p. 158.

23. Süssmuth, H., 'Luther 1983 in beiden deutschen Staaten. Kritische Rezeption oder ideologische Vereinnahmung?', p. 38.

24. Ibid., p. 39.

25. Ibid.

26. Rosenberg, A., *Protestantische Rompilger*, p. 84.

27. Diwald, H., *Luther. Eine Biographie*, pp. 9, 10.

28. Farin. K. and Seidel-Pielen, E., *Rechtsruck*, p. 31.

29. *Verfassungsschutzbericht* 1996.

10. The GDR and the Legacy of Prussian Political Ideals

1. Bartel, H., Bachmann, P., and Knoth, I., *Preußen – Legende und Wirklichkeit*, p. 296.

2. Liebknecht, K., Zum 'Jubelfest' der Hohenzollern, *Gesammelte Reden und Schriften*, Vol. 5, p. 392. For that matter, Liebknecht was not alone. In his study *Entlarvte Geschichte* of 1934, Hegemann argues that the German spiritual leaders of the time turned especially against the barbarism of Prussia, and quotes Winckelmann's remark that 'I would rather be a Turkish eunuch than a Prussian', and Lessing, who said, 'Prussia is the most slavish country in Europe'. Hegemann, *Entlarvte Geschichte*, 2nd edn, 1934, p. 118; quoted in: Popper, K. R., *The Open Society and Its Enemies*, Vol. 2, Hegel & Marx, p. 312.

3. Engels, F., Letter to Marx of 25 July 1866, *MEW*, Vol. 31, p. 241. Especially in the works of Friedrich Engels, anti-Slavic utterances can repeatedly be found. In his treatise 'Revolution and Counter-revolution in Germany', for example, Engels expressed the opinion that Pan-Slavism aimed at nothing less than the 'subjugation of the civilised West by the barbaric East, of the city by the country, of trade, industry and intellectual life by the primitive farming of Slavic serfs'. Engels, F., 'Revolution und Konterrevolution in Deutschland (1851/52)', in: *MEW*, Vol. 8, pp. 5–108, here: p. 53.

4. Marx, K., Letter to Engels of 2 December 1856, *MEW*, Vol. 29, pp. 89, 90.

5. See Hegel's *Philosophy of History* (transl. by J. Sibree, 1857, quoted from the edition of 1914), p. 418. The translator writes 'Germanised Sclaves', in Popper, K. R., *The Open Society and Its Enemies*, Vol. 2, Hegel & Marx, p. 50.

6. Kohn, H. *The Mind of Germany. The Education of a Nation*, quoted here from the Dutch translation: *'De Duitse geest. De vorming van een volk'*, p. 287.

7. Lange, F., 'Die Volkserhebung von 1813', Berlin, 1952, pp. 17, 18. The East German NDPD, in which former National Socialists were accommodated, attached great importance to Fichte, Jahn and Arndt. The National Democrat Siegfried Dallmann, for example, argues: 'The progressive heritage of these great Germans is quite rightly being preserved and cultivated in our German Democratic Republic.' Dallmann does not deny that the threesome has its shortcomings: 'In spite of predominant positive assessments of their contribution, historical truth obliges us to state that, in their case also, the class boundaries belonging to a bourgeois democratic national consciousness can be seen.' Nevertheless he very clearly stresses their positive sides. He describes Fichte as an 'important thinker of the democratic lower middle class'. Unfortunately his comments on the Germans in his *Speeches to the German Nation*, in which he had described them as an *Urvolk*, had offered 'the imperialist bourgeoisie many starting points for also turning him,

very wrongly, into an ancestor of the German nationalists, or even into a user of German fascist and imperialist systems of thought'. According to Dallmann, 'the focal point' of his *Speeches to the German Nation* was his 'demand for democratic and national education as a most important contribution to the development of a nation of equal citizens, a nation which serves the progress of mankind by liberating itself from the shackles of feudalism'. In the eyes of the National Democrats, Friedrich Ludwig Jahn, too, contributed to progress. He 'made a positive and highly noteworthy contribution to the progressive national cause by his efforts towards the cultivation of the German language; but especially by his founding of the gymnastics movement (*Turnbewegung*), which was an important factor in creating able-bodied men (*Wehrhaftmachung*), especially among the youth, for the fight against Napoleon'. According to Dallmann, Ernst Moritz Arndt's book *Geist der Zeit* 'still has a present-day validity, Arndt called for a fight for national independence and unity of Germany'. Dallmann, Siegfried, Im Bewußt-sein der Übereinstimmung mit den wahrhaft nationalen Traditionen unseres Volkes leisten wir unseren Beitrag zur nationalen Mission der DDR, pp. 63, 64.

8. Fichte, J. G., *Reden an die deutsche Nation*, pp. 96, 111, 114.

9. Quoted in: Farin, K. and Seidel-Pielen, E., *Rechtsruck*, pp. 33–4. Popper comments as follows: 'It may be remarked that an originally anti-German feeling is common to many of the founders of German nationalism; which shows how far nationalism is based on a feeling of inferiority. As an example, Anderson [Anderson, E. H., *Nationalism and the Cultural Crisis in Prussia 1806–1815*, 1939, p. 79, JHB] says about E. M. Arndt, later a famous nationalist: 'When Arndt travelled through Europe in 1798–99, he called himself a Swede because, as he said, the name German "stinks in the world"; not, he added characteristically, through the fault of the common people', Popper, K. R., *The Open Society and Its Enemies*, vol. 2, Hegel & Marx, p. 312.

10. Förtsch, E., Preußen-Bild und historische Traditionen in der DDR, p. 126.

11. Engelberg, E., *Lehrbuch der deutschen Geschichte*, Vol. 7, pp. 231, 233.

12. Vetter, K. and Vogler, G., *Preußen. Von den Anfängen bis zur Reichsgründung*, p. 139.

13. Engelberg, E., *Bismarck. Urpreuße und Reichsgründer*, p. 726.

14. As early as 1967 the editor-in-chief of *Die Zeit*, Marion Gräfin von Dönhoff, argued that the 'state-forming powers' in Prussia are the 'hope for a real state for Germans'. Dönhoff von, 'Vorbild Preußen? Zwanzig Jahre nach der Liquidierung', *Die Zeit*, no. 7, 17 February 1967. Writing in 1970, she expanded on this notion: 'The Federal Republic, with its open society and the possibility of living in it with human dignity and a fair measure of freedom, is a state which is worth con-tributing to and building – but a *Heimat*? It cannot be a *Heimat* for someone from the East. ... So, a farewell to Prussia? No, because spiritual Prussia must continue to exert its influence in this age of materialism – otherwise this state that we call the Federal Republic will not survive.' Dönhoff von, 'Ein Kreuz auf Preußens Grab', *Die Zeit*, 20 November 1970, in: Dönhoff, Marion Gräfin von, *Polen und Deutsche. Die schwierige Versöhnung*, Frankfurt am Main, pp. 54–8, here: p. 58. In

1973, a year after the *Grundlagenvertrag* between the GDR and the Federal Republic, the founder of the *Ostverträge*, Willy Brandt, propagated the setting-up of a German National Foundation. It was argued that in this the so-called *Stiftung Preußischer Kulturbesitz* could make a good start on keeping the legacy of East German culture alive. See Brandt, W., *Bulletin des Presse – und Informationsamtes der Bundesregierung*, Bonn, no. 6, 19 January 1973, p. 53. Genscher supported this aim in the same year. He also referred explicitly to the 'cultural works of the *Vertriebenen* and the refugees', i.e. the former German territories of East Prussia, Pomerania and Silesia. Genscher, 'Alte Heimat – neue Heimat', WDR-Radio Cologne of 6 April 1973, in: Heckel, E.; Ulle, D., and Kessler, H., *Kultur in den Kämpfen unserer Zeit. Zur ideologischen Klassenauseinandersetzung zwischen Sozialismus und Imperialismus auf dem Gebiet von Kultur und Kunst*, p. 140.

    15. Quoted in: Brinks, J.H. *Die DDR-Geschichtswissenschaft*, p. 274.

    16. Ibid., p. 289.

11. An Anti-'Anti-Fascist' Iconoclastic Fury?

    1. Venohr, W., *Die roten Preußen*, p. 21.

    2. Faulenbach, B., et al., *Empfehlungen zur Neukonzeption der brandenburgischen Gedenkstätten*, p. 24.

    3. Finn, G., *Sachsenhausen 1936–1950. Geschichte eines Lagers*, 1991 Preface.

    4. 'Antisemitismus', *Die Tageszeitung (TAZ)*, 30 January 1993.

    5. Schröder, G., *Rechte Kerle*, p. 11.

    6. 'Juden und Deutsche', *Spiegel Spezial 2*, 1992, p. 68.

    7. Richter, W., *Unfrieden in Deutschland*, pp. 148, 149.

    8. Ibid., pp. 142–58.

12. The *Historikerstreit*

    1. Nolte, E., 'Zwischen Geschichtslegende und Revisionismus? p. 29.

    2. Ibid., p. 33.

    3. Nolte, E., 'Vergangenheit, die nicht vergehen will', p. 45.

    4. Nolte, E., 'Zwischen Geschichtslegende und Revisionismus?', p. 24.

    5. This view can be traced back to two quotations which are considered to be of fundamental importance to both ideologies. Marx and Engels had maintained in their Communist Manifesto: 'the history of all hitherto existing society is a history of class struggle'. In: *A Handbook of Marxism*, edited by E. Burns, 1935, p. 22; quoted in: Popper, K. R., *The Open Society and Its Enemies*, Vol. 2, Hegel & Marx, p. 111. Hitler, on the other hand, believed that 'all events in world history are only the expression of the urge towards self-preservation of the races in the good or in the bad sense'. In: Hitler, Adolf, *Mein Kampf*, p. 324. This insight, like others, Hitler had not developed himself, since he derived most

of his knowledge from newspapers. Even in imperial Germany such views enjoyed great popularity. On 13 April 1913, for example, the *Deutsche Arbeitgeber-Zeitung* wrote: 'It is not class struggle as Marx and his supporters maintain that forms the most important content of history, but racial struggle.' Quoted in: Fischer, Fritz, *Krieg der Illusionen. Die Deutsche Politik von 1911–1914*, p. 365.

6. Nolte, E. *Nietzsche und der Nietzscheanismus*, p. 80.

7. Ibid., p. 277.

8. Nolte, E., *Geschichtsdenken im 20 Jahrhundert. Von Max Weber bis Hans Jonas*, pp. 328–9, 602.

9. Baring, A., *Deutschland was nun?*, p. 55.

10. Ibid., p. 58.

11. Ibid., pp. 105, 106.

12. Ibid., p. 166.

13. Wollenberg, J., 'Antisemitismus und Judenvernichtung', in: Butterwegge, C., and Isola, H., *Rechtsextremismus im vereinten Deutschland*, p. 47.

14. According to the Bulletin of the Federal Government of 2 February 1984, the chancellor said in the Knesset on 25 January: 'I add this as someone who could not become guilty in the Nazi period, because he had the grace of late birth and the good fortune of a very special parental home.' 'Juden und Deutsche', *Spiegel Spezial*, 2, 1992, p. 42.

15. Giordano, R., *Die zweite Schuld oder von der Last ein Deutscher zu sein*, p. 50.

16. Venohr, W., *Die roten Preußen*, p. 266.

17. Diwald, H., *Deutschland einig Vaterland*, p. 78.

18. Translated from German into English and quoted in: Assheuer, T., and Sarkowicz, H., *Rechtsradikale in Deutschland*, p. 107.

19. *Texte zur inneren Sicherheit*, p. 97.

20. Assheuer, T. and Sarkowicz, H., *Rechtsradikale in Deutschland*, pp. 107, 108.

21. Ibid., p. 108.

22. Diwald, H., *Geschichte der Deutschen*, pp. 164, 165.

23. Diwald, H., *Deutschland einig Vaterland*, p. 70.

24. Ibid., p. 82.

25. Ibid., pp. 84, 85.

26. Ibid., p. 381.

27. Assheuer, T. and Sarkowicz, H., *Rechtsradikale in Deutschland*, p. 191. Wolfgang Gessenharter also speaks of the New Right as a 'hinge between neo-conservatism and right-wing extremism'. Gessenharter, W., 'Das Freund-Feind-Denken der Neuen Rechten', in: Butterwegge, C. and Isola, H., *Rechtsextremismus im vereinten Deutschland*, p. 62.

28. Jaschke, H.-J., 'Politischer Konservatismus im vereinten Deutschland', in: Butterwegge, C. and Isola, H., *Rechtsextremismus im vereinten Deutschland*, p. 147.

13. The New Right

1. Gottfried Milde, minister of internal affairs for Hessen, in the preface to the annual report of the security services of 1989, quoted in: Butterwegge, C. and Isola, H., *Rechtsextremismus im vereinten Deutschland*, p. 103.

2. '5 Millionen Deutsche: "Wir sollten wieder einen Führer haben ...". Die Sinus-Studie über rechtsextremistische Einstellungen bei den Deutschen', Reinbeck 1981, in: Hacker, F., *Das Faschismus-Syndrom*, p. 19.

3. It is not only Roeder who campaigned for the greater influence of Germany in former East Prussia. In December 1997, for example, it also became known that the president of the Federal States party of the CSU in the Bundestag, Michael Glos, has announced his support for the right-wing radical *Schulverein zur Förderung der Rußlanddeutschen in Ostpreußen E.V.* In an article that he wrote on 20/21 April 1996 for this organisation, he argued among other things that this association continues with 'German traditions in this region and hence keeps history alive. You are making a contribution to the promotion and preservation of the cultural heritage of the Germans in Russia.' Glos was not the only German politician who praised this right-wing extremist association. Steffen Heitmann (CDU), Heinrich Lummer (CDU), Gebhard Glück (CSU), Jörg Haider (Freiheitliche Partei Österreichs) and the professors Ernst Nolte, Lothar Bossele, Dieter Blumenwitz and Werner Maser sent their best wishes. 'Glos schrieb Grußwort für rechtsextremen Verein', *SZ*, 13/14 December 1997.

4. 'Weihnachtsbotschaft für die Truppe', *SZ*, 24/25/26 December 1997.

5. In November 1997 the Military Intelligence Service investigated 760 cases in its own ranks which appeared to have a right-wing radical character; 138 suspected right-wing extremists were kept under observation. 'MAD ermittelt gegen rechtsextreme Soldaten', *SZ*, 10 November 1997.

6. 'Kampf gegen "Schmutzfinken"', *SZ*, 28 October 1997; also: 'Die Mär vom Heer. Mehr als die Hälfte der Bundeswehr-Studenten sieht sich politisch rechtsaußen, ohne rechtsextrem zu sein', *SZ*, 2/3 May 1998. Right-wing attitudes within the army can also be observed in the former GDR. In a *'Deliktkartei'* of the Stasi for the period 1965 to 1980, the GDR authorities had kept on file 700 offences arising from the glorification of the Third Reich by East German soldiers. According to research work by the Gauck authorities, cases were recorded of sergeants addressing each other as 'Hitler', 'Göring' and 'Goebbels'. A lieutenant argued that Hitler had not killed enough Poles, and an officer candidate expressed the view that the *Endlösung* of the *Judenfrage* has not been finished yet. Meinhardt, Birk, 'Braune Flecken im Internationalismus', *SZ*, 25 September 1998.

7. 'SPD: Nischen für Extremisten aufspüren', *SZ*, 17 December 1997.

8. *Verfassungsschutzbericht 1996.*

9. Quoted in: Assheuer, T. and Sarkowicz, H., *Rechtsradikale in Deutschland*, p. 178.

10. Baring, A., *Unser neuer Größenwahn*, p. 164.

11. Ibid., p. 7.

12. *Nation & Europa. Deutsche Monatshefte*, 10/96, p. 10, quoted in: *Verfassungs-schutzbericht, 1996.*

13. Assheuer, T. and Sarkowicz, H., *Rechtsradikale in Deutschland*, p. 63.

14. Butterwegge, C., 'Rechtsextremismus vor und nach der Wiedervereinigung. Grundlagen – Gefahren – Gegenstrategien', in: Butterwegge, C. and Isola, H., *Rechtsextremismus im vereinten Deutschland*, p. 16.

15. 'Nation & Europa', *Deutsche Monatshefte*, 9/96, pp. 5ff.; quoted in: *Verfassungsschutzbericht 1996.*

14. The Republikaner

1. Stöss, R., *Die 'Republikaner'*, p. 42.

2. Assheuer, T. and Sarkowicz, H., *Rechtsradikale in Deutschland*, p. 49.

3. Stöss, R., *Die 'Republikaner'*, p. 41.

4. Ibid., p. 43.

5. It was quite remarkable that after the European elections in June 1989 the Greens announced that they had lost voters particularly in the age groups from 18 to 23, some of whom had found their way to the Republikaner. In that age category an average of 7.9 per cent voted for the Republikaner. Assheuer, T., and Sarkowicz, H., *Rechtsradikale in Deutschland*, p. 49.

6. Quoted in: Stöss, R., *Die 'Republikaner'*, p. 19.

7. Ibid., p. 47.

8. Schomers, M., 'Die Republikaner von innen betrachtet', in: Butterwegge, C. and Isola, H., *Rechtsextremismus im vereinten Deutschland*, p. 81.

9. Ködderitzch, P., 'Republikaner in der ehemaligen DDR', in: Butterwegge, C. and Isola, H., *Rechtsextremismus im vereinten Deutschland*, p. 91.

10. The Republikaner are a party of men. But, argues the journalist Burckhard Schröder, sociological surveys have shown that many women also sympathise with their ideas. See Schröder, B., *Rechte Kerle*, p. 12.

11. Leggewie, C., 'REPs – die fünfte Partei', in: *Anno 1989*, Gütersloh/ München, 1990, p. 91; quoted in: Assheuer, T. and Sarkowicz, H., *Rechtsradikale in Deutschland*, pp. 48, 49.

12. Heitmeyer, W., 'Einig Vaterland – einig Rechtsextremismus?', in: Butterwegge, C. and Isola, H.,, *Rechtsextremismus im vereinten Deutschland*, p. 124. It does indeed look as though the Republikaner have a reasonable amount of support among the police. As early as May 1989 leading officials in the police union stated that they suspected that approximately 20 per cent of police officers in the Federal Republic sympathised with the Republikaner. They were afraid that in Bavaria this might be as high as 50 per cent. Stöss, R., *Die 'Republikaner'*, pp. 96, 97. On his own admission, the former leader of the Republikaner always had intensive contacts with high-ranking officers in the army. In an interview

with the *Süddeutsche Zeitung*, Schönhuber stated that both his official military advisor, General (ret.) Franz Uhle-Wettler and his deputy-chairman Rear-Admiral (ret.) Günter Poser, had 'gathered quite a large group of officers around them, through whom I was constantly in touch with the *Bundeswehr*'. 'Stets Kontakt zu hohen Offizieren', *SZ*, 12 December 1997.

13. Assheuer, T., and Sarkowicz, H., *Rechtsradikale in Deutschland*, p. 47.

14. Borchers, A., *Neue Nazis im Osten*, p. 101.

15. Schomers, M., 'Die Republikaner – von innen betrachet', in: Butterwegge, C., and Isola, H., *Rechtsextremismus im vereinten Deutschland*, pp. 84, 85.

16. Ibid., pp. 81, 82.

17. In: Stöss, R., *Die 'Republikaner'*, p. 44.

18. *Verfassungsschutzbericht, 1996.*

19. MK Report, 1/96, p. 1, quoted in ibid.

20. *Verfassungsschutzbericht, 1996.*

21. Ibid.

22. 'Schleichende Gefahr von rechts', *SZ*, 13 May 1997.

23. 'Etwas dagegenhalten', *Der Spiegel*, 16 March 1970, no. 12, pp. 106–7, here: p. 106. At present, however, a development is taking place that Strauß tried to prevent. In December 1997, for example, the Evangelical minister Heiner Kappel from Hessen left the FDP and together with 300 sympathisers founded the 'Offensive für Deutschland'. In this party Kappel wants to unite the national-conservative forces in Germany. Together with the 'Bund Freier Bürger' of Martin Brunner, they took part in the Bundestag elections in September 1998 under the name 'Offensive für Deutschland-Die Freiheitlichen'. This choice of name is not fortuitous, but refers to the party of the right-wing populist Jörg Haider in Austria. In the parliamentary elections in 1998 the endeavours of the 'Offensive für Deutschland-Die Freiheitlichen' failed. After the defeat of the conservatives, Michael Glos, chairman of the CSU group in the Bundestag, immediately stated that his party would continue its efforts to prevent the establishment of a party to the right of the CSU. In: 'CDU will sich von Grund auf erneuern', *SZ*, 30 September 1998.

24. Despite some points of contact between right-wing radicalism and the German conservatives there are essential differences, the most important of which is that the right-wing radicals are basically anti-Western, while the majority of German conservatives are not.

25. *Verfassungsschutzbericht, 1996.*

15. Anti-Semitism

1. ' "Wir wurden von allen verraten" ' *Der Spiegel*, no. 28, 1992, pp. 54–69. See also 'Juden und Deutsche', *Spiegel Spezial* 2, 1992, pp. 69, 70, 73.

2. Funke, H., *'Jetzt sind wir dran'*, p. 121.

3. This is also confirmed by statistics. According to the Ministry of Internal Affairs of Nordrhein-Westfalen, for example, a sharp increase in the number of anti-Semitic offences could be recorded in this Federal state alone in the first six months of 1997. In comparison with the same period in the previous year, the number rose by 28 cases to a total of 87. 'Mehr antisemitische Straftaten an Rhein und Ruhr', *SZ*, 7 November 1997. In 1997 seven right-wing extremists, among them six members of the 'Aktion Sauberes Deutschland', were arrested, having admitted to defiling Jewish cemeteries in Busenberg and in Neustadt an der Weinstraße. Among them was the leader of the 'Internationales Hilfs-kommitee für nationale politische Verfolgte', 'Friedhof-Schändungen in der Pfalz aufgeklärt', *SZ*, 20/21 December 1997.

4. In: *Allgemeine Jüdische Wochenzeitung*, Vol. 52, no. 25, Bonn, 11 December 1997.

5. Roll, Evelyn, 'Antisemitismus: "Da ist eine neue Qualität". Ein Schwein kennt keine Scham', *SZ*, 7 December 1998.

6. Assheuer, T., and Sarkowicz, H., *Rechtsradikale in Deutschland*, p. 93.

7. *Das III. Reich. Ein Volk, ein Reich, ein Führer. Eine historische Collage über den erregendsten Abschnitt deutscher Geschichte – in Wort, Bild und Ton 1933–1939*, Vols 1 and 2, here: Vol. 1, p. 3.

8. *Texte zur Inneren Sicherheit*, p. 60. Such slogans, it is true, were heard, for example, in the Netherlands, but given the pre-history of anti-Jewish feeling in Germany, they were given a certain added value.

9. *Vorwärts*, no. 27, 1983, p. 27; quoted in: Wollenberg, J., 'Antisemitismus und Judenvernichtung', in: Butterwegge, C. and Isola, H., *Rechtsextremismus im vereinten Deutschland*, p. 53.

10. 'Juden und Deutsche', *Spiegel Spezial* 2, 1992, p. 52.

16. The 'Debate on Asylum-seekers' and the Influence of the New Right

1. At the end of 1996 Germany was in third place in the European Union with 7.31 million foreigners, meaning that 9 per cent of the German population consisted of non-Germans. According to the Federal government, Luxembourg and Belgium occupy first and second places. One in four migrants comes from a member state of the EU. 1.43 million or 20.5 per cent of all foreigners were born in Germany. The number of foreigners living in Germany in 1996 consisted of 2.05 million Turks, 754,000 Yugoslavs, almost 600,000 Italians, 363,000 Greeks, 342,000 Bosnians, 283,000 Poles, 202,000 Croats and 185,000 Austrians. Two-thirds of Turks and Greeks had been living for ten years or more in the Federal Republic. For Italians the percentage was 71 per cent and for Spaniards 82 per cent. Of the 2.05 million Turks, 271,000 had limited residence permits and 534,000 had unlimited residence permits. Only 519,000 had the right of domicile. ('20 Prozent der Ausländer sind in Deutschland geboren', *SZ*, 9 January 1998.)

2. 'Zahl der Asylbewerber 1997 weiter gesunken', *SZ*, 14 January 1998.

3. Koepf, p. *Stichwort Asylrecht*, p. 75.

4. Ibid., pp. 8, 9.

5. Ibid., p. 75.

6. 'Schwacher Aufwind für CDU/CSU', *Der Spiegel*, no. 38, 1991, pp. 44–57, here: p. 50.

7. Assheuer, T., and Sarkowicz, H., *Rechtsradikale in Deutschland*, p. 38.

8. Quoted in: Borchers, A., *Neue Nazi's im Osten*, pp. 144, 145.

9. Farin, K. and Seidel-Pielen, S., 'Über die Mitverantwortung von Pädagogik und Jugendarbeit an der Rechtsorientierung Jugendlicher', in: Butterwegge, C. and Isola, H., *Rechtsextremismus im vereinten Deutschland*, p. 157.

10. 'Grüne: Behörde auf rechtem Auge blind', *SZ*, 20/21 December 1997.

11. 'Nichts wissen, nichts sagen', *SZ*, 26 May 1998.

12. Quinkert, A., and Jäger, S., *Die rassistische Hetze von 'Bild' gegen Flüchtlinge im Herbst 1991*, p. 12.

13. Ibid., p. 13.

14. 'CDU-Langmut gegen rechtsaußen', *TAZ*, 3 February 1993.

15. Since 1–2 June 1996 this Communist association has been known as the 'Vereinigung der Verfolgten des Naziregimes/Bund der Antifaschistinnen und Antifaschisten' and in that year had approximately 8,000 members. This made it, according to the German internal security services, the largest organisation in the spectrum of the 'left-wing extremist anti-Fascism' (*Verfassungsschutzbericht, 1996*).

16. 'Volksverherzung: Anzeige gegen CDU', *Die Tageszeitung* (TAZ), 7 October 1991.

17. 'Scheinasylanten blockieren fluchtlinge', *Berliner Morgenpost*, 6 August 1992.

18. 'Gewalt, "nur die Spitze eines Eisbergs"', *TAZ*, 11 April 1992.

19. Ibid.

20. *Texte zur Inneren Sicherheit*, p. 73. The assessment of another ministry spokesman was: 'The continuing stream of refugees, and the problems involved in finding accommodation, housing shortages and unemployment which are aggravated as a result, could, however, soon again become an effective base for agitation for the right-wing extremists. Particularly when the privations that the regained constitutional unity necessarily entails.' Ibid., p. 100.

21. Engelmann, B., *Du Deutsch?*, p. 22.

22. 'Initiative für doppelte Staatsbürgerschaft gescheitert', *SZ*, 11 December 1997.

23. 'Die CDU entdeckt die Türken', *SZ*, 13/14 December 1997.

24. 'Türkische Gemeinde hält Kohl Vorurteile vor', *SZ*, 31 October, 1/2 November 1997; also 'Kohl lehnt doppelte Staatsbürgerschaft ab', *SZ*, 27 October 1997.

25. 'Kebab, Bauchtanz, Bürgerrechte', *SZ*, 31 October, 1/2 November 1997.

26. 'Ausländer und Deutsche. Gefährlich fremd. Das Scheitern der multi-kulturellen Gesellschaft', *Der Spiegel*, no. 16, 14 April 1997.

27. 'Wasser auf die Mühlen der völkischen Stimmung', *SZ*, 15 April 1997.

28. 'Vorschläge Schröders als "Brandstiftung" kritisiert', *SZ*, 24 July 1997.

29. 'Ausländerbeauftragte attackiert Schröder', *SZ*, 4 August 1997.

30. Koepf, P., *Stichwort Asylrecht*, pp. 83, 84.

31. 'Die Eichhörnchen der CSU', *SZ*, 13 May 1998.

32. 'Experten warnen: Abschieben ist wie Sippenhaft', *SZ*, 6 May 1998.

33. 'Nur ein kleines bisschen stolz. Stoiber und sein Anteil am Sieg', *SZ*, 9 February 1999.

34. In September 1992 the *Berliner Morgenpost* newspaper quoted a survey conducted by the German bureau Infas. According to the survey, more than half of those interviewed felt that slogans like 'Germany for the Germans' were 'fully justified'; 26 per cent agreed with the call 'Foreigners out!'; 37 per cent believed that Germans should 'defend' themselves 'against the foreigners in their own country'. 'Jeder zweite für "Deutschland den Deutschen"', *Berliner Morgenpost*, 12 September 1992.

35. 'Paten für Flüchtlingsheime', *TAZ*, 8 October 1991.

17. Poland, the New Right, German Conservatives and 'Ordinary Germans'

1. See Klönne, A., 'Die Neue Rechte angesichts der deutschen Einheit', in Butterwegge, C. and Isola, H., *Rechtsextremismus im vereinten Deutschland*, p. 75.

2. In: Weber, Hermann, *Ulbricht fälscht Geschichte. Ein Kommentar mit Dokumenten zum 'Grundriß der Geschichte der deutschen Arbeiterbewegung'*, p. 98.

3. Venohr, W., *Die roten Preußen*, p. 295.

4. 'In Nordrhein-Westfalen vier schlafende Kinder mit Brandsätzen beworfen. Angriffe auf Ausländer werden immer brutaler', *SZ*, 4 October 1991.

5. 'Polenwitze: Kultur?', *SZ*, 19 November 1997. Tensions between Germans and Poles are also fostered by an unequal distribution of wealth, as a result of which many Poles, sometimes as moonlighters, try to find a position in Germany. In October 1998 the Polish Ministry of Economic Affairs criticised the German authorities for the treatment of Polish construction workers in Germany. Jaroslav Maka, director of the foreign sales department of the ministry, explained that in some cases 'Polish workers had been treated like dangerous criminals'. He could appreciate the endeavours of the German authorities to trace moonlighters. However, these inspections, according to Maka, should not end in a 'manhunt'. He announced counter-measures towards German companies in Poland if job opportunities for Polish building contractors in Germany were further restricted. 'Polnische Bauarbeiter wie Verbrecher behandelt', *SZ*, 10/11 October 1998.

6. Czaja, H., *Unsere sittliche Pflicht*, p. 66.

7. Information from the State Department from a member of Georgetown University, Washington/USA, in: Funke, H., *'Jetzt sind wir dran'*, p. 41.

8. 'Ostpreußen gehört zu Deutschland', *Das Ostpreußenblatt*, 2 October 1976.

9. 'CSU fordert Rückkehrrecht für Vertriebene', *SZ*, 14 July 1997.

10. Funke, H., *'Jetzt sind wir dran'*, p. 41.

11. Baring, A., *Deutschland, was nun?*, p. 167.

12. Urban, Thomas, *Deutsche in Polen. Geschichte und Gegenwart einer Minderheit*, p. 202.

13. But New Right and conservative views have some points of contact besides the Western Polish frontier. Opinions also seem sometimes to converge on the question of the Russian Germans. Most Russian Germans enjoy the protection of the German government as 'ethnic Germans', and it is relatively easy for them to apply for German citizenship. But the German authorities are trying to put a brake on the stream of immigrants from Russia. However, it now appears as if some German conservatives, New Right agitators and spokesmen of the Russian Germans see the former Königsberg in East Prussia as a suitable place for these immigrants. Since January 1991 the former Königsberg has been an open city again. Thousands of Russian Germans have already settled there with the support of the German government. According to the weekly *Der Spiegel*, the German government has provided a subsidy of DM 25 million to house Russian Germans from Kazakhstan in Kaliningrad. 'Die schwarze Serie', *Der Spiegel*, no. 51, 1997, pp. 22–8, here: p. 26. In parallel with this settlement, the Lutheran church in Kaliningrad is busily attempting to set up new congregations. Nevertheless many Russian Germans feel discriminated against by the German government. In 1992 one of their leaders said that they will turn *en masse* to the Republikaner if their wishes are not met. See '"Der Traum ist aus". Interview mit dem Führer der Rußlanddeutschen Heinrich Groth', *Der Spiegel*, no. 42, 12 October 1992, pp. 31–3. See also Brinks, J. H., 'The Miraculous Resurrection of Immanuel Kant: Germany's Breakthrough to Former East Prussia', *Political Geography*, Vol. 17, no. 5, June 1998, pp. 611–15.

14. Assheuer, T. and Sarkowicz, H., *Rechtsradikale in Deutschland*, p. 135.

15. The impression that this was not just a matter of German–Prussian culture was strengthened by the fact that the last wish of Frederick II was simply ignored by the German authorities. The king had given instructions that he was to be buried without ceremony at night among his dogs. However, the reinternment took place with military honours – and in the presence of Chancellor Kohl. Some Poles regarded this as simply insulting.

16. Gessenharter, W., 'Das Freund-Feind-Denken der Neuen Rechten', in: Butterwegge, C. and Isola, H., *Rechtsextremismus im vereinten Deutschland*, p. 69.

17. 'Grenzschutz sucht Amtshilfe am Taxistand', *SZ*, 17 December 1997. According to the *Forschungsstelle Flucht und Migration*, in Brandenburg alone more than 40 taxi drivers are being prosecuted for 'aiding and abetting illegal residence', 'Kleingärtner an der Neiße haben aufgerüstet', *SZ*, 27 March 1998.

18. Moreover, the DVU could count on votes not only in the new Federal territories but also in the old Federal Republic. During the elections for the parliament of Hamburg in 1997 the DVU gained 4.977 per cent of the vote and was 190 votes short of being represented in the parliament. The party was elected in four of the seven district assemblies: Hamburg-Mitte (8.5 per cent), Harburg (7.5 per cent), Bergedorf (5.5 per cent) and Wandsbek (5.5 per cent). 'DVU fehlen in Hamburg 190 Stimmen', *SZ*, 26/27 September 1997.

18. Weimar Revisited?

1. 'Minderheitsregierung in Sachsen-Anhalt. Höppner mit Stimmen der PDS wiedergewählt', *SZ*, 27 May 1998.

2. 'Deutschland teuerstes Land für Unternehmen', *SZ*, 13/14 December 1997. See also the joint study of the Heritage Foundation and the *Wall Street Journal* which in 1997 put Germany in 24th place among the 'free' economies and observed a falling tendency. 'Deutschlands Wirtschaft immer "unfreier"', *SZ*, 2 December 1997.

3. 'Rot–Grüne Mehrheiten in den Bezirken', *TAZ*, 25 May 1992.

4. 'Demokratiebekenntnis in 15 Sekunden', *SZ*, 22 May 1998; 'Bundestags-wahl 27 September 1998. Amtliches Ergebnis, *SZ*, 15 October 1998.

5. *Verfassungsschutzbericht, 1996.*

6. 'PDS wird sich im Osten halten', *SZ*, 16 April 1997.

7. PDS-Mitgliederzeitschrift 'Disput' no. 2/96/PDS-Pressedienst no. 5/6, 1996, in: *Verfassungsschutzbericht, 1996.*

8. PDS-Pressedienst, no. 46 of 15 November 1996, in: *Verfassungsschutzbericht, 1996.*

9. See Pareto, V., *Treatise on General Sociology*, section 1843 [English translation: *The Mind and Society*, 1935, Vol. III, p. 1281ff. Cf. also note 65, Chapter 10]. Quoted in: Popper, K. R., *The Open Society and Its Enemies*, Vol. 2, Hegel & Marx, p. 318.

Bibliography

Amnesty International, *Jahresbericht 1995*, Fischer, Frankfurt am Main, August 1995, pp. 163–6; *Jahresbericht 1996*, pp. 177–80; *Jahresbericht 1997*, pp. 176–80.

Assheuer, T. and Sarkowicz, H., *Rechtsradikale in Deutschland. Die alte und die neue Rechte*, Munich, 1992.

Baring, A., *Unser neuer Größenwahn. Deutschland zwischen Ost und West*, Stuttgart, 1988.

— *Deutschland. Was nun?*, Berlin, 1991.

Bartel, H., Bachmann, P. and Knoth, I., *Preussen Legende und Wirklichkeit*, Berlin (East), 1985.

Barth, K., Ein Brief nach Frankreich (1939), in: *Eine Schweizer Stimme 1938–1945*, Zürich, 1945, pp. 108–17.

Bayer, B., 'Wider die Monopolia' – Zu Luthers ökonomischen Erkenntnissen, Radio DDR/II. Programm. Redaktion Schulfunk, Sendung 22.4.1983/17.15 Uhr, Bd.–Nr.: Schf/3708.

Bebel, A., *Ausgewählte Reden und Schriften, 1863–1878*, Vol. 1, Berlin (E), 1983.

Becker, Howard, *German Youth: Bond or Free*, London, 1946.

Borchers, A., *Neue Nazis im Osten. Hintergründe und Fakten*, Weinheim, 1992.

Brinks, J. H., *Die DDR–Geschichtswissenschaft auf dem Weg zur deutschen Einheit. Luther, Friedrich II. und Bismarck als Paradigmen politischen Wandels*, Frankfurt am Main/New York, 1992.

Buber-Neumann, M., *Der kommunistische Untergrund. Ein Beitrag zur Geschichte der kommunstischen Geheimarbeit,* Institut für politologische Zeitfragen, Zürich, 1970.

Der Bundesminister des Innern, *Texte zur Inneren Sicherheit. Rechtsextremismus in der Bundesrepublik Deutschland. Aktueller Stand*, Presse- und Informationsamt der Bundesregierung, Bonn, 1991.

Butterwegge, C. and Isola, H., *Rechtsextremismus im vereinten Deutschland. Randerscheinung oder Gefahr für die Demokratie?*, Bremen/Berlin, 1991.

Czaja, H., *Unsere sittliche Pflicht. Leben für Deutschland*, Munich, 1989.

Dallmann, Siegfried, Im Bewußtsein der Übereinstimmung mit den wahrhaft nationalen Traditionen unseres Volkes leisten wir unseren Beitrag zur nationalen Mission der DDR, in: *Nation und Nationalbewußtsein. Einige Beiträge der*

National-Demokratischen Partei Deutschlands zur Entwicklung nationalen Denkens dabei Referat und Diskussionsbeiträge der Studientagung des Parteivorstandes am 28 September 1966 zur Eröffnung des Studienjahres 1966/67 der NDPD, Berlin (E), 1966, pp. 45–88.

Das III. Reich. Ein Volk, ein Reich, ein Führer. Eine historische Collage über den erregendsten Abschnitt deutscher Geschichte – in Wort, Bild und Ton 1933–1939, Vols 1 and 2, Hamburg, 1975.

Diwald, H., *Geschichte der Deutschen*, Berlin/Vienna, 1978.

— *Luther. Eine Biographie*, Bergisch Gladbach, 1982.

— *Deutschland, einig Vaterland*, Berlin, 1990.

Dreher, K., *Helmut Kohl. Leben mit Macht*, Stuttgart, 1998.

Ehrenburg, Ilya, *The Fall of Paris*, London, 1943.

Engelberg, E. von, *Lehrbuch der deutschen Geschichte.* (Beiträge), Vol. 7, Deutschland von 1849–1871. Von der Niederlage der bürgerlich-demokratischen Revolution bis zur Reichsgründung, Berlin (E), 1965.

— *Bismarck. Urpreuße und Reichsgründer*, Berlin, 1985.

Engelmann, B., *Du deutsch? Geschichte der Ausländer in Deutschland*, Göttingen, 1992.

Falter, J. W., *Hitlers Wähler*, Munich, 1991.

Farin, K. and E. Seidel-Pielen, *Rechtsruck. Rassismus im neuen Deutschland*, Berlin, 1992.

Faulenbach, B., Endlich, S., Graf, A., Leo, A., Lutz, T., Rürup, R. and Zimmerman, M., *Empfehlungen zur Neukonzeption der brandenburgischen Gedenkstätten*, January 1992.

Fichte, J. G., *Reden an die deutsche Nation*, Stuttgart, 1923.

Finn, G., *Sachsenhausen 1936–1950. Geschichte eines Lagers*, Bad Münstereifel, 1988 (third edition 1991).

Fischer, Fritz, *Krieg der Illusionen. Die Deutsche Politik von 1911–1914*, Düsseldorf, 1987.

Förtsch, E., Preußen-Bild und historische Traditionen in der DDR, Schriftenreihe der Gesellschaft für Deutschlandforschung, in *Die DDR und die Tradition*, Vol. IV, 1981, pp. 113–32.

Frei, Norbert, *Vergangenheitspolitik. Die Anfänge der Bundesrepublik und die NS-Vergangenheit*, Munich, 1996.

Funke, H., *'Jetzt sind wir dran'. Nationalismus im geeinten Deutschland. Eine Streitschrift*, Berlin, 1991.

— 'Demokratieaufbau Ost', *Blätter für deutsche und internationale Politik*, no. 6, Bonn, 1998, pp. 650–4.

Gauck, J., *Die Stasi-Akten. Das unheimliche Erbe der DDR*, Reinbek bei Hamburg, 1992.

Gerard, James W., *Face to Face with Kaiserism*, New York, 1918.

'Germany for Germans'. Xenophobia and Racist Violence in Germany, Human Rights Watch, Helsinki/New York, April 1995.

Geschichte Lehrbuch für Klasse 10, Berlin (E), 1985.

Gesellschaft zum Schutz von Bürgerrecht und Menschenwürde (GBM), ed. Richter, W., *Unfrieden in Deutschland. Weißbuch. Diskriminierung in den neuen Bundesländern*, Berlin, 1992.

Giordano, R., *Wenn Hitler den Krieg gewonnen hätte. Die Pläne der Nazis nach dem Endsieg*, Berlin, 1990.

— *Die zweite Schuld oder von der Last ein Deutscher zu sein*, Munich, 1990.

Gunther, J., *Inside Europe*, London, 1936.

Hacker, F., *Das Faschismus-Syndrom. Analyse eines aktuellen Phänomens*, Frankfurt am Main, 1992.

Hanke, H., Zur Rolle von Traditionen in Lebensweise und Kultur, *Weimarer Beiträge*, Vol. 1, 1980, year 26, pp. 35–58.

Heckel, E., Keßler, H. and Ulle, D., *Kultur in den Kämpfen unserer Zeit. Zur ideologischen Klassenauseinandersetzung zwischen Sozialismus und Imperialismus auf dem Gebiet von Kultur und Kunst*, Berlin (E), 1981.

Heiber, H., *Die Republik von Weimar*, Munich, 1969.

Herles, W., *Nationalrausch, Szenen aus dem gesamtdeutschen Machtkampf*, Munich, 1990.

Hitler, A., *Mein Kampf*, Munich, 1940.

Honecker, E., 'Unsere Zeit verlangt Parteinahme für Fortschritt, Vernunft und Menschlichkeit', *Martin Luther und unsere Zeit. Konstituierung des Martin-Luther-Komitees der DDR am 13 Juni 1980 in Berlin/GDR–Weimar*, 1980, pp. 9–18.

Hörnig, H., 'Sozialismus und ideologischer Kampf', *Zeitschrift für Geschichtswissenschaft*, no. 8, 1984, pp. 667–80.

Jarmatz, K., *Ravensbrücker Ballade oder Faschismusbewältigung in der DDR*, Berlin, 1992.

'Juden und Deutsche', *Spiegel Spezial 2*, 1992.

Kappelt, O., *Braunbuch DDR. Nazis in der DDR*, Berlin, 1981.

Klemperer, V., *LTI*. Notizbuch eines Philologen, Leipzig, 1982.

Kocka, J., 'Geteilte Erinnerungen. Zweierlei Geschichtsbewußtsein im vereinten Deutschland', *Blätter für deutsche und internationale Politik*, no. 1, Bonn, 1998, pp. 104–11.

Koepf, P., *Stichwort Asylrecht*, Munich, 1992.

Kohn, H., *De Duitse geest. De vorming van een volk*, Amsterdam, 1962 (transl. of *The Mind of Germany: the Education of a Nation*, New York, 1960).

Kremers, H. (ed.), *Die Juden und Martin Luther – Martin Luther und die Juden. Geschichte, Wirkungsgeschichte, Herausforderung* (with a foreword by Johannes Rau), Neukirchen-Vluyn, 1985.

Kuhrt, E. and Von Löwis, H., *Griff nach der deutschen Geschichte*, Erbeaneignung und Traditionspflege in der DDR, Paderborn, 1988.

Lange, F., *Die Volkserhebung von 1813. Drei Aufsätze über die Notwendigkeit aus der eigenen Geschichte zu lernen*, Berlin, 1952.

'Lehren aus dem Prozeß gegen das Verschwörerzentrum Slansky'. Beschluß des

Zentralkomitees der Sozialistischen Einheitspartei Deutschlands. December 20, 1952, in: *Matern, Hermann, Über die Durchführung des Beschlusses des ZK der SED 'Lehren aus den Prozeß gegen das Verschwörerzentrum Slansky', 13 Tagung des Zentralkomitees der Sozialistischen Einheitspartei Deutschlands*, 13–14 May 1953, pp. 48–70.

Lehrpläne für die Grund- und Oberschulen in der Sowjetischen Besatzungszone Deutschlands. Geschichte, 1 July 1946, Berlin.

Leonhard, W., *Die Revolution entläßt ihre Kinder*, Frankfurt am Main, 1976.

Lessing, T., *Geschichte als Sinngebung des Sinnlosen*, Munich, 1983.

Liebknecht, K., *Gesammelte Reden und Schriften*, Vol. 5, Berlin (E), 1977.

Luther, M., 'Von den Juden und Ihren Lügen' (1543), in: *Martin Luthers Werke, Kritische Gesamtausgabe*, Vol. 53, Weimar, 1919/1920, pp. 412–552.

Maaz, H.-J., *Der Gefühlsstau. Ein Psychogramm der DDR*, Berlin, 1990.

— *Das gestürzte Volk oder die unglückliche Einheit*, Berlin, 1991.

'Mann ohne Gewissen'. Ulbricht als unbefugter Richter – Die rote Diktatur löste nur die braune ab. Eine bemerkenswerte Vergangenheit. *Bulletin des Presse- und Informationsamtes der Bundesregierung*, 12 May 1960, no. 89, pp. 875–6.

Mann, Thomas, *Reden und Aufsätze*, part 2, Stockholmer Gesamtausgabe der Werke von Thomas Mann, Oldenburg, 1965.

Marx Engels Werke, Vol. 1, Berlin (East), 1983; Vol. 31, Berlin (East). 1986; Vol 8, Berlin (East), 1982 and Vol. 29, Berlin (East), 1978.

Meier, H. and Schmidt, W., 'Tradition und sozialistisches Bewußtsein', *Einheit*, Vol. 12, 1978, pp. 1220–7.

Meyers, P., *Friedrich II. von Preußen im Geschichtsbild der SBZ/DDR. Ein Beitrag zur Geschichte der Geschichtswissenschaft und des Geschichtsunterrichts in der SBZ/DDR mit einer Methodik zur Analyse von Schulgeschichtsbüchern*, Studien zur internationalen Schulbuchforschung, Schriftenreihe des Georg-Eckert-Instituts, Vol. 35, Braunschweig, 1983.

Mikolajczyk, S., *The Rape of Poland. Pattern of Soviet Aggression*, Westport, CT, 1948; Dutch transl. by Otto G. Peyl as *Verkracht volk. In de greep van Soviet Rusland*, Bilthoven, 1949.

Mitscherlich, A. and M., *Die Unfähigkeit zu trauern*, Munich, 1977.

Mohler, A., *Die konservative Revolution in Deutschland 1918–1932*, Ein Handbuch, Darmstadt, 1994.

Nationalrat der Nationalen Front des Demokratischen Deutschland. Dokumentationszentrum der Staatlichen Archivverwaltung der DDR. *Braunbuch. Kriegs- und Naziverbrecher in der Bundesrepublik. Staat. Wirtschaft. Armee. Verwaltung. Justiz. Wissenschaft*, Berlin (E), 1965.

Neuhäußer-Wespy, U., Von der Urgesellschaft bis zur SED. Anmerkungen zur 'Nationalgeschichte der DDR', *Deutschland-Archiv*, no. 2, 1983, pp. 145–60.

Nolte, E., Zwischen Geschichtslegende und Revisionismus? Das Dritte Reich im Blickwinkel des Jahres 1980', in: *'Historikerstreit'. Die Dokumentation der Kontroverse um die Einzigartigkeit der national-sozialistischen Judenvernichtung*, Munich, 1987, pp. 13–35.

— Vergangenheit die nicht vergehen will. Eine Rede, die geschrieben, aber nicht gehalten werden konnte', in: *'Historikerstreit'. Die Dokumentation der Kontroverse um die Einzigartigkeit der national-sozialistischen Judenvernichtung*, Munich, 1987, pp. 39–47.

— *Nietzsche und der Nietzscheanismus*, Frankfurt am Main/Berlin, 1990.

— *Geschichtsdenken im 20 Jahrhundert. Von Max Weber bis Hans Jonas*, Berlin/Frankfurt am Main, 1992.

Norden, A., *Um die Nation. Beiträge zu Deutschlands Lebensfrage*, Berlin, 1952.

NVA-Kalender 1987, Militärverlag der Deutschen Demokratischen Republik, Berlin (E), 1986.

Popper, K.R., *The Open Society and Its Enemies*, Vols 1 and 2, London, 1969, 1973.

Programm der Sozialistischen Einheitspartei Deutschlands. Einstimmig angenommen auf dem IX Parteitag der Sozialistischen Einheitspartei Deutschlands, Berlin (East), 18–22 May, 1976.

Quinkert, A. and Jäger, S., *Die rassistische Hetze von 'Bild' gegen Flüchtlinge im Herbst 1991*, Duisburger Institut für Sprach- und Sozialforschung, Duisburg, 1991.

Rathenau, W. *Von Kommenden Dingen*, Berlin, 1918.

— *Was Wird Werden?*, Leipzig, Berlin, 1920.

Rauschning, H., *The Voice of Destruction*, New York, 1940.

Richter, W. (ed.) *Unfrieden in Deutschland. Weissbuch. Diskriminierung in den neuen Bundesländern*, Berlin, 1992.

Röhl, K. R., *Nähe zum Gegner. Kommunisten und Nationalsozialisten im Berliner BVG-Streik von 1932*, Frankfurt am Main/New York, 1994.

Rosenberg, A., *Protestantische Rompilger. Der Verrat an Luther und der Mythus des 20 Jahrhunderts*, Munich, 1937.

Schröder, B., *Rechte Kerle. Skinheads, Faschos, Hooligans*, Reinbek bei Hamburg, 1992.

Siegler, B., *Auferstanden aus Ruinen. Rechtsextremismus in der DDR*, Berlin, 1991.

Stalin, J., *Werke*, Vol. 2, Berlin, 1950.

Stock, M. and Mühlberg, P., *Die Szene von innen. Skinheads, Grufties, Heavy Metals, Punks*, Berlin, 1990.

Stöss, R., *Die 'Republikaner'. Woher sie kommen; Was sie wollen; Wer sie wählt; Was zu tun ist*, Cologne, 1990.

Strasser, G., *Kampf um Deutschland. Reden und Aufsätze eines Nationalsozialisten*, Munich, 1932.

Süssmuth, H., 'Luther 1983 in beiden deutschen Staaten, Kritische Rezeption oder ideologische Vereinnahmung?', in: Süssmuth, H. (ed.), *Das Luther-Erbe in Deutschland. Vermittlung zwischen Wissenschaft und Öffentlichkeit*, Düsseldorf, 1985, pp. 16–40.

Theses on Martin Luther, *Zeitschrift für Geschichtswissenschaft*, no. 10, 1981, year 29, pp. 879–93.

Treitschke, H. von, 'Unsere Aussichten', *Preußische Jahrbücher*, 15 November 1879, Vol. 44, Berlin, 1879, pp. 559–76.

— 'Luther und die deutsche Nation', *Preußische Jahrbücher*, no. 52, Berlin, 1883, pp. 469–86.

Ulbricht, W., *Zur Geschichte der neuesten Zeit. Die Niederlage Hitlerdeutschlands und die Schaffung der antifaschistisch-demokratischen Ordnung*, Vol. 1, 1 half-binding, Berlin, 1955.

— 'Grundsätze der sozialistischen Ethik und Moral, in: Zur Geschichte der Deutschen Arbeiterbewegung', Vol. 7, *Reden und Aufsätze, 1957–1959*, Berlin (E), 1964, pp. 376–8.

Urban, Thomas, *Deutsche in Polen. Geschichte und Gegenwart einer Minderheit*. Munich, 1994.

Venohr, W., *Die roten Preußen. Aufstieg und Fall der DDR*, Frankfurt am Main/ Berlin, 1992.

Verbeeck, G., *Geschiedschrijving en politieke cultuur. DDR-historici over 'De weg naar het fascisme' in het geschiedenisbeeld van de DDR*, Leuven, 1992.

Verfassungsschutzbericht 1996, Bundesamt für Verfassungsschutz, Bonn.

Vetter, K. and Vogler, G., *Preußen. Von den Anfängen bis zur Reichsgründung*, Cologne, 1981.

Viereck, P., *Metapolitics. The Roots of the Nazi Mind*, New York, 1961.

Weber, H., *Der Deutsche Kommunismus. Dokumente*, Cologne/Berlin, 1963.

— *Ulbricht fälscht Geschichte. Ein Kommentar mit Dokumenten zum 'Grundriß der Geschichte der deutschen Arbeiterbewegung'*, Cologne, 1964.

— *DDR: Grundriß der Geschichte, 1945–1990*, Hannover, 1991.

West, Rebecca, *The Meaning of Treason*, London, 1949.

Wiesenthal, W., *Die gleiche Sprache: Erst für Hitler – jetzt für Ulbricht*. Pressekonferenz von Simon Wiesenthal am 6 September 1968 in Wien. Eine Dokumentation der Deutschland-Berichte. Jüdisches Dokumentationszentrum, Simon Wiesenthal Centre, Vienna, Austria.

Wippermann, W., *Antifaschismus in der DDR: Wirklichkeit und Ideologie, Beiträge zum Thema Widerstand*, 16, Informationszentrum Berlin. Gedenk- und Bildungsstätte Stauffenbergstraße, Berlin, 1980.

— *Der 'Deutsche Drang nach Osten'. Ideologie und Wirklichkeit eines politischen Schlagwortes*, Darmstadt, 1981.

Wolf, Markus, *Spionagechef im geheimen Krieg. Erinnerungen*, Munich, 1998.

Wörterbuch der Geschichte, A-K, Berlin (E), 1984.

Wörterbuch der Geschichte, L-Z, Berlin (E), 1984.

Index

Abusch, Alexander, 55
Adenauer, Konrad, 4, 10, 11, 12, 63, 86, 126; *Die roten Preuen*, 5
Alternative Liste, 116
American Jewish Committee, 57, 98
Amnesty International, criticism of German police, 28
Anne Frank, diaries of, 107
anti-Americanism, 113, 114, 127
anti-anti-fascism, in GDR, 61, 93–100
anti-fascism, 114, 156, 159; in GDR, xvi, 69–71 (as foundation myth, xvii, 68; legitimisation of, 59–68)
anti-Marxism, 113
anti-Semitism, x, xvi, 9, 25, 31, 51, 75, 79, 89, 93, 103, 123, 124–8; in GDR, 51–8, 97, 125; of Martin Luther, 73, 74, 80
anti-Slav sentiment, xvi, 9, 89; of Marx and Engels, 83–4
anti-Zionism, 54, 55
Arab–Israeli War, attitude of GDR, 53
Arndt, Ernst Moritz, 86
Arnold, Richard, 53–4
Article 131 of German Constitution, 63
Assheuer, T., 118, 152
Asylant, use of term, 135
Asylum Act, Germany, 141
Asylum in the Church organisation, 138
asylum law in Germany, 130; emended in Constitution, xv, 130, 131
asylum-seekers, 30, 96, 128, 153; allegedly false, 135; attacks on, viii; debate on, xiv, xvii, 129–42, 160

Auschwitz concentration camp, 128; killings denied, 108
Aussiedler, use of term, 135
Aust, Hans Walter, 65
Austria, 150
Autonomen, 28, 33
Axe, Hermann, 55

Ball, Kurt Herwart, 54
Baring, Arnulf, 105, 152; *Deutschland was nun?*, 104; *Unser neuer Großenwahn*, 112
Barth, Karl, 72, 76
Bästlein, Bernhard, 98
Bautzen concentration camp, 94
Bayer, Brigitte, 78
Bebel, August, 6
Becher, Johannes, 98
Beckstein, Günther, 150–1
Benjamin, Georg, 98
Benz, Wolfgang, 127
Berlin, 'miracle' of, 115
Berlin Public Transport Company, strike at, 40
Berlin Wall: building of, 26, 46, 69; fall of, x, xi, xvi, 12, 14, 24, 26, 32, 41, 49, 50, 93, 94, 106, 131, 141, 143, 148, 154
Biedenkopf, Kurt, 25
Bild Zeitung, 135–6
Bisky, party chairman of PDS, 158–9
von Bismarck, Otto, 12, 83, 87, 88; restoration of, 145
Bittburg cemetery, reception of Ronald Reagan, 105
von Bittenfeld, Hans Herwarth, 5

Lutheranism, legacy of, in GDR, 72–81

Maaz, Hans Joachim, 20, *Der Gefhlsstau*, 19
Magdeburg, rioting in, 27
Mann, Thomas, 72
Marshall Aid, 15
Marx, Karl, 6, 7, 78, 83, 104; anti-Slav sentiment of, 83–4 *see also* anti-Marxism
Marxism-Leninism, 10
Mengele, Josef, xvii
Merker, Paul, 56
Micksch, Jürgen, 136
Mielke, Erich, 55
Mikolajczyk, Stanislaw, 67
militarism, xv; in GDR, 45–58 *see also* Prussia
Mitscherlich, Alexander, xvii, 20, 61
Mitscherlich, Margarete, xvii, 20, 61
Mitteldeutsche Neueste Nachrichten, 54
Mittenzwei, Ingrid, 88–9
Modrow, Hans, 19, 26, 146
Moeller van der Bruck, Arthur, 111
Mölln, attacks in, vii
Mommsen, Hans, 108
Moricone, Ennio, 'Play Me the Song of Death', 115
Müller, Vincenz, 46, 47
Müntzer, Thomas, 79

Nachama, Andreas, 58, 95
Nation & Europa-Deutsche Monatshefte, 114
National Demokratische Partei Deutschlands (NDPD), 29, 41, 53, 54, 67, 68
'national liberated zones' in East Germany, 31
National Socialism, 29, 38, 40, 46, 62, 66, 75, 111, 126, 127; as reaction to Stalinism, 102; defined as fascism, 61; equated with communism, 98, 100, 101
National-Conservative Deutschland Forum, 133
National-Zeitung, 68

Der nationale Demokrat, 53
Nationale Offensive, 29
Nationale Volksarmee, xvii; founding of, 46; oath-taking for, 93
nationalism, German, 11, 32 (nineteenth-century, 9)
Nationalistische Front, 29
Nationalkomitee Freies Deutschland, 47, 64
Nationalsozialistische Deutsche Arbeiterpartei (NSDAP), 30, 37, 39, 54, 63, 74, 156; former members in GDR *Volkskammer*, 64–5
Nazi symbolism, xii; use of, 147
Nazism, x, 161; amnesty laws for, 63; de-nazification, 63, 67, 126; drawing line under *see* Third Reich; internment of functionaries, 94; sentences for crimes of, 63
Neo-Nazism, x, 42, 100, 117; organisations banned, 29; programme of, 36
Neue Zeit, 54
Neuengamme concentration camp, 94
Neues Deutschland, 53
Neues Forum movement, 19
Neumann, Heinz, 40
Neumann, Margarete, 40, 66
New Right, xiii, xiv, 109, 110–14, 118, 119, 129–42, 143–54, 150, 153, 160, 161
Nietzsche, Friedrich, 104
Niggemeier, Horst, 133
Night of the Long Knives, 37
Noll, Dieter, *The Adventures of Werner Holt*, 60
Nolte, Ernst, 102, 103, 105, 107; *Geschichtsdenken im 20 Jahrhundert*, 104; *Nietzsche und der Nitzscheanismus*, 104
Norden, Albert, 55; *Um die Nation*, 8

Oder–Neiße frontier, 144, 153
Ostbiete, 148; loss of, 143, 145, 147; recovery fantasies, 149
Ostmarkverein, 85
Ostpolitik, ix